SEVEN YEARS TO A BETTER TOMORROW

2011 TO 2018

GOD'S LONGSUFFERING CONTINUES…

During Great Tribulation

©MARTY CATTUZZO

A *2011studies* Publication

Seven Years to a Better Tomorrow-2011 to 2018-God's Longsuffering Continues During Great Tribulation

By Marty Cattuzzo

Printed in the United States of America

ISBN: 9780692304969

The observations in this book are based on the continued study of God's holy and inspired Word, the Bible. The principle method of Bible study used is comparing Scripture with Scripture to arrive at truth. This book is also a result of prayer following God's principle of asking for wisdom when our meager understanding falls short of truth. Bible quotations are taken from the King James Version of the Bible.

Disclaimer: Many of the Bible studies in this book were originally presented on the YouTube™ channel entitled: *2011studies* and are currently being presented there freely.

Therefore, the copyrights of these individual studies predate the release date of this book entitled: *Seven Years to a Better Tomorrow.*

Author's Note:

The readers of this book are invited to join the YouTube channel entitled: *2011studies* (one word). Any new information coming forth form God's Word will be presented on *2011studies*, which features Bible study videos along with ongoing music videos. A new web site entitled: *www.lettersofpeaceandtruth.com* is available for word studies. A new blog site entitled: *www.1335days.com* is also available for all people who are looking for the coming of Christ on the *last day* in *power and great glory.*

> **Habakkuk 2:14: For the earth shall be filled with the knowledge of the glory of the LORD, as the waters cover the sea.**
>
> **2 Peter 3:9: The Lord is not slack concerning his promise, as some men count slackness; but is longsuffering to us-ward, not willing that any should perish, but that all should come to repentance.**
>
> **2 Peter 3:15: And account *that* the longsuffering of our Lord *is* salvation; even as our beloved brother Paul also according to the wisdom given unto him hath written unto you...**

I would like to offer a heartfelt thanks to my family and friends who have been a true source of encouragement and support in writing this book. God is merciful and longsuffering. The studies continue...

- What happened in the year 2011 as the worldwide announcement of Judgment Day came upon the world?
- Is God's longsuffering the reason we passed the 7,000-year anniversary of the flood?
- How does God use Biblical history to illustrate key events of the final years of history?
- Does the Bible mention a *tribulation* period and <u>also</u> a final *great tribulation* period encompassing seven years? Is this period of time shortened by God?
- Will the believers in Jesus Christ be here on earth when He returns in *power and great glory* on the *last day*?
- Does 2 Peter 3 contain important information regarding the promise of Christ's return?
- Did the Apostle Paul know something that is referenced by Peter that all believers should know?
- Are church leaders proclaiming the soon coming of Jesus on the last day or are they suggesting "no man knows the day or hour"?
- Were Daniel's and the disciple's inquiries about the things of the end shunned by God or were they given end-time information by God?
- Will the churches "glory" be despised in the coming years as a judgment from God?
- Is there a historical example of a 7-year period called the time of *great tribulation*?
- Does Joel 2 speak of a time when God removes Satan and at that time God is magnified?

- When will God remove the *strength of the kingdoms of the nations* and *shake the heavens and earth*? Is the year 2015 an important turning point in the final seven years?
- Why are Elijah and Job mentioned in the book of James as our examples to learn from *unto the coming of the Lord?*
- Does God repeat the prophecy of *blessed is he that waits and comes to the 1,335th day* in the final seven years of history (2011-2018)?
- Will Satan be *removed* by God during the final years of history?
- Is the task to *consume and destroy* the kingdom of Satan given to the believers worldwide?
- Will judgment come upon the fallen houses of God according to the historical account of Moab who was a hireling of the King of Assyria?
- How exactly has God fit so many historical patterns within the final seven years of history including the *time, times and half time* (3 ½ years) from the book of Daniel?
- Are the Biblical years of King Darius showing us the rebuilding of God's eternal house in which believers worldwide are living stones?
- Are we all living in the final seven years of history awaiting the glorious coming of Jesus in *power and great glory?*

These important questions will be answered in this book, *Seven Years to a Better Tomorrow-2011 to 2018*. This is a Bible study book and being such, the Word of God will be presented to show how God's salvation plan will become the governing force in these final seven years. God's Word will cover the earth and He alone will be magnified in a great way beginning in the year 2015. There is much information coming forth from God's Word at this present time, and it shows this is truly a time in which *knowledge* is increasing by God's Spirit granting wisdom and understanding:

> **Daniel 12:4: But thou, O Daniel, shut up the words, and seal the book, _even_ to the time of the end: many shall run to and fro, and knowledge shall be increased.**

I believe Daniel, as well as the disciples, are our examples for being inquisitive. They asked God for wisdom and understanding concerning the things of the end. In Daniel 12, God's Word proclaims that *knowledge* shall be increased. What knowledge is God referring to? When studying the Bible, we compare Scripture with Scripture and word with identical word. The Hebrew word (*daath* H1847) translated as *knowledge* in Daniel 12:4 relates to the knowledge of God and His Word. Below are two verses which use the same Hebrew word for knowledge as found in Daniel 12:4:

> **Hosea 6:6: For I desired mercy, and not sacrifice; and the knowledge of God more than burnt offerings.**

> **Habakkuk 2:14: For the earth shall be filled with the knowledge of the glory of the LORD, as the waters cover the sea.**

Yet, there is also the truth that glory can be changed to shame for lack of knowledge of God and His Word:

> **Hosea 4:6: My people are destroyed for lack of knowledge: because thou hast rejected knowledge, I will also reject thee, that thou shalt be no priest**

to me: seeing thou hast forgotten the law of thy God, I will also forget thy children.

Hosea 4:7: As they were increased, so they sinned against me: *therefore* will I change their glory into shame.

With this established truth concerning the knowledge of God and His Word, we can now forge on to gain understanding concerning the final events in what is very possibly the final seven years of history (2011-2018). Expect to be amazed how God has orchestrated everything according to past Biblical history. There is nothing new under the sun:

Ecclesiastes 1:9: The thing that hath been, it *is that* which shall be; and that which is done *is* that which shall be done: and *there is* no new *thing* under the sun.

Note: In this study of God's Word we will be using the King James translation. We will also be using an electronic Biblical concordance[1] for the Greek and Hebrew words. Quick example: If we are studying the English word *life* in the Greek text, there will be the original Greek word listed along with the concordance number: *life- Zoe* (G2222). The same will apply if we are studying the Hebrew text: *life-Chay* (H2416). The "G" and the "H" are representing Greek and Hebrew accordingly. The computer software for Bible study is available free online. The *References* page will list the sites for free download. In front of the *References* page, there will be charts which relate to the final seven years including the second fulfillment of *Blessed is he that waits and comes to the 1,335th day* in the year 2015. Please refer to these charts should any questions arise concerning the timeline of the final seven years.

Table of Contents

Preface

It was the year 2011 and a grand worldwide announcement of Judgment Day was upon us all. The media ran with this announcement; the weekend TV comedy shows performed skits with the *rapture* as the topic of mocking. Even at sporting events, large banners hung by stadium fans read: "Raptured." Billboards worldwide were placed by concerned believers proclaiming that we were approaching Judgment Day at the 7,000[th] year anniversary of the flood (4990 B.C.) on May 21, 2011. What happened? Was something missed as we studied the infamous chapter of 2 Peter 3? Truly, the flood of Noah's day is mentioned in 2 Peter 3, and in this context it is related to the *promise of His coming*:

> **2 Peter 3:6: Whereby the world that then was, being overflowed with water, perished: 7: But the heavens and the earth, which are now, by the same word are kept in store, reserved unto fire against the day of judgment and perdition of ungodly men. 8: But, beloved, be not ignorant of this one thing, <u>that one day is with the Lord as a thousand years, and a thousand years as one day.</u>**

Since God compares a thousand years as one day (possibly day one) then it would make sense that 7,000 years since the flood on May 21, 2011 would be (to say the least) an important marker in history. Since much evidence of the great *falling away* seen today worldwide (as mentioned in 2 Thessalonians) matched Jesus' words of the *abomination that makes desolate*, surely we are not going to have to wait another thousand years before the promise of His coming arrives. So what did happen in the year 2011?

Seven Years to a Better Tomorrow is a Bible study book that features how God has established historical patterns and then incorporated them within a 23-year *tribulation* period <u>and a final seven-year *great tribulation*</u>. There was something about 2 Peter 3 that led myself and other Bible students back to Bible study. Certain chapters in the Bible, such as Habakkuk 2, really needed more study. The prophet stands upon his watch and wonders what to answer when he is reproved (questioned/corrected). Then God makes sure we understand one huge truth: though the vision lingers or hesitates wait for it, for it will not be slack or delay longer; it will surely come, Habakkuk 2 also mentions how the just (justified by Christ) shall live by His faith:

> **Habakkuk 2:2: And the LORD answered me, and said, Write the vision, and make *it* plain upon tables, that he may run that readeth it. For the vision *is* yet for an appointed time, but at the end it shall speak, and not lie: <u>though it tarry, wait for it; because it will surely come, it will not tarry</u>. 4: Behold, his soul which is lifted up is not upright in him: but <u>the just shall live by his faith</u>.**

This Hebrew word translated as faith (*emunah* H530) is also translated as stability or faithfulness:

> **Isaiah 33:5: The LORD is exalted; for he dwelleth on high: he hath filled Zion with judgment and righteousness. 6: And <u>wisdom and knowledge shall be the stability of thy times</u>, *and* strength of salvation: the fear of the LORD *is* his treasure.**

> **Lamentations 3:22: *It is of* the LORD'S mercies that we are not consumed, because his compassions fail not. 23: *They are* new every morning: <u>great *is* thy faithfulness</u>.**

Through asking God for wisdom and continued study of His Word, God has revealed much information concerning the final years of history. These truths from God's Word are not absent from opposition since many of today's church leaders are proclaiming "no man knows the day of hour." Yet, with patience we continue to pray that God will eventually stir up some pastors to begin searching these truths coming from the Bible. I am dedicating an entire final chapter to the "no man knows the day or hour" topic, so please read the chapter in light of this entire book. How did the churches stray so far from seeking the truth concerning the coming of Christ? Daniel wanted to know about the things of the end, and God gave him *wisdom* and *understanding*. The disciples also were very interested in *the sign of thy coming and the end of the world*:

> **Matthew 24:3: And as he sat upon the mount of Olives, the disciples came unto him privately, saying, Tell us, when shall these things be? and what *shall be* the sign of thy coming, and of the end of the world? 4: And Jesus answered and said unto them, Take heed that no man deceive you. 5: For many shall come in my name, saying, I am Christ; and shall deceive many.**

By Christ proclaiming that many will come in His name saying: "I am anointed" (Christ in Greek means anointed), we can know this is how the deception comes. Today, some leaders of large religious gatherings are proclaiming that they are *anointed* by God's Spirit and performing what the Bible calls *lying signs and wonders*. By this activity, we can know we are in the time just prior to Christ coming in *power and great glory* on the *last day*.

So why are the words "no man knows the day or hour" repeated over and over by church leaders? I believe the Bible gives evidence that this is for a good reason as history has shown. God is going to reveal certain truths first to the believers in Christ who have departed out of the fallen houses of God for a good reason. Our first *tribulation* was mirrored after the 70-year captivity of Judah. God has an order in which He gives understanding to get His Word out. Those who did depart out of the fallen houses of during the first *tribulation* period have a connection with historical Judah:

> **Zechariah 12:7: <u>The LORD also shall save the tents of Judah first</u>, that the glory of the house of David and the glory of the inhabitants of Jerusalem do not magnify *themselves* against Judah.**

> **Hosea 11:12: Ephraim compasseth me about with lies, and the house of Israel with deceit: but <u>Judah yet ruleth with God, and is faithful with the saints.</u>**

We also must be keenly aware that a message of 'peace, peace" will be coming forth from the houses of God when there is no peace in what they are proclaiming:

> **Ezekiel 13:10: Because, even because they have seduced my people, saying, Peace; and *there was* no peace; and one built up a wall, and, lo, others daubed it with untempered *morter*:**

Both *Peace and safety* are going to be a proclaimed by the leaders in the fallen houses of God before sudden destruction comes (1Thessalonians 5:3). Proclaiming that judgment is coming on the fallen houses of God is never popular, but it must be proclaimed because it will come to pass. Daniel chapter 11 declares that there are certain believers in Christ who will be granted understanding by God. Along with the understanding and wisdom comes the difficult task to warn. In order to arrive at a *better tomorrow* we must first declare the truth of God's Word. In the book of Daniel, the believers are instructed to warn. Before we get into the first chapter of *Seven Years to a Better Tomorrow*, I would like to demonstrate how God's Word needs to be studied in order to arrive at truth. The study verse will be Daniel 12:3 with a focus on the word *shine*:

> **Daniel 12:3: And they that be wise shall <u>shine</u> as the brightness of the firmament; and they that turn many to righteousness as the stars for ever and ever.**

The Hebrew word translated as *shine* by the King James translators is the word *Zahar* (H2094). When this word is used in other places in God's Word, it can mean to admonish, to warn, or to teach. Underlined below are two examples from the Bible where *Zahar* is used:

> **Exodus 18:20: And thou shalt <u>teach</u> them ordinances and laws, and shalt shew them the way wherein they must walk, and the work that they must do.**

> **Ezekiel 3:19: Yet if thou <u>warn</u> the wicked, and he turn not from his wickedness, nor from his wicked way, he shall die in his iniquity; but thou hast delivered thy soul.**

By fully reading and studying Daniel 12, we can know that God has given wisdom and understanding concerning the things of the end. We can also know that the believers in Jesus who have understanding are to *warn* or *teach*. This will be the ongoing focus of this book, *Seven Years to a Better Tomorrow*.

In this book, Biblical history will be used to illustrate how God is drawing from history to illustrate the conditions of the end just prior to Christ's return in *great power and great glory*. Using God's Word, it will be shown how the pattern of the 8,400 days, ending on May 21, 2011, was correct based on Judah's historical captivity of 840 months or 70 years.[2] It will also be demonstrated that after the original pattern of Judah/Jerusalem's 70-year captivity in Babylon, a rebuilding process begins. Also, in Zechariah 1:13 *good and comfortable words* were given by God and Jerusalem was rebuilt. Thus, we can know how the final seven years past the year 2011 are a time for rebuilding and sending forth the Gospel into the entire world.

Throughout this study it is important to show how important Biblical markers of the timeline of history relate to our time. There are important patterns that God has set up to illustrate how the Kingdom of Christ and the Kingdom of Satan engage in warfare prior to the return of Christ on the last day. There are two *tribulation* periods as illustrated in the chart below. The first one is illustrated by Judah/Jerusalem's captivity by the King of Babylon. The second one is the *great tribulation* mentioned in the Bible, the time of famine in Canaan. This was the 7-year period in which Jacob was saved out of *great tribulation*:

Date	Event	Relationship
609 B.C.	Josiah killed in battle-Judah loses independence. Thus, the 70-Yr/840 month *tribulation* period begins	1988-Satan assaults the houses of God during the first *tribulation* of 23 yrs-8,400 days ending May 21, 2011
587 B.C.	Judah's *tribulation* continues: Judah/Jerusalem destroyed by the King of Babylon	The *falling away* in the houses of God continues with *lying signs and wonders*, prosperity gospels etc... Believers flee.
539 B.C.	Captivity of Judah ends. The kingdom given to the Mede and the Persian by God.	Believers who have fled the fallen churches are made aware of the Years of Darius.
Nisan 538 B.C.	The official years of Darius begin. Time to rebuild the temple- The historical picture of God's eternal houses made up of believers worldwide.	Nisan 2012 lines up with the official first year of Darius. Darius' six years fit within the final 7 years.
1879 B.C.	The 7-year *great tribulation* of Joseph/Jacob's time.	The final seven years of history. 2011 to 2018 in which many events fit inside a 7-year period.

We will look closely at the years of Darius since the Babylonian kingdom was given to the Mede (Darius) and the Persian (Cyrus) in the year 539 B.C.[3] The mirror of the years of Darius in our time, which comes after the year 2011, will be shown to be a time of sending forth the *Gospel of the Kingdom*. This is the spiritual aspect of building God's eternal house that was established for us with the temple building during the original years of Darius.

We will also be studying key phrases such as: *unto the coming of the Lord.* Why does God want us to look at Elijah and Job as examples for us *unto the coming of the Lord*? It has been a constant amazement for me to study and observe how the Lord has fit so much Biblical history into a final seven years of time. The Lord has done this for our understanding so that we can be ready for His return and on that great day to be able to stand and hear:

> **Matthew 25:21: His lord said unto him, Well done, *thou* good and faithful servant: thou hast been faithful over a few things, I will make thee ruler over many things: enter thou into the joy of thy lord.**

My prayer is that God will bless this writing. I believe many people worldwide will become saved by His Spirit and then realize God's longsuffering, forbearance, and mercy. The writing of this book *Seven Years to a Better Tomorrow* began in January of the year 2014. In the next couple of years, God will be magnified in a great way. This writing is a foreshadowing of great things to come so that when God is magnified, people worldwide will know the Bible is truth. Is this not how God has revealed truth in the past?

> **Amos 1:1: The words of Amos, who was among the herdmen of Tekoa, which he saw concerning Israel in the days of Uzziah king of Judah, and in the days of Jeroboam the son of Joash king of Israel, <u>two years before the earthquake.</u>**

> **2: And he said, The LORD will roar from Zion, and utter his voice from Jerusalem; and the**

habitations of the shepherds shall mourn, and the top of Carmel shall wither.

The believers in Jesus, who are the branches, humbly admit that we know nothing outside of what the Lord, as the vine, has given us. We can only produce fruit if we abide in Him. Believers, like God who is the husbandman of the vineyard, wait patiently for the *precious fruit of the earth*. Salvation worldwide is coming on the horizon and the pattern is Pentecost 33 A.D. All years within the 7-year timeline are important, yet 2015 stands out as the mirror or duplicate of the prophecy from Daniel 12:12 in God's Word:

Daniel 12:12: Blessed *is* he that waiteth, and cometh to the <u>thousand three hundred and five and thirty days.</u>

13: But go thou thy way till the end *be*: for thou shalt rest, and stand in thy lot at the end of the days.

About the Book

Since the passing of the 153 days that fell between May 21, 2011 and October 21, 2011, it became clear to me that the years following 2011 would be a time of *feeding Christ's sheep*. I began recording video Bible studies to show why it was that we passed the important year of 2011. The studies have been posted on the YouTube channel *2011studies*. God willing, these video Bible studies will continue even after this book is complete. I thought it would be important to share these studies in the form of a book for those who may not be following the video Bible studies.

In this book, I am setting out to show how God draws from past Biblical history in order to illustrate to us the things of the end. For example, Bible students followed how the historical pattern of Judah's 840 months/70-year captivity related to the 8,400 days of *tribulation* ending on May 21, 2011. However, we would also need to understand what transpired *after the 70 years* of Judah's historical *tribulation* period. This is why the years of Darius now have become so critical to understand. The years of Darius followed Judah's 70-year captivity.

Therefore, instead of being a time of dodging any questions concerning the year 2011 being the 7,000th year anniversary of the flood, it was a time to pray and to continue studying God's Word. A few years before the year 2011, I came across the terms *good words and comfortable words* in Zechariah 1:13 that God had promised after the seventy years of Judah's captivity had passed. That became the original focus of why we passed the 8,400 days without Judgment Day coming upon the world. Further study amplified the truth that God is longsuffering toward us and He is not willing that any would perish (2 Peter 3:9). 2 Peter 3 became a very important aspect of further study of God's Word. Peter, under the inspiration of God's Spirit, suggested that we all need to understand what Paul understood concerning God's longsuffering. Why would Peter be so concerned that we grasp something Paul understood? Why would this concern be in the context of *the promise of His Coming?*

The studies continued as well as asking God for wisdom and understanding. The questions continued: How did the *good and comfortable words* relate to our time? Why are the years of Darius so precisely outlined after God gave Babylonia to the Mede and Persian (Darius and Cyrus)? I will be presenting these topics and many more topics in this book, *Seven Years to A Better Tomorrow*. In order to arrive at a better tomorrow, the time of *great tribulation*, which is patterned after the *great affliction* of Jacob's 7-year period, must occur. The good news is that Jacob, who represents the Israel of God (all believers), will be saved out of the time of Jacob's trouble (Jeremiah 30:7).

Judgment upon the fallen houses of God (where self-glorification will be despised) will ensue midway through the seven years. Following this judgment upon the fallen houses of God, a final worldwide salvation by God's Spirit will occur. God and His Word will be magnified. Some people may ask why God has done this to His *land and to His house:*

> **1Kings 9:8: And at this house, *which* is high, every one that passeth by it shall be astonished, and shall hiss; and they shall say, Why hath the LORD done thus unto this land, and to this house?**

> **1Kings 9:9: And they shall answer, <u>Because they forsook the LORD their God</u>, who brought forth their fathers out of the land of Egypt, and <u>have taken hold upon other gods, and have worshipped them, and served them</u>: therefore hath the LORD brought upon them all this evil.**

I know from the past that the opposition of piecing together God's Word has come from people who will claim that the above verses were only speaking to national Israel many years ago. The problem with this kind of logic is that God has written His Word in a very special way. What happened to national Israel back then is happening today within the fallen houses of God. What happened in Christ's day? The temple was overrun with moneychangers. They had turned His Father's house into a *house of merchandise*, and Christ overthrew the moneychangers:

> **John 2:16: And said unto them that sold doves, Take these things hence; <u>make not my Father's house an house of merchandise</u>.**

> **Psalm 92:7: When the wicked spring as the grass, and <u>when all the workers of iniquity do flourish</u>; *it is* that they shall be destroyed for ever: 8: But thou, LORD, art most high for evermore.**

In order to make the case of how we should study and compare scripture with scripture and spiritual with spiritual, we need to review some important verses. Let us first look at a prophecy from the book of Hosea and then compare it to the book of Revelation as Christ addresses the *seven churches*. Both verses are addressing false worship, and we know the *seven churches* encompass the fullness of all churches worldwide. In Hosea 10:8, the high places of *Aven* (idolatry) are where false worship occurred many years ago, yet the Lord re-introduces this in the book of Revelation. There is no new thing under the sun:

> **Hosea 10:8: The high places also of Aven, the sin of Israel, shall be destroyed: the thorn and the thistle shall come up on their altars; and they shall say to the mountains, Cover us; and to the hills, Fall on us.**

> **Revelation 6:16: And said to the mountains and rocks, Fall on us, and hide us from the face of him that sitteth on the throne, and from the wrath of the Lamb:**

Historical judgment occurs at the hands of the enemy. God sends judgment on Israel for committing abominations with the Philistines:

> **1Samual 13:6: When the men of Israel saw that they were in a strait, (for the people were distressed,) then the people did hide themselves in caves, and in thickets, and in rocks, and in high places, and in pits.**

When Jesus was being tried while walking the path to His crucifixion, He mentioned something I believe relates to the coming judgment on the houses of God:

> **Luke 23:27: And there followed him a great company of people, and of women, which also bewailed and lamented him. 28: But Jesus turning unto them said, Daughters of Jerusalem, weep not for me, but weep for yourselves, and for your children. 29: For, behold, the days are coming, in the which they shall say, Blessed *are* the barren, and the wombs that never bare, and the paps**

which never gave suck. 30: <u>Then shall they begin</u> <u>to say to the mountains, Fall on us; and to the hills,</u> <u>Cover us.</u> 31: For if they do these things in a green tree, what shall be done in the dry?

All of this information is found within God's Word, but, in order to understand this information, we all need to understand how God has orchestrated past history. Then we can grasp how He uses past Biblical history to show us the two *tribulation* periods prior to the *last day*. The first was the 8,400 days ending on May 21, 2011. The final *great tribulation*, which is a 7-year period, is where we are today, and the focus is upon the fallen houses of God.

It will be shown in this book how one prophecy found in the book of Daniel relates to the 3 ½ years of Christ ministry, but also, how it relates to the first 3 ½ years of the final seven years of history. Thus, at the time of the cross, Jesus was projecting a coming judgment to the *dry tree* which would match the end of the 3 ½ years near the anniversary date of the cross.

There is much information to cover in this book, but first, I would like to address every reader concerning how this information coming forth from God's Word, the Bible, needs to be shared with many people.

A Letter to the Reader

I want to thank every reader of this book for looking into this information coming forth from God's Word. I expect when certain events discussed in this book begin to take place, the readers, such as yourself, will need to be able to explain further to family, friends or anyone else in your circle of influence. The first thing I would suggest is asking God for wisdom and understanding. God places understanding of His Word as a top priority and wisdom is available for those who are not *double minded* but rather sincere:

> **James 1:5: If any of you lack wisdom, let him ask of God, that giveth to all *men* liberally, and upbraideth not; and it shall be given him**.

I originally set-up the YouTube channel *2011studies* as a continuance of my first book: *Countdown to the Last Day*. However, as time went on past the year 2011, so much information was coming forth that I felt this book was needed to get the word out rapidly. Please feel free to join the YouTube channel *2011studies* (one word). God willing, continued study will be posted in video form on that channel along with hymns and original songs.

I am always open to suggestions in getting this message out since we are all coming very close to the glorious return of Jesus in *power and great glory*. If you have any ideas email your suggestions to: sevenyearsbook2018@gmail.com with a cc to: *2011studies@gmail.com*. I am very confident that this information will be understood more and more as we approach the year 2015. As believers in Christ, we do need to warn, teach and admonish for it will be the task of the believers to *consume and destroy* the Kingdom of Satan as God and His Word will be magnified in a great way. This reversal by God comes after the *time, times and half a time* or the 3 ½ year halfway mark of the final seven years:

> **Daniel 7:25: And he shall speak *great* words against the most High, and shall wear out the saints of the most High, and think to change times and laws: and they shall be given into his hand <u>until a time and times and the dividing of time. 26: But the judgment shall sit, and they shall take away his dominion, to consume and to destroy it unto the end.</u> 27: And the kingdom and dominion, and the greatness of the kingdom under the whole heaven, shall be given to the people of the saints of the most High, whose kingdom *is* an everlasting kingdom, and all dominions shall serve and obey him.**

According to the second year of Darius, we are commanded by God to *work for He is with us*. We are promised that God will bless this work.[4] Let us redeem the time wisely that God has given us during these final years. Let us also put away disagreements and love one another. I suspect once we get closer to the 1,335[th] day, all believers in Christ will be in *one accord* as it was at the first Pentecost in 33 AD:

> **1 John 4:10: Herein is love, not that we loved God, but that he loved us, and sent his Son *to be* the propitiation for our sins. 11: Beloved, <u>if God so loved us, we ought also to love one another.</u>**

> **Acts 2:1: And when the day of Pentecost was fully come, <u>they were all with one accord</u> in one place.**

Chapter 1—The Worldwide Announcement of the Coming of Christ in 2011 A.D.

The world experienced a strange phenomenon in the year 2011, which really was propelled by the world media. Whatever the motivation of exposing the proclamation of Judgment Day being announced, the world ran with this topic in a huge way. Weekend comedy shows spoofed the theme of being *raptured*. People at soccer events mocked as huge banners of "Raptured" were hung over the stadium balconies. I personally saw news reports from various countries of the world speaking of May 21, 2011 as Judgment Day.

As recent as October 20, 2013, Troy Anderson wrote an article entitled, *Billy Graham Sounds Alarm for 2nd Coming*.[5] In this article Billy Graham spoke of Harold Camping's Judgment Day announcement on May 21, 2011. He, however, brought up other well-known people who also believe we are living in the last days. Mr. Anderson quoted Benjamin Netanyahu from the United Nations General Assembly stating, "Biblical prophecies are being realized." Mr. Anderson also quoted Rep. Michele Bachmann R-Minn, as well as musician Charlie Daniels.

There was one topic brought up in this article to which I have decided to dedicate an entire chapter in this book. The topic is the *Blood Moon Tetrad of 2014 and 2015*. I do believe the *Blood Moon Tetrad* (eclipses) in the years 2014 and 2015 are significant since they land precisely on Biblical feast celebrations. However, while some pastors are proclaiming a warning to national Israel, I really believe the tetrad completion is indicating a soon to be experienced judgment on the fallen houses of God. Whether there is a parallel to national Israel and *Jerusalem* or the fallen houses of God this is yet to be seen.

However, even before fully understanding how these blood moons were projected for 2014 and 2015, the year 2015 has been projected in my online studies as the precise midway point of the seven years. I have been warning how 2015 seems to be the year in history that lines up with judgment coming upon the houses of God. This judgment (*despising of their glory)* of the fallen houses of God will be a theme of interest in this book and discussed in various chapters. This topic is so significant that I believe many more people besides Prime Minister Benjamin Netanyahu, Rep. Michele Bachman, Billy Graham, and Charlie Daniels will be wondering what happened to God's houses of worship worldwide:

> **Ezekiel 38:23: Thus will <u>I magnify myself, and sanctify myself; and I will be known in the eyes of many nations</u>, and they shall know that I *am* the LORD.**

There are so many Biblical illustrations God has given as historical patterns that anyone who is serious about Bible study can understand, by God's Spirit, how this coming judgment has been foretold in prophecy. We can also know how God uses the names *Israel, Jerusalem,* and *Sodom and Egypt* to represent something from the past which relates to the fallen houses of God.

So why did this awakening in 2011 take place? In my studies of the Bible, I have come to learn that God is the one who *sets up kings, and removes kings.* He is the one who *stirs up the spirit of the Medes* and also stirred up the spirit of Zerubbabel to accomplish His will (Haggai 1:14). The grand announcement of the coming of Christ in the year 2011 was by no means an accident. 2011 A.D. was the 7,000[th] year anniversary of the flood. 2 Peter 3 proclaimed the importance of the Noachian Flood in relationship to the *promise of His coming* (*parousia*). So what happened? In the precise context of the *promise of His coming* found in 2 Peter 3, there are three very important points. Some people who have studied the Biblical Calendar of History[6] overlooked God's longsuffering in regards to the year 2011 being the 7,000[th] anniversary of the flood. These following points will each be covered in this book:

1. God is *longsuffering to usward not willing that any would perish.* Peter was directing us to Paul's writings so that we may know how Paul was the pattern of God's longsuffering. This was written to let us know that salvation by God's Spirit is still going forth.

2. The mocking of *Where is the promise of His coming?* had to take place. Some people could make the point that those individuals who do not profess Christ as Savior had their time of mocking, especially in the media. However, the language of 2 Peter 3 suggests that the mocking would come from those who profess creation as a viable truth:

2 Peter 3:3: Knowing this first, that there shall come in the last days scoffers, walking after their own lusts, 4: And saying, Where is the promise of his coming? For since the fathers fell asleep, <u>all things continue as they were from the beginning of the creation.</u> 5: For this they willingly are ignorant of, that by the word of

God the heavens were of old, and the earth standing out of the water and in the water...

I believe there was equal opposition and mocking coming forth from the leaders in the houses of God. Twice in the Bible, the Greek word for *scoffers* is used. *Empaiktes* (G1703) is the Greek Word for *derider/scoffer* and this word is used in 2 Peter 3, but also in the book of Jude. In Jude, God speaks of mockers in the last time in the context of those who are *murmurers*, complainers, and those who speak *great swelling words* and desire the admiration of men rather than God. These mockers have gone the way of Cain and ran after greedy motives:

> **Jude 1:11: Woe unto them! For they have gone in the way of Cain, and ran greedily after the error of Balaam for reward, and perished in the gainsaying of Core.**

It makes sense then that the mocking is coming from those who are concerned about *profiting*. This was the condition with the temple of Christ's day as He expelled the money changers who had turned His Father's house into a *house of merchandise*. In our day, the fallen houses of God worldwide have been corrupted by greed. I suspect that some people of the media may have mocked simply out of fear of the topic of Judgment Day. However, some leaders in the houses of God who should be as the Bereans, willing to look at Biblical information concerning the greatest event in our time (i.e.; the coming of Christ in *power and great glory*), rather settled on being *willingly ignorant* concerning Jesus' return on the *last day*:

> **2 Peter 3:5: For this they willingly are ignorant of, that by the word of God the heavens were of old, and the earth standing out of the water and in the**

water: 6: Whereby the world that then was, being overflowed with water, perished: 7: But the heavens and the earth, which are now, by the same word are kept in store, reserved unto fire against the day of judgment and perdition of ungodly men.

If the majority of the houses of God were professing the glorious return of Jesus on the *last day* instead of the fable of "you will be left behind," more people would be concerned about the *last day*. Instead, there is a *peace and safety* message and a real lack of concern of Jesus coming as the judge on the *last day*. Will this condition of *sleep* continue to be prevalent in the houses of God? In the next couple of years, as the glory of the houses of God becomes despised, more people will have a keen interest in God's Word and the topic of Judgment Day coming upon the world. After all, if judgment comes first on God's established churches, then what will be on the horizon for the entire world?

3. The third point that many Bible students missed concerning the year 2011 is that there are two *tribulation* periods in Biblical history. Admittedly, it was hard to understand if Jesus, in the Gospels, was warning of the *tribulation* and *great tribulation* as one and the same event. However, further study shows how *great tribulation* historically related to the 7-year famine of Joseph's time.

   Therefore, the 8,400 days ending on May 21, 2011 was, in fact, a true pattern of the 840 months of Judah's historical *tribulation* period. Once the Hebrew people came out of captivity, the years of Darius were at the forefront of rebuilding what had been destroyed by the King of Babylon. Likewise, what follows the year 2011 (the end of the 8,400-day *tribulation* period), based on the years of Darius and Joseph's 7-year famine is the time of *great affliction* or *great tribulation.*

Act 7:11: Now there came a dearth over all the land of Egypt and Chanaan, and great affliction: and our fathers found no sustenance. 12: But when Jacob heard that there was corn in Egypt, he sent out our fathers first.

This time of *great tribulation* was spoken of by Jesus as He warned of the difficulty of fleeing out once the abomination is seen in the houses of God. He proclaimed that we should pray that our *flight be not in the winter*, the time of the *great tribulation:*

Matthew 24:20: But pray ye that your flight be not in the winter, neither on the sabbath day: 21: For then shall be great tribulation, such as was not since the beginning of the world to this time, no, nor ever shall be. 22: And except those days should be shortened, there should no flesh be saved: but <u>for the elect's sake those days shall be shortened.</u>

Are we to even suggest that *great tribulation* comes upon the houses of God? Actually, yes, this is what Jesus was also warning of in the book of Revelation. In Revelation 2:20 Christ mentions Jezebel in the context of *great tribulation:*

Revelation 2:20: Notwithstanding I have a few things against thee, because thou sufferest that woman Jezebel, which calleth herself a prophetess, to teach and to seduce my servants to commit fornication, and to eat things sacrificed unto idols.

21: And I gave her space to repent of her fornication; and she repented not. 22: Behold, I will cast her into a bed, and them that commit adultery with her into great tribulation, except they repent of their deeds.

The mentioning of Jezebel as a warning to the church in Thyatira is a huge warning to the worldwide houses of God who adulterate the house of worship with false worship of man. Historically, Jezebel and her husband Ahab led Samaria into false worship; thus, God sent judgment:

1Kings 16:31: And it came to pass, as if it had been a light thing for him to walk in the sins of Jeroboam the son of Nebat, that he took to wife Jezebel the daughter of Ethbaal king of the Zidonians, and went and served Baal, and worshipped him. 32: And he reared up an altar for Baal in the house of Baal, which he had built in Samaria. 33: And Ahab made a grove; and Ahab did more to provoke the LORD God of Israel to anger than all the kings of Israel that were before him.

In Revelation 2, the Lord is giving fair warning for the houses of God to turn from false worship or else experience the fate of *great tribulation*. In Hosea 7, God speaks of chastising His people:

Hosea 7:1: When I would have healed Israel, then the iniquity of Ephraim was discovered, and the wickedness of Samaria: for they commit falsehood; and the thief cometh in, *and* the troop of robbers spoileth without...

> **Hosea 7:11: Ephraim also is like a silly dove without heart: they call to Egypt, they go to Assyria. 12: When they shall go, I will spread my net upon them; I will bring them down as the fowls of the heaven; <u>I will chastise them, as their congregation hath heard.</u>**

Incidentally, the two men who are mentioned in the book of James in the context of *unto the coming of the Lord* are Elijah and Job. Elijah was pursued by Jezebel and her evil actions. Elijah's prayer for no rain for the space of 3 ½ years, where false worship was occurring, is one reason why we are to look to Elijah as an example. The 3 ½ pattern of Elijah's prayer for no rain is repeated during the first half of the final seven years. During these 3 ½ years of abomination, the glory of the houses of God will be despised by the nations, especially towards the year 2015. This judgment on the fallen houses of God is patterned after the *glory of Moab being contemned*:

> **Isaiah 16:14: But now the LORD hath spoken, saying, <u>Within three years, as the years of an hireling, and the glory of Moab shall be contemned</u>, with all that great multitude; and the remnant *shall be* very small *and* feeble.**

> **Isaiah 21:16: For thus hath the Lord said unto me, <u>Within a year, according to the years of an hireling, and all the glory of Kedar shall fail</u>: 17: And the residue of the number of archers, the mighty men of the children of Kedar, shall be diminished: for the LORD God of Israel hath spoken *it*.**

The Almighty Lord of Heaven who, of course, has had the greatest scope of past Biblical history is allowing us to know, through His Word, that judgment upon the fallen houses of God is coming. The year 2015 will be highly important in bringing low the self-glorification of the fallen houses of God. God is no respecter of persons; what applies to the fallen houses of God as a whole, also applies to each individual as the Apostle Paul declares by God's Spirit:

> **Romans 2:9: Tribulation and anguish, upon every soul of man that doeth evil, of the Jew first, and also of the Gentile; 10: But glory, honour, and peace, to every man that worketh good, to the Jew first, and also to the Gentile: 11: For there is no respect of persons with God.**

Why all this language of judgment and tribulation? Is this book not about reaching a better tomorrow? I suspect that God, in His mercy, brings chastisement in order to get our wandering attention back to the straight and narrow. The Lord Jesus came to give life, incredible abundant life. If He needs to chastise His people to bring them back to a better place, then chastisement, while never easy to experience, produces an end result which is for our benefit.

A few years back as I studying the year 2011, I came across a verse which really caught my attention since it mentioned the *waters of Noah*.

<u>God Hides His Face—As the Waters of Noah</u>

Isaiah 54:7: For a small moment have I forsaken thee; but with great mercies will I gather thee. 8: In a little wrath I hid my face from thee for a moment; but with everlasting kindness will I have mercy on thee, saith the LORD thy Redeemer.

> **9: For this *is as* the waters of Noah unto me: for *as* I have sworn that the <u>waters of Noah</u> should no more go over the earth; so have I sworn that I would not be wroth with thee, nor rebuke thee.**

There are times in God's Word where He illustrates why He will hide His face. He will turn away from sin because He is righteous and holy, yet honorably, He returns and shows mercy.

False worship can cause God to hide His face which is the opposite of blessing.

> **Ezekiel 39:21: And I will set my glory among the heathen, and all the heathen shall see my judgment that I have executed, and my hand that I have laid upon them. 22: So the house of Israel shall know that I *am* the LORD their God from that day and forward.**

> **23: And <u>the heathen shall know that the house of Israel went into captivity for their iniquity</u>: because they trespassed against me, <u>therefore hid I my face from them, and gave them into the hand of their enemies</u>: so fell they all by the sword.**

> **24: According to their uncleanness and according to their transgressions have I done unto them, <u>and hid my face from them.</u>**

Since both the *tribulation* of the 8,400 days and the *great tribulation* of these current seven years intersect at the 7,000th year anniversary of the flood, perhaps this is why God relates the hiding of His face to *the waters of Noah*. Perhaps also, this is why after a short time God's mercy returns to save His people. Once Noah and his family exited the ark, they were instructed to be *fruitful and multiply*. Do you know that being fruitful and multiplying can relate to God saving people and increasing His people by His saving Spirit? These same words of *fruitful and multiply* are seen elsewhere in God's Word:

> **Genesis 9:1: And God blessed Noah and his sons, and said unto them, <u>Be fruitful, and multiply</u>, and replenish the earth.**

> **Leviticus 26:9: For I will have respect unto you, <u>and make you fruitful, and multiply you</u>, and establish my covenant with you.**

> **Ezekiel 37:26: Moreover I will make a covenant of peace with them; it shall be an everlasting covenant with them: and <u>I will place them, and multiply them</u>, and will set my sanctuary in the midst of them for evermore. 27: My tabernacle also shall be with them: yea, I will be their God, and they shall be my people. 28: And the heathen shall know that I the LORD do sanctify Israel, when my sanctuary shall be in the midst of them for evermore.**

Current Interest in the Noachian Flood

There seems to be much interest in the Noachian flood of 4990 B.C. Recently, I saw a trailer to the 2014 movie entitled, *Noah*.[7] I cannot speak of the accuracy of this movie since it is rare that Biblical truth is depicted honestly in movies anymore. There was one scene, however, which depicted the waters of the flood coming forth from the earth itself. That much of the movie is accurate as the Bible records how the *fountains of the great deep* or abyss were *broken up*:

Genesis 7:11: In the six hundredth year of Noah's life, in the second month, the seventeenth day of the month, the same day were <u>all the fountains of the great deep broken up</u>, and the windows of heaven were opened. 12: And the rain was upon the earth forty days and forty nights.

There is a creator who is righteous and looking upon the earth. He sees how His creation has turned their backs on Him. *Violence* filled the land, and judgment for this *violence* came as God brought the flood upon the entire earth:

Genesis 6:12: And God looked upon the earth, and, behold, it was corrupt; for all flesh had corrupted his way upon the earth. 13: And God said unto Noah, The end of all flesh is come before me; <u>for the earth is filled with violence</u> through them; and, behold, I will destroy them with the earth.

Prior to the year 2011, I had studied this Hebrew word for *violence* which is *chamas* (H2555 in the concordance). This word is highly related to false worship and turning away from the creator. The Hebrew word *chamas* is also found in the following verse where God is speaking to His people:

Micah 6:12: For the rich men thereof are full of <u>violence</u>, and the inhabitants thereof have spoken lies, and their tongue *is* deceitful in their mouth. 13: Therefore also will I make *thee* sick in smiting thee, in making *thee* desolate because of thy sins.

The Day of the Lord-A Time Period of Judgment

The *day of the Lord* is a term used in the Bible that is associated with judgment that falls on the fallen houses of God due to their *violence* or wrong doing. The *day of the Lord* is also known as a time in which God judges the *heathen* who represent the people of the nations. God, at this precise time in history, which may well be the reversal in the year 2015, renders recompense. Below are three verses that speak of this recompense. The first one from Zephaniah speaks of the judgment on the fallen houses of God. The second and third verses predict a time of the *heathen* or nations. This is when God sends recompense in such a way that only God can bring to pass such a massive event:

> **Zephaniah 1:7: Hold thy peace at the presence of the Lord GOD: for <u>the day of the LORD *is* at hand</u>: for the LORD hath prepared a sacrifice, he hath bid his guests. 8: And it shall come to pass in the day of the LORD'S sacrifice, that <u>I will punish the princes, and the king's children, and all such as are clothed with strange apparel.</u> 9: In the same day also will I punish all those that leap on the threshold, <u>which fill their masters' houses with violence and deceit.</u>**

> **Ezekiel 30:3: For the day *is* near, even the day of the LORD *is* near, a cloudy day; it shall be the time of the heathen.**

> **Obadiah 1:15: For the day of the LORD *is* near upon all the heathen: <u>as thou hast done, it shall be done unto thee: thy reward shall return upon thine own head.</u> 16: For as ye have drunk upon my holy mountain, *so* shall all the heathen drink continually, yea, they shall drink, and they shall**

swallow down, and they shall be as though they had not been.

It will be at this time, a time like no other in history, where God is recompensing for the evil that was done to His truths and His people. Yet, God is not glossing over the wrong done in the fallen houses of God either. God uses the word violence in relationship to what occurs within the fallen houses of God.

Violence and Deceit in the Fallen Houses of God

There seems to be a real connection with the violence or wrong doing in the days of Noah to similar activity within the fallen houses of God where deceit and wrong doing (*violence*) occurs. Both Jeremiah and Zephaniah prophesied against this deceit:

> **Jeremiah 9:6: Thine habitation is in the midst of deceit; <u>through deceit they refuse to know me,</u> saith the LORD.**
>
> **Zephaniah 1:9: In the same day also will I punish all those that leap on the threshold, which fill their masters' houses with <u>violence and deceit</u>.**

The Hebrew word *chamas* (H2555) is translated as violence and is related to the earth being corrupt and full of violence prior to the flood; Ezekiel also connects this word with false worship. Was there false worship prior to the flood? Most definitely there was. The Hebrew word translated as *corrupt* is associated with *stumbling at the law* and *corrupting the covenant* (Malachi 2: 8). In Ezekiel 45, God speaks to the princes of Israel and demands that equity is practiced and not violence and oppression. That was then, but now this false worship is addressed to the fallen houses of God:

Ezekiel 45:9: Thus saith the Lord GOD; Let it suffice you, O princes of Israel: remove violence and spoil, and execute judgment and justice, take away your exactions from my people, saith the Lord GOD.

Satan, who is the *king of fierce countenance* spoken of by Daniel, is the chief instigator of this deceit (*craft*) and *violence* as explained in Daniel 8:25 and Ezekiel 28:16:

Daniel 8:25: And through his policy also he shall cause <u>craft</u> to prosper in his hand; and he shall magnify *himself* in his heart, and by peace shall destroy many: he shall also stand up against the Prince of princes; but he shall be broken without hand.

Ezekiel 28:16: By the multitude of thy merchandise they have filled the midst of thee <u>with violence</u>, and thou hast sinned: therefore I will cast thee as profane out of the mountain of God: and I will destroy thee, O covering cherub, from the midst of the stones of fire.

The good news is that with all of Satan's self-glorying and prospering of deceit within God's houses of worship, there comes a time when he is removed by God. It is then that God is magnified (does *great things*) and this world will experience a time of salvation. God tells us to rejoice for what He will do:

Joel 2:20: But I will remove far off from you <u>the northern</u> *army*, and will drive him into a land barren and desolate, with his face toward the east sea, and his hinder part toward the utmost sea, and his stink shall come up, and his ill savour shall

51

come up, because he hath done great things. 21: Fear not, <u>O land; be glad and rejoice: for the LORD will do great things.</u>

God mentions very similar language that is found in the book of James *unto the coming of the Lord*. He creates a time of *rain*, which I believe is a time of understanding His Word, so that many will turn to Him for salvation. It will be a great time of blessing. Joel chapter 2 speaks of this great time that we are rapidly approaching:

Joel 2:22: Be not afraid, ye beasts of the field: for the pastures of the wilderness do spring, for the tree beareth her fruit, the fig tree and the vine do yield their strength. 23: Be glad then, ye children of Zion, and rejoice in the LORD your God: for he hath given you the former rain moderately, and <u>he will cause to come down for you the rain, the former rain, and the latter rain</u> in the first *month*.

So when is this time of blessing coming? This topic is most fascinating because in the book of James, God depicts Himself as the husbandman who waits for the precious fruit of the earth. However, first must come the *early and latter* seasonal rain of understanding. Remember also how this language found in James 5 is in the context of *unto the coming of the Lord*:

James 5:7: Be patient therefore, brethren, unto the coming of the Lord. Behold, the husbandman waiteth for the precious fruit of the earth, and hath long patience for it, <u>until he receive the early and latter rain.</u> 8: Be ye also patient; stablish your hearts: for the coming of the Lord draweth nigh.

How then does this relate to the seven years of *great tribulation* (2011 to 2018) that follows the 8,400 days ending on May 21, 2011? Do you remember when we discussed earlier the 3 ½ years of Elijah who prayed for no rain where false worship was occurring? We know by further reading of James chapter 5 that Elijah prayed yet again and rain came forth! The rain produced fruit! In the verse below, we see how Elijah (*Elias* in Greek) prays yet again and God sends rain:

> **James 5:17: Elias was a man subject to like passions as we are, and he prayed earnestly that it might not rain: and it rained not on the earth by the space of three years and six months. 18: <u>And he prayed again, and the heaven gave rain, and the earth brought forth her fruit.</u>**

Is God here alerting us to the truth that after 3 ½ years He will send the rain of understanding and great worldwide salvation will be the result? The patience of Job is also mentioned in the book of James. It is the parable of Job that ties the *latter rain* to something mankind will be very thirsty for- wisdom and understanding:

<u>Mankind Will be Thirsty for Wisdom & Understanding</u>

The book of Job has some great clues of the time of *latter rain.* This is where God grants understanding to His Word and salvation plan. When people begin to fear God this is when people begin to have wisdom. It is also important to depart from evil in order to have understanding. Since the duplication of *blessed is He that waits and comes to the 1335ᵗʰ day* is very significant in the year 2015, this does seem to be the time of *latter rain* as mentioned in the parable of Job 29:22-23:

> **Job 28:28: And unto man he said, Behold, the fear of the Lord, that is wisdom; and to depart from evil is understanding.**
>
> **Job 29:1: Moreover <u>Job continued his parable</u>, and said...**
>
> **Job 29:22: After my words they spake not again; and my speech dropped upon them. 23: And <u>they waited for me as for the rain; and they opened their mouth wide as for the latter rain.</u>**

In order for the precious fruit of the earth to come forth (salvation of souls), first must come the fear of God and with that comes wisdom and understanding. Salvation will be desired; knowledge of God's Word will be thirsted after. How can we know that the *precious fruit of the earth* is related to salvation of people worldwide?

Besides having a repeating of a worldwide Pentecost in the year 2015 which duplicates the first Pentecost (more on this later), the Greek word translated as precious is *Timios* (G5093). It is related to a believer's faith that is tried by fire which is called precious by God, but we also know the blood of Christ is precious. Let us look at these two verses for further understanding of the *precious fruit of the earth*:

> **1Peter 1:7: That <u>the trial of your faith, being much more precious than of gold that perisheth</u>, though it be tried with fire, might be found unto praise and honour and glory at the appearing of Jesus Christ: 8: Whom having not seen, ye love; in whom, though now ye see him not, yet believing, ye rejoice with joy unspeakable and full of glory: 9: Receiving the end of your faith, even the salvation of your souls.**

The blood of Christ is most precious for the remission of sins and hope of eternal life:

> **1 Peter 1:18: Forasmuch as ye know that ye were not redeemed with corruptible things,** *as* **silver and gold, from your vain conversation** *received* **by tradition from your fathers; 19: <u>But with the precious blood of Christ</u>, as of a lamb without blemish and without spot: 20: <u>Who verily was foreordained before the foundation of the world, but was manifest in these last times for you</u>, 21: Who by him do believe in God, that raised him up from the dead, and gave him glory; that your faith and hope might be in God.**

One could spend a lifespan stacking gold piece upon gold piece creating a massive mountain of gold, but that would be worthless if life itself was not granted. How precious is the blood of Christ? One would have to ask, how precious is the free gift of eternal life? How precious is the glorious new world to come where perfect peace and righteousness will reign? How precious is a Savior who draws a person out of the grave and raises them to eternal life? I would plead with anyone that true life everlasting is the single most precious thing we can possess.

The Bible uses language of Jesus as the *true vine*, and if we *abide in Him*, we are *the branches* that produce fruit. This truth is very similar to language found in Isaiah as the spirit of judgment comes to purge *Jerusalem* or the houses of God:

> **Isaiah 4:2: In that day shall the branch of the LORD be beautiful and glorious, and <u>the fruit of the earth</u>** *shall be* **excellent and comely for them that are escaped of Israel.**

> **John 15:1: I am the true vine, and my Father is the husbandman. 2: Every *branch* in me that beareth not fruit he taketh away: and every branch that beareth fruit, he purgeth it, that it may bring forth more fruit. 3: Now ye are clean through the word which I have spoken unto you. 4: Abide in me, and I in you. As the branch cannot bear fruit of itself, except it abide in the vine; no more can ye, except ye abide in me. 5: I am the vine, ye *are* the branches: <u>He that abideth in me, and I in him, the same bringeth forth much fruit: for without me ye can do nothing.</u>**

The casting forth of the Gospel, like seed, produces fruit, and when fruit comes forth, it is harvest time. The parable of casting seed given by Christ is found in Mark 4. This parable really illustrates why God, as the husbandman, is being so patient and forbearing with His creation while awaiting the fruit:

> **Mark 4:26: And he said, So is the kingdom of God, as if a man should cast seed into the ground; 27: And should sleep, and rise night and day, and the seed should spring and grow up, he knoweth not how. 28: For the earth bringeth forth fruit of herself; first the blade, then the ear, after that the full corn in the ear. 29: But <u>when the fruit is brought forth, immediately he putteth in the sickle, because the harvest is come.</u>**

As we study the glorious return of Jesus on the *last day*, we must remember what the book of James is teaching concerning *unto the coming of the Lord*. We are to understand that God, as *the husbandman*, is waiting patiently for the *precious fruit of the earth*. Once we understand that the prayer of Elijah for no rain, which resulted in 3 ½ years of no rain, fits the first half of the final seven years, then we can accept how the last 3 ½ years will be a time of *rain* and *fruit* will come forth:

> **James 5:17: Elias was a man subject to like passions as we are, and he prayed earnestly that it might not rain: and it rained not on the earth by the space of three years and six months. 18: And <u>he prayed again, and the heaven gave rain, and the earth brought forth her fruit.</u>**

The books of the New Testament are full of clues that when we find them, we can then compare the verses to the original source:

> **1Kings 17:1: And Elijah the Tishbite, *who was* of the inhabitants of Gilead, said unto Ahab, *As* the LORD God of Israel liveth, before whom I stand, there shall not be dew nor rain these years, but according to my word.**

At this time, I would suggest a continued study in 1 Kings 17 and onward to see how the rain came, how the prophets of Baal are defeated, and what resulted with Jezebel and her evil works. There was also something that Elijah did not discern and that fact was how he was not alone; God had reserved unto Himself 7,000 people who did not bow the knee to Baal and false worship. Once we reach the 2015 mark, I believe a real separation will be seen in this world; God's power will be magnified in a great way.

The year 2011 A.D. was an extremely important year as it was the 7,000[th] anniversary of the Noachian flood. It was also a turning point to show that God is longsuffering. God has used both the time of Judah's 70-year captivity and also

Jacob's seven years of *great tribulation* as our examples to understand the timing of the end. Let us study further to see how these two historical accounts are separate *tribulation* periods just prior to *the coming of the Lord*.

Chapter 2—The Separation of the 8,400-Day Tribulation, & the Final 7-Year Great Tribulation

The most incredible aspect of studying the Bible is that God seems to reveal truths very close to the proximity of the events that are about to take place. Many of us who were studying the year 2011 and how that year lined up with the 7,000th anniversary of the flood, did not fully understand one thing: God has divided the 8,400 days of *tribulation* (which was a short version of Israel's 840 month captivity) from the time of *great tribulation*. Once that truth was better understood, then we had a great outline of seven years past the year 2011. Why seven years?

In the Bible, the term *great tribulation* and *great affliction* are one and the same. Jesus spoke of *great tribulation* in the book of Revelation but also in Matthew chapter 24. In the book of Acts, we see yet another mention of the term *great affliction* and how that related to Joseph storing up food in Egypt and his family coming to Egypt to live in the land of Goshen.

> **Act 7:11: Now there came a dearth over all the land of Egypt and Chanaan, and <u>great affliction</u>: and our fathers found no sustenance. 12: But when Jacob heard that there was corn in Egypt, he sent out our fathers first.**

> **Genesis 41:53: And the seven years of plenteousness, that was in the land of Egypt, were ended.**
>
> **54: And the seven years of dearth began to come, according as Joseph had said: and the dearth was in all lands; but in all the land of Egypt there was bread.**

When we follow on in study, we learn by Jesus' words that this time of *great tribulation* is a time of real spiritual famine in the land. Jesus warned of this time prior to His coming (*parousia*) on the *last day*:

> **Matthew 24:21: For then shall be great tribulation, such as was not since the beginning of the world to this time, no, nor ever shall be. 22: And except those days should be shortened, there should no flesh be saved: but for the elect's sake those days shall be shortened.**

Much like the time of Joseph where food supplies were stored up in Egypt, during this present *great tribulation;* the people who were studying God's Word during the 8,400 days would have plenty of spiritual food. In the book of Amos, God tells us that He will send a famine of *hearing the words of the LORD*. In Amos 8, God also mentions the sin of Samaria. We have learned previously that Ahab and Jezebel brought false worship to Samaria. God once again is showing how this historical account of *famine in the land* relates to His Word being scarce where false worship is taking place.

> **Amos 8:11: Behold, the days come, saith the Lord GOD, that <u>I will send a famine in the land, not a famine of bread, nor a thirst for water, but of hearing the words of the LORD</u>: 12: And they**

shall wander from sea to sea, and from the north even to the east, they shall run to and fro to seek the word of the LORD, and shall not find *it*.

Them of Understanding…

We also can know that before the end of this present world, there are certain people who *understand* the truths coming forth from God's Word. The Bible uses the term *them of understanding*. The book of Daniel speaks of those who *understand* these truths from God's word:

> **Daniel 11:33: And <u>they that understand among the people shall instruct many</u>: yet they shall fall by the sword, and by flame, by captivity, and by spoil, *many* days. 34: Now when they shall fall, they shall be holpen with a little help: but many shall cleave to them with flatteries. 35: And *some* <u>of them of understanding shall fall</u>, to try *them*, and to purge, and to make them white, *even* to the time of the end: because *it is* yet for a time appointed.**

The same Hebrew word translated as *understanding* is also the identical word used in relation to Daniel and his fellow companions in captivity. The Hebrew word is *sakal* (H7919) and is translated as *skill* in Daniel 1:17:

> **Daniel 1:17: As for these four children, God gave them knowledge and <u>skill in all learning</u> and wisdom: and Daniel had understanding in all visions and dreams.**

So where does this *skill* or *understanding* come from? The phrase *skill in all learning* can be translated by the concordance as *intelligence in all the writing or book*. In fact, Daniel 1 states that God gave them *knowledge and skill in all learning.* By this information in God's Word, and with Daniel as an example, we can understand that there is a two-step process to coming to understanding in God's Word. First we must ask God for wisdom and understanding of His Word just as Daniel asked to understand the things of the end:

> **Daniel 10:12: Then said he unto me, Fear not, Daniel: for from the first day that thou didst set thine heart to understand, and to chasten thyself before thy God, thy words were heard, and I am come for thy words.**

Then we must wait patiently for God to grant wisdom:

> **Daniel 10:13: But the prince of the kingdom of Persia withstood me one and twenty days: but, lo, Michael, one of the chief princes, came to help me; and I remained there with the kings of Persia.**

Twenty One Days Daniel had to Wait

Why would God want us to know about the spiritual warfare in the above verse that hindered Daniel from being granted the understanding that he desired? Twenty one days is not a long time to wait for understanding. Yet, what is God showing us with this number? One truth I have come to understand about the time of the end is that God will not reveal information concerning the end before it is time for the specific truth to be understood. The entire 8,400 days, which ended May 21, 2011, is 4 x 2,100. From the Jubilee year in 1994 to 2015 it is 21 years. Therefore, the end of the first *tribulation* period that ended May 21, 2011 and also the year 2015 are both important times when God gave and will give more understanding.

All in One Accord- Pentecost 2015

The year 2015 is a crucial aspect in this study because this is the year in which a repeating of *blessed is he that waits and comes to the 1,335ᵗʰ day* occurs. We will study how this prophecy is related to both the first Pentecost in 33 A.D., but also how it relates to a worldwide Pentecost in the upcoming year 2015 A.D. First, however, I would like to show how at Pentecost in 33 A.D. understanding came forth by Peter. Peter was given understanding by God to explain what had transpired from the betrayal of Christ to the resurrection of the Lord. Peter stood up at Pentecost and began explaining God's Word. In Acts chapter 1, we have the account of the disciples, Mary, and the other women being in *one accord* in prayer and supplications:

> **Act 1:14: These all continued with <u>one accord</u> in prayer and supplication, with the women, and Mary the mother of Jesus, and with his brethren.**

It was then that Peter stood up and began to explain something concerning a prophecy from the book of Psalms that foretold of Judas' desolation:

> **Acts 1:16: Men *and* brethren, this scripture must needs have been fulfilled, <u>which the Holy Ghost by the mouth of David spake before concerning Judas</u>, which was guide to them that took Jesus. 17: For he was numbered with us, and had obtained part of this ministry.**

> **Acts 1:18: Now this man purchased a field with the reward of iniquity; and falling headlong, he burst asunder in the midst, and all his bowels gushed out. 19: And it was known unto all the dwellers at Jerusalem; insomuch as that field is**

called in their proper tongue, Aceldama, that is to say, the field of blood. 20: <u>For it is written in the book of Psalms,</u> Let his habitation be desolate, and let no man dwell therein: and his bishoprick let another take.

Peter was expounding from the Word of God how Judas' actions (as the *son of perdition*), was a direct fulfillment of God's Word. I really believe that this explaining by Peter is showing us considerable information. With the repeating of the 1,335 prophecy being fulfilled for the second time in the year 2015, many are going to understand by the expounding of God's Word how the *son of perdition* (Satan) sought to destroy God's houses/people during the time of the *abomination which makes desolate*.

In the case of the year 2015, Satan's *last end of the indignation* (3 ½ years) will have expired and many will understand what God's Word has been proclaiming. In other words, the 21 years from 1994 to 2015 will be finally reached and many more people will understand God's Word. I also suspect that believers worldwide will be in *one accord*. Being of one accord would also include understanding of what Satan has done during this time of *great tribulation*. We can know this because both Judas and Satan are termed the *son of perdition*.

Judas as the *son of perdition*:

John 17:12: While I was with them in the world, I kept them in thy name: those that thou gavest me I have kept, and <u>none of them is lost, but the son of perdition; that the scripture might be fulfilled.</u>

Satan as the *son of perdition*:

> **2 Thessalonians 2:3: Let no man deceive you by any means: for** *that day shall not come,* **except there come a falling away first, and that man of sin be revealed,** <u>the son of perdition</u>**; 4: Who opposeth and exalteth himself above all that is called God, or that is worshipped; so that he as God sitteth in the temple of God, shewing himself that he is God.**

The day of Christ shall not come unless there is a falling away first and the *man of sin* is revealed. We are in the final years of the *falling away*. Satan is called the *son of perdition* and the *man of sin*. The Lord is called a *man of war*.

> **Exodus 15:3: The LORD** *is* **a man of war: the LORD is his name. 4: Pharaoh's chariots and his host hath he cast into the sea: his chosen captains also are drowned in the Red sea.**

Some teachers of God's Word have suggested the *man of sin* to be antichrist who is to come. Yet, the Bible teaches that many antichrists are already in the world:

> **1 John 2:18: Little children, it is the last time: and as ye have heard that antichrist shall come, even now are there many antichrists; whereby we know that it is the last time.**

In Revelation 21:17, God's word interchanges the measure of a man with that of an angel:

> **Revelation 21:17: And he measured the wall thereof, an hundred** *and* **forty** *and* **four cubits,** *according to* **the measure of a man, that is, of the angel.**

When studying to understand the things of the end, it is important to see how Satan operated at the time of Christ.

65

Satan came with the Word of God tempting Christ. Satan also had control of the temple as the house of God had become the *house of merchandise*. Satan entered into Judas and Judas did his bidding. It does not take much observation by anyone in this world to know that the abomination which makes desolate has been occurring in the fallen houses of God.

A close look at the houses of God will show that the falling away has been and is now occurring. Whether observing the sin of greed, false worship, or the prosperity gospels etc., one can tell that something is not right in the houses of God. Further, it does not take much to view online the falling away as extreme activity of *signs and lying wonders* is occurring. Jesus spoke about this when He answered the disciples about the *sign of His coming and the end of the world* (age):

> **Matthew 24:4: And Jesus answered and said unto them, Take heed that no man deceive you. 5: For many shall come in my name, saying, I am Christ; and shall deceive many.**

Many Deceivers Come in Jesus' Name Saying: "I am Anointed"

Many will come in Jesus name and say *I am Christos*. In Greek, the name *Christos* means *anointed*. Truly, Jesus was the Lord from Heaven, the anointed one. However, the disguised ministers of evil who are coming in Jesus name proclaiming: "I have the anointing of the Holy Spirit," and then proceeding to practice *signs and lying wonders*, will encounter the judgment of the true Christ. When will this judgment come? I believe the next couple years will be the timing of the Lord judging the fallen houses of God.

It is one thing to see this strange activity in the churches, yet, even more incredible is the understanding that God has set up historical patterns so we will realize when judgment comes. God uses the following terms/warnings which, when studied, reveal much about this judgment that will fall upon the fallen houses of God:

1. *Babylon has fallen, has fallen.*
2. The *Glory of Moab* will be despised.
3. The *Day of the Lord is at Hand.*
4. The *Glory of Kedar will fail.*
5. When the people in the churches say: "peace and safety," then comes sudden destruction.
6. They will also say "peace, peace" when there is no peace.
7. The *falling away* must come first.
8. The *abomination that makes desolate* will be seen.

If Jesus did not hold back judgment on the temple in His day for becoming *a house of merchandise,* what will be the outcome when the fallen houses of God worldwide come under judgment? In the year 2011, which was the 7,000[th] year anniversary of the flood, God could have judged the entire world at that point. However, God's longsuffering and His salvation plan govern when judgment will come.

What Comes After the 8,400 Days?

One of the difficult things to understand concerning the 8,400 days, which ended in the year 2011, was the question of what comes next. The signs of the great *falling away* in the houses of God were seen and understood by many Bible students. Yet, God, in His mercy, slowly started to reveal more from His Word. Not only was there the pattern of Judah's 70-year *captivity/tribulation* (the 8,400 days), but God also used the historical *great tribulation* to show us all how there would be a final 7-year extension of time. God placed the historical 7-year famine of Joseph's time in the Bible to let us know about the spiritual famine that was to come upon the houses of God at the end of time.

Once the dividing of the 8,400 day *tribulation* period and the 7-year *great tribulation* period was understood, then many other timelines fit perfectly. The final 7-years encompass many Biblical events:

1. Elijah prays for no rain and for the space of 3 ½ years no rain occurs where there is false worship.
2. Within three years the *Glory of Moab* will be despised according to *the years of a hireling*.
3. Within one year the *Glory of Kedar* will fail.
4. The *last end of the indignation* is when Satan is only given a final *time, times and half time* (3 ½ years).
5. *Blessed is He that waits and comes to the 1,335th day.*
6. The spiritual wickedness during Christ's 3 ½ year ministry is repeated from 2011-2015.
7. There is a repeating of the 1,290 days to the 1,335th day from Trumpets 2011 to Pentecost 2015.
8. The blood moon tetrad falls on precise feast days in 2014 and 2015 indicating the Lord's judgment coming upon the fallen houses of God.
9. Directly after the 840 months, God gave Babylon to the Mede and the Persian. After the 8,400 days, the mirror of the years of Darius the Mede would then repeat during the final 7-years.
10. The rebuilding process after the captivity, in which the temple was complete in the sixth year of Darius, follows the timeline to the year 2018.

11. God's promise to *shake heavens and earth* and to *overthrow the strength of the kingdoms of the heathen* occurs during the years of Darius.
12. The early and latter rains are promised by God in both Joel 2 and also in the book of James, *unto the coming of the Lord.*

One Day is as a Thousand Years

2 Peter 3 is full of great information concerning the coming of Jesus on the last day. The patient waiting, the enduring unto the end is all important. There is something that does seem to relate to creation itself and that is how God views time:

2 Peter 3:8: But, beloved, be not ignorant of this one thing, that one day *is* with the Lord as a thousand years, and a thousand years as one day.

The ISA renders the last part of 2 Peter 3:8 as: *and a thousand years is as day one.* Is God relating every 1000 years as day one? Since the context of 2 Peter 3 is the world perishing at the time of the flood, then the year 2011 was significant in being the 7,000[th] year anniversary of the flood. God told Noah with a final advance warning that there would be *yet seven days* before He would destroy the world with the flood. Is God now warning the world, from the year 2011, *yet seven years?* Since the context of 2 Peter 3 is also about God's longsuffering, then this does seem to be what God has established with the number 7 during the final seven years.

There is no doubt that God has precisely fit many events within the final seven years of history. Is there any good news within all of these strong declarations coming from God's Word? Yes, there is good news! Once we reach the halfway mark of the final seven years in the year 2015, God performs a great reversal and is magnified in a great way.

> **Joel 2:21: Fear not, O land; be glad and rejoice: for the LORD will do great things.**

In Jeremiah 4:23, God speaks of a time when the earth is without form and void. This sounds very much like the language of Genesis 1:2:

> **Genesis 1:2: And the earth was without form, and void; and darkness *was* upon the face of the deep. And the Spirit of God moved upon the face of the waters.**

The similarities are really quite amazing. The phrase *without form* can be translated as desolate based on the Hebrew word *tohu* (H8414). The earth was desolate and empty/void in the beginning. However, Jeremiah 4:23 speaks of a time of *destruction upon destruction* and yet God sees the world in the same way as in Genesis 1:2. The times of *tribulation* produce desolation and emptiness. Jeremiah 4 seems to be speaking of the times of *tribulation* as *they have none understanding: they are wise to do evil, but to do good they have no knowledge.*

Another key phrase in Jeremiah 4 is how the *fruitful place* became *a wilderness.* We can know this is significant by a close study of Isaiah 32:15. It is there that the wilderness is turned into a fruitful field:

> **Isaiah 32:15: <u>Until the spirit be poured upon us from on high</u>, and the wilderness be a fruitful field, and the fruitful field be counted for a forest.**

Let us take a close look at the book of Joel and the importance of the reversal God performs according to His Word. When does God perform this great reversal?

Chapter 3—God is Magnified as Judgment Comes Upon the Fallen Houses of God

I really do not think there is a book in the Bible that in some way does not relate to what is happening in this present time. Genesis speaks of the sun and the moon being for signs, seasons, days and years:

> **Genesis 1:14: And God said, Let there be lights in the firmament of the heaven to divide the day from the night; and let them be for signs, and for seasons, and for days, and years...**

The blood moon eclipses of 2014 may be indicating a real pre-warning of judgment on the fallen houses of God worldwide. This could mean that the time of judgment will come according to the proper associated feast in which the eclipses occur. The blood moons do fall on precise *seasons* in God's perfect calendar (Passover and Tabernacles). Passover is connected to the judgment time of Christ as the Passover lamb. The feast of Tabernacles represents the coming out of Egypt. Thus, Passover in 2015 would represent the time of judgment upon the fallen houses of God, and Tabernacles would represent the fleeing out of what is spiritually called *Sodom and Egypt* (the fallen houses of God). What are a few examples that show how certain books of the Bible relate to our time?

In the book of Exodus, the journey out of Egypt displays how God's people near Christ's return would come out of *Sodom and Egypt* (the fallen houses of God) and flee to God.

Jeremiah became the weeping prophet who was under stocks showing the *captivity* of the end.

The book of Daniel outlines some very precise times concerning the things of the end, including the *last end of the indignation*. The book of Joel is no different. It depicts a time in which evil comes against Israel for their sin. Then God, in His mercy, reverses this evil and He alone is magnified. Could God be using the language of Joel to show us today how the evil comes upon the houses of God? How has this evil *barked His tree*? How does God then reverse the evil for His magnification? Joel is a most fascinating book that only has three chapters. In those three chapters there is such a great detailed outline of the time we are all living.

Joel chapter one opens with a warning to the *drunkards* and describes how a *fierce nation* has come upon the land and *barked His fig tree*. The fig tree is bare, the vine wasted, and the land is left desolate:

> **Joel 1:6: For a nation is come up upon my land, strong, and without number, whose teeth *are* the teeth of a lion, and he hath the cheek teeth of a great lion. 7: He hath laid my vine waste, and barked my fig tree: he hath made it clean bare, and cast it away; the branches thereof are made white.**

The timing of this historical event is the King of Babylon coming up against Judah for their sins. This can be shown by a parallel verse in Jeremiah 30. One key phrase used both in Joel and Jeremiah involves God *returning/reversing the captivity of Israel and Judah*:

> **Jeremiah 30:3: For, lo, the days come, saith the LORD, that <u>I will bring again the captivity of my</u>**

**people Israel and Judah, saith the LORD: and I
will cause them to return to the land that I gave to
their fathers, and they shall possess it.**

**Joel 3:1: For, behold, in those days, and in that
time, when I shall bring again the captivity of
Judah and Jerusalem,**

God uses the term *the Northern* as being the invader. Thus,
the king of Babylon was involved in this invasion of Judah.
We know from the book of Isaiah (Isaiah 14:4) that God
compares the King of Babylon with Satan himself. Therefore,
the historical language of *the captivity of Judah and Jacob's
trouble* does identify with the 8,400 days first and then
finally the *last end of the indignation*. Satan was given a final
assault period of a *time, times and half time* (3 ½ years) in
which he wages a final war on the houses of God. In Joel 2,
God is placing a strong emphasis on the house of God and
the priests. There is a warning to those people who are *drunk
with wine* similar to what is found in the book of Amos:

**Amos 2:8: And they lay *themselves* down upon
clothes laid to pledge by every altar, and they
drink the wine of the condemned *in* the house of
their god.**

In Jeremiah 30:7, we learn that Jacob is saved out of *great
tribulation* and also the reversal God eventually performs.
How, though, can we be sure this is speaking of a time of
great tribulation or, in other words, the 3 ½ years from 2011
to 2015? Within the chapter of Jeremiah 30 that mentions
God reversing the captivity, we have language that separates
this time from any other time in history. The language below
sounds very similar to the warning Jesus gave in Matthew of
great tribulation. Let's compare these verses:

Jeremiah 30:7: Alas! For that day *is* great, <u>so that none *is* like it: it *is* even the time of Jacob's trouble</u>; <u>but he shall be saved out of it</u>. 8: For it shall come to pass in that day, saith the LORD of hosts, that I will break his yoke from off thy neck, and will burst thy bonds, and strangers shall no more serve themselves of him: 9: But they shall serve the LORD their God, and David their king, whom I will raise up unto them.

Matthew 24:21: For then shall be <u>great tribulation, such as was not since the beginning of the world to this time, no, nor ever shall be.</u> 22: And except those days should be shortened, there should no flesh be saved: but for the elect's sake those days shall be shortened.

We now have three major connections with the timeline of Joel. We have the time of *Jacob's trouble* (a spiritual reliving of the seven year famine of Joseph's time) spoken of in Jeremiah 30. We have both Joel and Jeremiah proclaiming that God will perform a reversal of the captivity. By God's Word proclaiming the time of *Jacob's trouble,* we can see a real care by God saying Jacob (God's people) will be saved out of it. This truth is also seen in Isaiah 33:2:

Isaiah 33:2: O LORD, be gracious unto us; we have waited for thee: be thou their arm every morning, <u>our salvation also in the time of trouble</u>. 3: At the noise of the tumult the people fled; at the lifting up of thyself the nations were scattered.

The Mystery of Matthew 24:22

Matthew 24:22 has been a puzzle to many Bible students, myself included. In Matthew 24:22, the days are shortened for the elect's sake. This places a heavy emphasis on God's salvation plan governing the length of time Satan is allowed to desolate the houses of God. After the period of the first half of the seven years, God's salvation plan multiplies worldwide. The time of *Jacob's trouble* was a full seven years, yet we know that Satan is given a precise time of 3 ½ years, which is called *the last end of the indignation*:

> **Daniel 8:19: And he said, Behold, I will make thee know what shall be in the last end of the indignation: for at the time appointed the end shall be.**

> **Daniel 12:7: And I heard the man clothed in linen, which *was* upon the waters of the river, when he held up his right hand and his left hand unto heaven, and sware by him that liveth for ever that <u>*it shall be* for a time, times, and an half</u>; and when he shall have accomplished to scatter the power of the holy people, all these *things* shall be finished.**

We will discuss Daniel 12 in a dedicated chapter. I, however, want to discuss how it is possible that the shortened time of *great tribulation* is limited to 3 ½ years. God uses very precise words in Matthew 24:22 when He mentions: *And except those days should be shortened, there should no flesh be saved: but for the elect's sake those days shall be shortened.* Why would God use the word *flesh in Matthew 24:22*? I feel the answer can be found in 1 Peter where God refers to mankind as *flesh*. Flesh is like the grass that fades away. In this context, God is highlighting *being born again by the Word of God*. It is salvation and the Word of God that endures forever:

> **1 Peter 1:23: Being born again, not of corruptible seed, but of incorruptible, by the word of God,**

> **which liveth and abideth for ever. 24: <u>For all flesh</u>
> *<u>is</u>* <u>as grass, and all the glory of man as the flower</u>
> <u>of grass.</u> The grass withereth, and the flower
> thereof falleth away: 25: But the word of the Lord
> endureth for ever. And this is the word which by
> the gospel is preached unto you.**

All flesh is as grass, and all the glory of man as the flower of the grass. Neither one lasts forever, not the flesh and certainly not the glory of man. By Christ *shortening* the days, He may be proclaiming that His election plan of saving man (flesh) will go forth. Satan's plan of destruction will leave desolation, but God is going to reverse the situation. This truth matches perfectly with the *Gospel of the kingdom* going forth before the end comes:

> **Matthew 24:14: And this <u>gospel of the kingdom</u>
> shall be preached in all the world for a witness
> unto all nations; and then shall the end come.**

With the onset of the worldwide geo-engineering of the upper atmosphere (hazardous chemical spraying), we can't escape that when man attempts to act like God, he fails miserably. There is a possibility that if the days were not shortened no flesh would be saved could have a physical reality. However, I believe the first meaning of God shortening the days is for the purpose of God saving people by His Spirit.

What is the Gospel of the Kingdom?

The *gospel of the kingdom* is defined in the Bible by the actions of Jesus as He went forth preaching *the gospel of the kingdom.* By His words, we can know the *gospel* (good news) *of the kingdom* is initiated by *repent and believe the gospel:*

Mark 1:14: Now after that John was put in prison, Jesus came into Galilee, preaching the gospel of the kingdom of God, 15: And saying, The time is fulfilled, and the kingdom of God is at hand: repent ye, and believe the gospel.

Jesus, after John was put in prison, was really focusing on the time having arrived. It is time to repent (think differently) and believe the Gospel (good news) of the kingdom. We know that Jesus emphasized that the kingdom of God is within us as we experience salvation. In the following verse, however, He seems to be really placing a strong emphasis on the *kingdom of heaven* being near.

Matthew 4:16: The people which sat in darkness saw great light; and to them which sat in the region and shadow of death light is sprung up. 17: From that time Jesus began to preach, and to say, Repent: <u>for the kingdom of heaven is at hand</u>.

Why would Jesus begin saying this during His 3 ½ year ministry when His return on the *last day* would not be for many years to come? I can hear people argue, "You see the Bible is not accurate; it was many years ago that Jesus proclaimed the *kingdom of heaven is at hand.*" Please be patient though, as we will begin to see in this study how God has repeated both the time of desolation of the house (s) of God, and also His great plan of salvation, which lines up with Pentecost in 33 A.D. This is why the reversal in the book of Joel is so important. Double fulfillment of scripture means the time truly is *at hand* when the prophecy is fulfilled the second time in history, very near the coming of Jesus on the last day.

Joel is not merely an historical account of judgment upon Judah and Jerusalem. It is an illustration of what happens to

79

the houses of God and also God's people near the timing of Christ's return. Now it is much easier to understand Jesus' proclamation that *the kingdom of heaven is at hand*. He commanded people to think different and believe. He taught the disciples to preach the same *Gospel of the kingdom:*

> **Matthew 10:7: <u>And as ye go, preach, saying, The kingdom of heaven is at hand</u>. 8: Heal the sick, cleanse the lepers, raise the dead, cast out devils: freely ye have received, freely give.**

We are in the midst of the repeating of the 3 ½ years from 29 A.D. to 33 A.D. These seven years that follow the 8,400 days, which ended May 21, 2011, truly will experience a double fulfillment of more than one Bible prophecy. The *kingdom of heaven* most definitely is *at hand*.

How Will God be Magnified?

The book of Joel is truly an incredible study. God speaks of *the Northern* who at some point in time is *removed*. It is then that God Himself is magnified. This comes after the time of the barking of the *fig tree*. Once *the Northern* is removed into a *barren and desolate* place, it is then God's time to be magnified. The reproach upon God's people will no longer be something the believers must endure:

> **Joel 2:18: Then will the LORD be jealous for his land, and pity his people. 19: Yea, the LORD will answer and say unto his people, Behold, I will send you corn, and wine, and oil, and ye shall be satisfied therewith: and <u>I will no more make you a reproach among the heathen</u>...**

> **Joel 2:20: <u>But I will remove far off from you the northern *army*, and will drive him into a land</u>**

barren and desolate, with his face toward the east sea, and his hinder part toward the utmost sea, and his stink shall come up, and his ill savour shall come up, because he hath done great things. 21: Fear not, O land; be glad and rejoice: for the LORD will do great things.

God, in other passages of the Bible, speaks of Satan who lifts himself up to be as God:

2 Thessalonians 2:4: Who opposeth and exalteth himself above all that is called God, or that is worshipped; so that he as God sitteth in the temple of God, shewing himself that he is God.

Revelation 13:5: And there was given unto him a mouth speaking great things and blasphemies; and power was given unto him to continue forty *and* two months. 6: And he opened his mouth in blasphemy against God, to blaspheme his name, and his tabernacle, and them that dwell in heaven.

During the time of the 8,400 days and also during the 42 months or a *time, times and half time*, Satan is given a certain time to cause desolation. The *last end of the indignation* is a period of 42 months or 3 ½ years. Satan, in his feeble attempt to be *as God,* speaks *great things* and magnifies himself. In Joel 2, the words *great things* have a meaning of being *magnified.* It applies first to *the Northern* who does *great things* and then to God Himself as He promises to do *great things* once *the Northern* is removed.

The Hebrew word for *magnified* is *gadal* (H1431) in the Bible concordance. There are two verses in which this same word is used. I feel these verses give a very proper understanding of being magnified. First, Abraham's name was made large:

> **Genesis 12:2: And I will make of thee a great nation, and I will bless thee, and <u>make thy name great</u>; and thou shalt be a blessing...**

Second, Isaac was blessed of God and became very great (*gadal*):

> **Genesis 26:12: Then Isaac sowed in that land, and received in the same year an hundredfold: and the LORD blessed him. 13: And the man waxed great, and went forward, and grew until <u>he became very great</u>:**

So we now have two great examples of God's blessing to make one *great*. However, in Joel 2 it is God Himself who will be magnified and a grand showing of His eternal magnification will be seen by the world. So much so that God proclaims that there should be no more fear in the land:

> **Joel 2:21: Fear not, O land; be glad and rejoice: for the LORD will do great things. 22: Be not afraid, ye beasts of the field: for the pastures of the wilderness do spring, for the tree beareth her fruit, the fig tree and the vine do yield their strength.**

All the Trees of the Field

Let's go back to Joel 1 and review the language of the *vine* and the *fig tree*. There is also language that is very similar to the words of Jesus in the Gospels when He mentions: *all the trees of the field.* God is the one who sends the judgment that dries up the trees and their produce. This is a righteous judgment for the sins of His people. Israel was the historical example of what God does to His houses of worship at the end of time. Yet, there seems to be a promise of a great reversal. Let us examine this language of judgment from God:

> **Joel 1:12: The vine is dried up, and the fig tree languisheth; the pomegranate tree, the palm tree also, and the apple tree, *even* all the trees of the field, are withered: because joy is withered away from the sons of men.**

The book of Habakkuk also uses very similar language of the destruction of God's houses. There is also a big time clue mentioned in Habakkuk. *In the midst of the years* a plea is made to *revive thy work*:

> **Habakkuk 3:2: O LORD, I have heard thy speech, *and* was afraid: O LORD, <u>revive thy work in the midst of the years, in the midst of the years make known; in wrath remember mercy.</u>**

This is very exciting language because Habakkuk also speaks of the failing of the fruitful trees and vines:

> **Habakkuk 3:17: Although the fig tree shall not blossom, neither *shall* fruit *be* in the vines; the labour of the olive shall fail, and the fields shall yield no meat; the flock shall be cut off from the fold, and *there shall be* no herd in the stalls.18: Yet I will rejoice in the LORD, I will joy in the God of my salvation.**

Perhaps Habakkuk could still rejoice because he understood of the coming magnification of God. Perhaps he understood how the reviving of God's work would take place in the *midst of the years*. This does line up very well with the 3 ½ years which began the final seven years of *Jacob's trouble*. I believe this time is truly from 2011 to 2018 with a mid-way point in the year 2015. Joel 2 and Habakkuk 3 have much in common, and we can learn much from these chapters concerning the final years of history. We also need to look at the words of Jesus now as He mentions the following:

> **Luke 21:29: And he spake to them a parable; <u>Behold the fig tree, and all the trees</u>; 30: When they now shoot forth, ye see and <u>know of your own selves that summer is now nigh at hand.</u> 31: So likewise ye, when ye see these things come to pass, <u>know ye that the kingdom of God is nigh at hand.</u>**

Jesus is relating the *shooting forth* of the fig tree and all the trees to *summer being at hand*. This parable is showing us that when we see these things in Luke 21 that the *kingdom of God is nigh at hand*.

We know from Matthew 24 that Jesus related the time of *great tribulation* to *winter*. There, we are instructed to pray that our flight out of the fallen houses of God would not be during the time of *winter*, indicating that it would be a hard exit out. Then we have the language in Joel 2 of God being magnified. Also, Habakkuk speaks of God reviving His work in the *midst of the years*. I have read many commentaries on *the fig tree* representing national Israel becoming a nation in the year 1948. However, the great reversal by God in the *midst of the years* may represent God's people bringing the Gospel into the entire world to produce fruit. All the trees of the field begin to shoot forth, spiritual winter is over and fruitful summer is on the way.

The Vine and the Fig Tree

God first established the vine and the fig tree as a blessing of safety and peace:

1 Kings 4:25: And Judah and Israel dwelt safely, every man under his vine and under his fig tree from Dan even to Beersheba, all the days of Solomon.

The *vine* and the *fig tree* are also related to people of the nations coming to *the mountain of the house of the Lord* and seeking out God in the last days:

Micah 4:1-4: But <u>in the last days</u> it shall come to pass, *that* the mountain of the house of the LORD shall be established in the top of the mountains, and it shall be exalted above the hills; and people shall flow unto it. 2: And many nations shall come, and say, Come, and let us go up to the mountain of the LORD, and to the house of the God of Jacob; and <u>he will teach us of his ways, and we will walk in his paths:</u> for the law shall go forth of Zion, and the word of the LORD from Jerusalem. 3: And he shall judge among many people, and rebuke strong nations afar off; and they shall beat their swords into plowshares, and their spears into pruninghooks: nation shall not lift up a sword against nation, neither shall they learn war any more. 4: But <u>they shall sit every man under his vine and under his fig tree; and none shall make *them* afraid</u>: for the mouth of the LORD of hosts hath spoken *it*.

Micah 4 mentions how many nations will begin to desire the Lord's *ways and paths* as they come up to the *mountain of the house of the Lord.* This seems opposite of the time of *great tribulation* when there is *nation rising against nation* and *kingdom against kingdom* (Matthew 24:7).

Zechariah 3 and the Years of Darius

The book of Zechariah also speaks of the *vine* and the *fig tree*, which, by the verses listed above, we can understand how God has used these words as a blessing from Him. A time of spiritual growth and a time of salvation are related to the *vine* and the *fig tree* producing fruit. Zechariah 3 is so important in the timeline of the final years (2011-2018) because it is within the context of the second year of Darius. We will study the *years of Darius* in a future chapter, but, for now, the second year of Darius lines up with the years 2013-2014.

In Zechariah 3, the following takes place:

1) *Jerusalem* is declared to be the *brand that was plucked out of fire.*
2) Joshua, in filthy garments, is given clean garments.
3) Satan begins his accusations in opposition to God's actions.
4) God forecasts the future rebuking of Satan, and then he is not found accusing again in Zechariah 3.
5) Joshua is told that if he will walk in God's ways and keep His charge that he will judge or rule His house.
6) The stone laid before Joshua had *seven eyes*.
7) A promise is given that *the Branch*, who is Christ, would come forth.
8) The promising language of the *vine* and the *fig tree* comes to pass.

   Zechariah 3:10: In that day, saith the LORD of hosts, shall ye call every man his neighbour under the vine and under the fig tree.

God Will Shortly Rebuke Satan

I believe Zechariah 3 is a dramatic illustration of what happens during the final years of history (2011-2018). As we approach the year 2015, there is a good possibility that Satan will be rebuked by God. The ISA renders the words of rebuking as: *Yahweh to the adversary- He shall rebuke.* This would mean that Satan, as he stands as the *accuser of the brethren,* is warned that his rebuking is coming. The word *rebuke* is never a trivial non-effective word in the Bible. When we study this word, and especially because the Lord is the one who does the rebuking, we find that the result of His rebuking is dramatic. Here are some examples from God's Word which feature God performing a rebuke:

When the Lord Rebukes (*Gaar*- H1605):

> **Psalms 106:9: <u>He rebuked</u> the Red sea also, and <u>it was dried up</u>: so he led them through the depths, as through the wilderness. 10: And he saved them from the hand of him that hated *them*, and redeemed them from the hand of the enemy.**

> **Isaiah 17:13: The nations shall rush like the rushing of many waters: but <u>*God* shall rebuke them</u>, and they shall flee far off, and shall be chased as the chaff of the mountains before the wind, and like a rolling thing before the whirlwind.**

God Rebukes the Devourer (Satan):

> **Malachi 3:11: And <u>I will rebuke the devourer</u> for your sakes, and he shall not destroy the fruits of your ground; neither shall your vine cast her fruit before the time in the field, saith the LORD of hosts. 12: And all nations shall call you blessed:**

for ye shall be a delightsome land, saith the LORD of hosts.

The above examples alone should be enough to illustrate to us that when God rebukes, it is powerful. Satan must have known this as he stood accusing Joshua. This warning of being rebuked by God would have caused a real fear. If God dried up the Red (reed) sea to allow for escape from the enemy, what will be the outcome when Satan is rebuked by God? What will be the end result when God removes *the Northern* as found in Joel chapter 2? God will be magnified and God's people will no longer be a reproach to the non-believer (Ezekiel 36:15).

Prior to May 21, 2011, the information concerning God removing *the Northern* was presented in the book *Countdown to the Last Day*. However, at that time, the years of Darius, the rebuking of Satan, the reversal *in the midst of the years*, and many other timeline issues were simply not fully understood. In my studies, I have learned that God will increase understanding a couple of years prior to the event. Is there evidence for this? I believe so as God gave information to Amos two years before the earthquake:

> **Amos 1:1: The words of Amos, who was among the herdmen of Tekoa, which he saw concerning Israel in the days of Uzziah king of Judah, and in the days of Jeroboam the son of Joash king of Israel, <u>two years before the earthquake.</u>**

Amos 1 introduces the *two years before the earthquake* and then goes on to describe God's judgment coming upon many historical lands. Jesus will *roar from Zion* and *the habitations of the shepherds shall mourn*. How are we to understand this language? This is, yet again, an example of how God uses past history to illustrate the coming judgment on the *habitations* of those who are supposed to be shepherding God's flock. God also mentions the top of Carmel in Amos:

> **Amos 1:2: And he said, The LORD will roar from Zion, and utter his voice from Jerusalem; and the habitations of the shepherds shall mourn, and the top of Carmel shall wither.**

The top of Carmel is mentioned in Amos 9 as a hiding place, but there is no hiding place from God's judgment:

> **Amos 9:3: And though they hide themselves in the top of Carmel, I will search and take them out thence; and though they be hid from my sight in the bottom of the sea, thence will I command the serpent, and he shall bite them. 4: And though they go into captivity before their enemies, thence will I command the sword, and it shall slay them: and I will set mine eyes upon them for evil, and not for good.**

I really believe God is drawing from past history to illustrate how His judgment will come upon the fallen houses of God, whose sin is like that of Samaria (Ahab and Jezebel's propagating false worship). This is why Elijah prayed for no rain, and for 3 ½ years there was no rain. When he began to anticipate rain, he went up to the top of Carmel and sent forth a messenger to examine toward the sea:

> **1Kings 18:42: So Ahab went up to eat and to drink. And Elijah went up to the top of Carmel; and he cast himself down upon the earth, and put his face between his knees, 43: And said to his servant, Go up now, look toward the sea. And he went up, and looked, and said, there is nothing. And he said, <u>Go again seven times.</u>**

The rain came; in fact, the Bible calls it *great rain* (1 Kings 18:45). Rain is also one aspect of the book of Joel. When God removes *the Northern*, the land is blessed. God promises an abundance of rain:

> **Joel 2:23: Be glad then, ye children of Zion, and rejoice in the LORD your God: for he hath given you the former rain moderately, and he will cause to come down for you the rain, the former rain, and the latter rain in the first *month*. 24: And the floors shall be full of wheat, and the fats shall overflow with wine and oil. 25: And I will restore to you the years that the locust hath eaten, the cankerworm, and the caterpillar, and the palmerworm, my great army which I sent among you.**

The Rain of Understanding that Leads to Salvation

Since Elijah's prayer for no rain is mentioned in the book of James, within the context of *unto the coming of the Lord,* believers in Jesus should take note of this information. When we study the *early* and *latter rain,* we also really need to look at Job's parable concerning *latter rain.* I believe this parable is speaking of a real desire to understand God's Word. People will be thirsting for the truth of God's Word. Further, the judgment upon the fallen houses of God may create this thirst for truth:

> **Job 29:21: Unto me *men* gave ear, and waited, and kept silence at my counsel. 22: After my words they spake not again; and my speech dropped upon them. 23: <u>And they waited for me as for the rain; and they opened their mouth wide *as* for the latter rain.</u>**

Now let us compare the book of James and the mention of the *early* and *latter rain*:

> **James 5:7: Be patient therefore, brethren, unto the coming of the Lord. Behold, the husbandman waiteth for the precious fruit of the earth, and hath long patience for it, <u>until he receive the early and latter rain.</u> 8: Be ye also patient; stablish your hearts: for the coming of the Lord draweth nigh.**

Is it a mere coincidence that the Bible mentions both Elijah and Job in the book of James with the focus on rain? Not at all, God's Word is the perfection of truth and His Word is as rain which comes to give understanding to His people:

> **Deuteronomy 32:1: Give ear, O ye heavens, and I will speak; and hear, O earth, the words of my mouth. 2: <u>My doctrine shall drop as the rain, my speech shall distil as the dew, as the small rain upon the tender herb, and as the showers upon the grass:</u> 3: Because I will publish the name of the LORD: ascribe ye greatness unto our God. 4: *He is* the Rock, his work *is* perfect: for all his ways *are* judgment: a God of truth and without iniquity, just and right *is* he.**

In this chapter, we have examined how the language of Joel declares a time of reversal from the *years of destruction.* During this time Satan has desolated the fallen houses of God. The comparisons between past historical judgment and future judgment are an amazing aspect of how God wrote His Word. The good news is that Satan's power will be diminished in the year 2015 and eventually destroyed at the powerful coming of Jesus on the last day. Is there any evidence of the past that shows this great reversal? Yes, I believe God has revealed some incredible truths concerning the 3 ½ years of Jesus ministry. The ultimate result of the cross in 33 A.D. can very possibly become a worldwide re-living of Pentecost in the year 2015. Judgment arose first and then came the result of the cross, which was a time of great salvation. You may be asking the question: How can the historical events of the cross and Pentecost in 33 A.D. possibly relate to the year 2015? We must examine this most incredible discovery which is coming forth from God's Word.

Chapter 4—Blessed is He that Waits: The Double Fulfillment of Prophecy- 33 A.D. & 2015 A.D.

The study of God's Word, the Bible, may be new to some readers. Other people may have been active in Bible study for years now. No matter where you are in the study of God's Word, one thing we must understand is that God must perform the unveiling of truth. In the year 2013, a good friend mentioned to me how Pentecost in 33 A.D. may be an important link in the year 2015 A.D. As I listened, I wondered how this information would relate to the seven years from 2011 to 2018. It did seem important, but it was not until I received an email outlining this information from my friend that I understood how important this timeline would be.

Is it possible that God has caused to come to pass a prophecy, not just once, but twice in the timeline of His salvation plan? This idea became really exciting to me because I had always puzzled how a prophecy seemed related to the time of Christ (7 B.C. to 33 A.D.), but then it shifted to language of the last days. How can this be? This would mean that what happened at the time of Pentecost in 33 A.D. would repeat worldwide in 2015. It was at Pentecost that God's Spirit saved about 3,000 people in one day:

> **Acts 2:38: Then Peter said unto them, Repent, and be baptized every one of you in the name of Jesus Christ for the remission of sins, and ye shall receive the gift of the Holy Ghost. 39: For the**

promise is unto you, and to your children, and to all that are afar off, *even* **as many as the Lord our God shall call. 40: And with many other words did he testify and exhort, saying, <u>Save yourselves from this untoward generation</u>. 41: Then they that gladly received his word were baptized: and the same day there were added** *unto them* **about three thousand souls.**

The Untoward Generation

In Acts chapter 2, Peter proclaimed *be ye being saved from the crooked generation* as translated in the Interlinear Scripture Analyzer (ISA). *Save yourselves* is really not a proper translation in the King James Bible. The ISA has it as: *be ye being saved.* This matches the truth of God's Spirit *baptizing* for the remission of sins. I want to point out the similarities between the time prior to Pentecost in 33 A.D. and also the time leading up to 2015. How does the Bible define the *crooked generation*?

The Greek word for crooked/untoward is *skolios* (G4646). There is a promise in the Bible that God will make the *crooked straight* and the *rough ways smooth.* Isaiah's prophecy of this action from God is seen when John the Baptist cries out *prepare the way of the Lord, make his paths straight.* This command was given as people came to be baptized by John in the year 29 A.D.

Yet, the *making straight* related to salvation at Pentecost as God's Spirit saved about 3,000 and Peter declared: *Be ye being saved from this crooked generation* (ISA). The very act of God's Spirit saving is defined *making the crooked straight.* The prophecy in Isaiah 40:4 declares the following:

- Every valley exalted

- Every mountain and hill made low
- The crooked made straight
- The rough places made plain

In Isaiah 41, God gives more information about what He does in the plains and valleys:

> **Isaiah 41:17: *When* the poor and needy seek water, and *there is* none, *and* their tongue faileth for thirst, I the LORD will hear them, I the God of Israel will not forsake them. 18: I will open rivers in high places, and <u>fountains in the midst of the valleys:</u> I will make the wilderness a pool of water, and the dry land springs of water.**

In Deuteronomy 15, God gave the command to take care of *the poor and needy*, for they will always be *in the land*. The Bible also speaks of the oppressor who will be judged by God for mistreating the *poor and needy:*

> **Psalm 72:3: The mountains shall bring peace to the people, and the little hills, by righteousness. 4: He shall judge the poor of the people, <u>he shall save the children of the needy, and shall break in pieces the oppressor.</u> 5: They shall fear thee as long as the sun and moon endure, throughout all generations. 6: <u>He shall come down like rain upon the mown grass: as showers *that* water the earth.</u>**

The reversal that God speaks about throughout His Word seems to be lined up with the time of Pentecost in 33 A.D. However, what if we could show that the time of Pentecost is repeated in the year 2015 by examining God's important feast days and the prophecy spoken of in Daniel 12? We would then have much to look forward to in the year 2015!

The 1,335 Day Prophecy of Daniel

The book of Daniel has an incredible prophecy of blessing which comes when a precise timeline is reached. That timeline is 1,335 days in length. Part of that timeline includes the mention of 1,290 days. I believe the 1,290 days fits within the 1,335 days. The 1,290 days is all about desolation, and coming to the 1,335[th] day means the waiting is over; God reverses things in a huge way.

I would like to now go back a couple of years and quote something that I presented in the book: *Countdown to the Last Day.* In the book *Countdown,* I attempted to show how some really good Bible study work was presented in the book: *Time Has and End—A Biblical History of the World, by Harold Camping—Vantage Press.*[8] This Bible study work showed how the first prophecy of the 1,335 days started with the time of Jesus' baptism by John and went to the time of Pentecost. After this quote, I will present some new information concerning how the 1,335 day prophecy also relates to our time and will have fulfillment in the year 2015. The following is from the book *Countdown to the Last Day* (pages 237- 239):

> It has been established that once the time of the end is entered, God would give understanding of the things of the end. In the book, Time Has an End- A Biblical History of the World- 11,013 BC-2011 AD, Harold Camping gives one of the best explanations, though not fully conclusive, of the 1,290 to 1,335-day prophecy of Daniel when he states on page 320:
>
> "When we include both the day of Christ's baptism and the day of Pentecost, we end up with precisely 1,335 days. When we examine the 1,335 days we can

> *pinpoint that period on the calendar. The end of it is*
> *on Pentecost in A.D. 33." ~Harold Camping~*

Likewise, in the book *1994?*, Camping[9] lists on pages 412-413 a very precise answer to the 1,335-day prophecy starting with Jesus' baptism on September 28, 29 A.D. (Feast of Trumpets) to May 24, 33 A.D. (Pentecost). The original *blessed is he that waits* prophecy saw fulfillment on Pentecost in 33 A.D. when God saved about 3,000 people. The above detailed information cannot be a mere coincidence when showing the number 1,335, which implies *blessed is he that waits*.

> Quote from *Countdown* continued: *There indeed was a great blessing of salvation at the time of Pentecost. That was a fairly significant bit of information that Camping recorded, yet when we look at the exact prophecy of the 1,290 days to the 1,335th day, something seems to be missing when we read Daniel 12:11:*
>
> **Daniel 12:11: And from the time that the daily sacrifice shall be taken away, and the abomination that maketh desolate set up, there shall be a thousand two hundred and ninety days. 12: Blessed is he that waiteth, and cometh to the thousand three hundred and five and thirty days.**
>
> *Camping saw that the 3 ½ literal years of Christ's ministry was 1,278 days, then he added 5 days from Palm Sunday to the Cross, plus the 1 day from the cross to Saturday in the tomb, plus the Saturday of the crucifixion to Pentecost (a waiting period of 50 days). This does equate to 1,335 days inclusive. However, when we look at the prophecy of Daniel, we see that God is mentioning the "abomination that*

makes desolate." In Matthew 24, Christ referred us to the book of Daniel and the "abomination of desolation." This is in regards to the events prior to His return in power and great glory. Was Camping incorrect with this very precise, detailed answer to the 1,335 day prophecy? <u>There is something I am seeing with some of the prophecies and that is, they have a double fulfillment in history.</u>

Camping's summation seems to be very accurate. One thing that we know is that Satan's taking over the temple in Christ's day was the result of this same kind of "abomination." The activity of devils was very prevalent during Christ's time on earth as He cast out devils. Then in God's Word we learn that Christ mentioned that He must bind the strong man, only to be loosed again during the little season of the end.

~End of quotes from *Countdown to the Last Day, Time Has an End,* and *1994?* ~

In reviewing my own words from my last book *Countdown,* it would have been better if I had said: *the result of Satan taking control of the temple in Christ's time produced the evidence of the abomination.* The same is true for today. Satan, who is an evil fallen angel, is given a *little season* to bring about desolation as he seeks worship in the houses of God. Satan works through *his ministers* who come with *signs and lying wonders* and who glory in themselves:

2 Corinthians 11:12: But what I do, that I will do, that I may cut off occasion from them which desire occasion; <u>that wherein they glory</u>, they may be found even as we. 13: For such *are* false apostles, deceitful workers, transforming themselves into the apostles of Christ. 14: And no marvel; for

Satan himself is transformed into an angel of light. 15: Therefore *it is* no great thing if his ministers also be transformed as the ministers of righteousness; whose end shall be according to their works.

Paul said in the above verse, *But what I do, that I will do* in order to *cut off* opportunity of those who gloried in themselves. He used very strong language of *false apostles* and *deceitful workers*. Paul was obviously concerned that he should not be a burden to the Corinthians, and therefore, gained support from the brothers in Christ from Macedonia. There was an obvious problem with those *deceitful workers* in Corinth who gloried in themselves for gain. Paul decided the best way to *cut off* opportunity of this activity was to continue doing what he was doing, bringing the Gospel without deceit:

2 Corinthians 11:9: And when I was present with you, and wanted, I was chargeable to no man: for that which was lacking to me the brethren which came from Macedonia supplied: and in all *things* I have kept myself from being burdensome unto you, and *so* will I keep *myself.*

Paul was encountering the activity of Satan who was working through *deceitful workers* in Corinth. Paul knew that by staying on course and continuing to bringing the truth of the Gospel, without burdening the hearers with his personal needs (he was a tent maker), that this would eventually win souls. Thus, by his truthful actions, Paul was causing the *deceitful workers* to eventually be exposed. Paul himself exposed one *child of the devil* who was attempting to sway one away from the truth of the true Gospel:

> **Acts 13:8: But Elymas the sorcerer (for so is his name by interpretation) withstood them, seeking to turn away the deputy from the faith. 9: Then Saul, (who also *is called* Paul,) filled with the Holy Ghost, set his eyes on him, 10: And said, O full of all subtilty and all mischief, *thou* child of the devil, *thou* enemy of all righteousness, wilt thou not cease to pervert the right ways of the Lord?**

Satan has not changed his game plan. He has set out to turn many away from the faith. This true saving faith is what Christ gives freely. He will use people to bring about *subtlety* (deceit). Christ warned that this would be the activity prior to His return. The false Christ's will come in the name of Jesus but then proclaim *I am anointed* and glory in themselves for profit by performing *signs and lying wonders.*

We now know the nature of the deception that takes place within the fallen houses of God near the end. We also understand that from the baptism of Christ to Pentecost in the year 33 A.D. there was 1,335 days, thus, partially fulfilling the prophecy of Daniel concerning the 1,335 days. I say *partially* because if we know that Satan will be loosed for a *little season* to accomplish desolation, then the 1,290 days ending with 1,335 days should have a dual fulfillment in the year 2015. How is that possible?

The All Important Feast Celebrations

The feast days that God has pre-established many years ago can help us understand the double fulfillment of the 1,335 days. The reason why God established the feast celebrations in the Old Testament is because they were pointing to every fulfillment in Christ and also the atonement of His work on the cross. However, the feast days go beyond the first coming of Christ. There are two very significant feast days which are related to the 1,290 and 1,335 day prophecy: the *Feast of Trumpets* and the *Feast of Weeks/Pentecost*. John the Baptist announced Jesus on a precise feast day—the *Feast of Trumpets*. This was the grand announcement of Jesus as a voice from Heaven declared the reality of who He was:

> **Matthew 3:16: And Jesus, when he was baptized, went up straightway out of the water: and, lo, the heavens were opened unto him, and he saw the Spirit of God descending like a dove, and lighting upon him: 17: And lo a voice from heaven, saying, This is my beloved Son, in whom I am well pleased.**

The Feast of Trumpets was set forth in the book of Leviticus:

> **Leviticus 23:24: Speak unto the children of Israel, saying, in the seventh month, in the first *day* of the month, shall ye have a Sabbath, a memorial of blowing of trumpets, an holy convocation.**

This memorial of a *shout* was foreshadowing the rest/ Sabbath in the Christ. It was set aside for a *meeting of holiness*. If there was ever an example of the holiness of Christ, it was from the mouth of John as he proclaimed:

> **Matthew 3:13: Then cometh Jesus from Galilee to Jordan unto John, to be baptized of him. 14: But John forbad him, saying, I have need to be baptized of thee, and comest thou to me? 15: And Jesus answering said unto him, Suffer *it to be so* now: for thus it becometh us to fulfil all righteousness. Then he suffered him.**

This introduction of Christ by John the Baptist was a *holy meeting* as the Spirit of God descended upon Christ when He ascended out of the river Jordan. The Feast of Weeks (Pentecost) was also a *holy convocation* (meeting) as the Spirit of God saved about 3,000 souls.

> **Numbers 28:26: Also in the day of the firstfruits, when ye bring a new meat offering unto the LORD, after your weeks *be out*, ye shall have an holy convocation; ye shall do no servile work...**

From the Feast of Trumpets in 29 A.D. to the Feast of Weeks (Pentecost) in 33 A.D., there were 1,335 days. The 7 weeks of 49 days followed by the 50th day of Pentecost really did show a mini-jubilee. The jubilee year was after every 49th year; thus, the 50th year was the year of Jubilee. Jubilee was significant as it was a proclamation to set the captives free; it was a time of liberty:

> **Leviticus 25:10: And ye shall hallow the fiftieth year, <u>and proclaim liberty throughout *all* the land unto all the inhabitants thereof</u>: it shall be a jubilee unto you; and ye shall return every man unto his possession, and ye shall return every man unto his family.**

Jesus came to proclaim true liberty. The realization of this liberty is salvation by God's Spirit as seen at the time of Pentecost. About 3,000 souls were delivered from death at the time of Pentecost:

> **Luke 4:17: And there was delivered unto him the book of the prophet Esaias. And when he had opened the book, he found the place where it was written, 18: The Spirit of the Lord *is* upon me, because he hath anointed me to preach the gospel**

to the poor; he hath sent me to heal the brokenhearted, to preach deliverance to the captives, and recovering of sight to the blind, <u>to set at liberty them that are bruised</u>, 19: To preach the acceptable year of the Lord.

The year 2015 is such an important year in the timeline of God's salvation plan. Why? Because I believe the information my friend in Christ sent me fits perfectly with my personal studies of the final seven years. Not only is Pentecost 2015 important, but what follows the 1,335[th] day is equally important since salvation will continue. The example of this is found in the book of Acts. Once God's Spirit saved the people unto eternal life, they continued in the doctrine of the disciples and God added to the church (eternal church) daily. Talk about setting the captives free!

This time of salvation in 33 A.D. was so significant that if 2015 mirrors this great time after the cross, then this world will experience a special historical event of God being magnified. Forget about the antichrist sentiment of today, this time will be different. The *Northern* (Satan) will have been removed. This magnification of God is after the 3 ½ years of the *last end of the indignation.* Satan was only given *a time, times and half time* (3 ½ years) to complete the *last end of the indignation.* After the 3 ½ years, God will do *great things,* which comes after Satan's work of *great things* i.e., lifting himself up as God.

I want to now look at the prophecy of Daniel and the 1,335 days. Then I want to compare how, incredibly, Pentecost in 33 A.D. will be repeated at Pentecost in 2015, except now on a worldwide scale. This would also mean that the *Day of the Lord,* which is a time of darkness and not light, is repeated during the *time, times and half time* that Satan has to desolate the fallen houses of God. We are all awaiting the time in the year 2015 when we arrive at the second fulfillment of this prophecy from Daniel 12:

> **Daniel 12:11: And from the time *that* the daily *sacrifice* shall be taken away, and the abomination that maketh desolate set up, *there shall be* a thousand two hundred and ninety days. 12: Blessed *is* he that waiteth, and cometh to the thousand three hundred and five and thirty days.**

The 1,260, 1,290 and the 1,335 Days

In my studies of God's Word, I have found the double fulfillment of God's Word to be the most plausible answer to more than one prophecy. For instance, in the book of Joel, we have prophecy that was directly spoken of by Peter as the fulfillment of the book of Joel:

> **Acts 2:15: For these are not drunken, as ye suppose, seeing it is *but* the third hour of the day. 16: But this is that which was spoken by the prophet Joel; 17: And it shall come to pass in the last days, saith God, I will pour out of my Spirit upon all flesh: and your sons and your daughters shall prophesy, and your young men shall see visions, and your old men shall dream dreams...**

Peter continues:

> **Acts 2:20: The sun shall be turned into darkness, and the moon into blood, before that great and notable day of the Lord come: 21: And it shall come to pass, *that* <u>whosoever shall call on the name of the Lord shall be saved.</u>**

We can know that there was a promise of Elijah coming before the great and terrible (dreadful) day of the Lord. Jesus wanted His people to know how John the Baptist, or the voice of John, fulfilled this prophecy.

> **Malachi 4:5: Behold, I will send you Elijah the prophet before the coming of the great and dreadful day of the LORD: 6: And he shall turn the heart of the fathers to the children, and the heart of the children to their fathers, lest I come and smite the earth with a curse.**

> **Matthew 11:13: For all the prophets and the law prophesied until John. 14: And if ye will receive *it*, this is Elias, which was for to come.**

In Amos chapter 5, God relates the *day of the Lord* as a time of darkness. It is a time when God despises their feasts, not hearing their songs of melody, and Bethel (house of God) coming to nothing. Then we read in verse 7 how God causes those who engage in false worship to go into captivity. It is a time of God issuing forth judgment and righteousness:

> **Amos 5:24: But let judgment run down as waters, and righteousness as a mighty stream.**

Therefore, we can associate the *day of the Lord* with the desolation of the temple and the impact of judgment. The time somewhere between the beginning of the 1,335 days from when Jesus was baptized by John in 29 A.D. to Pentecost in 33 A.D. did see fulfillment of the *day of the Lord.* This timing was most likely the time of the cross:

> **Luke 23:44: And it was about the sixth hour, and there was a darkness over all the earth until the ninth hour. 45: And the sun was darkened, and the**

veil of the temple was rent in the midst. 46: And when Jesus had cried with a loud voice, he said, Father, into thy hands I commend my spirit: and having said thus, he gave up the ghost. 47: Now when the centurion saw what was done, he glorified God, saying, certainly this was a righteous man.

The 1,260, the 1,290 and the 1,335 fit the timing of when Jesus' 3 ½-year ministry was fulfilled. *Note: See charts in the back section of this book.* This time was also a time of heavy wickedness from Satan and his army. The activity of Christ casting out devils and Satan's involvement with the apostate temple gives us a pattern to follow. Jesus' 3 ½-year ministry began with the Feast of Trumpets and went to the cross. Then 50 days later was Pentecost, which completed the 1,335 days. This exact pattern is repeated from 2011 to 2015. In our time of *great tribulation*, the *day of the Lord* is about judgment coming on the fallen houses of God. The *last end of the indignation* or *time, times and half a time* (3 ½ years) is the time in which Satan is allowed to desolate.

The following chart shows something very special. Carefully note how the specific feast celebrations in 2015 (Trumpets to Pentecost) are an exact duplication to the time of Jesus' ministry (29 A.D. to 33 A.D.). The chart on the following page shows this duplication of the 1,335 day prophecy found in the book of Daniel.

The Pattern of the 1,335 Days Repeats from 2011 to 2015!		
Feast of Trumpets 9-28-0029 (Jesus is Baptized)	←1,335 Days→	Pentecost 5-24-0033 About 3,000 saved
Feast of Trumpets 9-28-2011	←1,335 Days→	Pentecost 5-24-2015 Great time of salvation worldwide

This is one of the most important pieces of information God has revealed post 2011. This is a duplication of the 3 ½-year ministry of Jesus with a repeating of Satan being given a *time, times and half time* (3 ½ years)—1,260 days. Many of the time periods of the end such as Elijah's 3 ½ years of no rain, the 1,260, the 1,290 of desolation, all seem to fit very well within the 1,335 day period. During this time ending in the year 2015, we should see an increase in the *spirit of antichrist,* in which many people come against Christ and even His disciples (His foundation). *Note: The charts in the back of the book diagram these precise timelines that are mentioned though out this book. Please reference the charts when needed.*

I have seen much evidence of this online as attacks on the Apostle Paul have been waged claiming he was the definition of a *ravening wolf*. Ironically, the very ones who are the *ravening wolves* are waging these attacks on Paul. The human foundations such as Paul were chosen by Jesus in a dramatic way. If Satan wanted to disrupt God's salvation then an attempt to discredit Paul would be the first plan of attack, since His attempt to tempt Jesus failed. This is why Jesus warned in Matthew 7 of these false prophets:

> **Matthew 7:15: Beware of false prophets, which come to you in sheep's clothing, but inwardly they are ravening wolves.**

These verbal attacks on the Apostle Paul and his writings are done to cause confusion. The spirit of antichrist does work through men and women in an attempt to disrupt God's salvation plan. The Bible speaks of *many antichrists,* so these attacks will come from many people who are against Christ and His foundations whom He chose. When looking at the term *ravening wolves,* the Bible does mention where these attacks will come from. Since nothing is new under the sun, the prophecy of the *bloody city* or Jerusalem in Ezekiel 22 is a picture of what would happen within the fallen houses of God:

> **Ezekiel 22:1: Moreover the word of the LORD came unto me, saying, 2: Now, thou son of man, wilt thou judge, wilt thou judge the bloody city? Yea, <u>thou shalt shew her all her abominations.</u>**

The *princes in the midst* are *the ravening wolves:*

> **Ezekiel 22:27: Her princes in the midst thereof <u>*are* like wolves ravening the prey</u>, to shed blood, *and* to destroy souls, <u>to get dishonest gain</u>. 28: And her**

prophets have daubed them with untempered *morter*, seeing vanity, and divining lies unto them, saying, Thus saith the Lord GOD, when the LORD hath not spoken.

What did the early church believe about Paul? When we study God's Word, we understand the unity of the early believers once truth was agreed upon under the control of God's Spirit. Peter called Paul *beloved* and pointed to Paul's understanding of God's longsuffering:

2 Peter 3:15: And account *that* the longsuffering of our Lord *is* salvation; <u>even as our beloved brother Paul also according to the wisdom given unto him</u> hath written unto you; 16: As also in all *his* epistles, speaking in them of these things; in which are some things hard to be understood, which they that are unlearned and unstable wrest, as *they do* also the other scriptures, unto their own destruction.

Peter points us to Paul's writings. Peter is underscoring that Paul was given wisdom. God is the one who gives this wisdom. Peter also knew that the information in Paul's epistles would be hard to understand. Those people who are *unlearned* in God's Word and *unstable* wrench or *turn* the Scriptures unto their own destruction. Peter was directly pointing us to Paul and his writings. This turning of the Scriptures is part of the nature of the time of God's *longsuffering* near the end. Those who are twisting God's Word and attacking the very epistles of Paul are doing so unto their own destruction. It is no small thing that Paul spoke in advance of this destruction that comes upon those who attack God's Word:

> **Romans 9:22:** *What* **if God, willing to shew** *his* **wrath, and to make his power known, endured with much longsuffering the vessels of wrath** <u>fitted to destruction</u>**: 23: And that he might make known the riches of his glory on the vessels of mercy, which he had afore prepared unto glory...**

The Greek word for destruction is *apoleia* (G684) and is defined as *ruin.* It is something that Paul forewarned against, so if we see the evidence of what Paul was speaking of, we can know that this *ruin* will also come. People may think their attack on God's Word will go unanswered but God is simply being longsuffering so that the *vessels appointed unto glory* will experience God's salvation.

Note: The Greek word *apoleia* (destruction/ruin) is very similar to the Greek word *apollyon* (destroyer):

> **Revelation 9:11: And they had a king over them,** *which is* **the angel of the bottomless pit, whose name in the Hebrew tongue** *is* **Abaddon, but in the Greek tongue hath** *his* **name Apollyon.**

How long will God allow the attack on His Word to go unanswered? There is something that the Lord mentioned concerning the *prince of this world* being *cast out*. Does the timing of the first casting out of Satan relate and follow the pattern of the time of the cross in 2015? After all, God promises to remove *the Northern* in Joel 2.

<u>The Prince of this World is Cast Out</u>

Prior to the cross, Jesus mentioned something I believe also occurs twice in history. He proclaimed that the *prince of this world* will be *cast out*. This is very similar to God removing *the Northern* to bring about God's magnification:

John 12:31: Now is the judgment of this world: now shall the prince of this world be cast out.

I believe it is safe to say that the *prince of this world* is Satan himself who is the *prince of the power of the air*:

Ephesians 2:1: And you *hath he quickened*, who were dead in trespasses and sins; 2: Wherein in time past ye walked according to the course of this world, <u>according to the prince of the power of the air</u>, the spirit that now worketh in the children of disobedience...

John 14:30: Hereafter I will not talk much with you: <u>for the prince of this world cometh, and hath nothing in me.</u> 31: But that the world may know that I love the Father; and as the Father gave me commandment, even so I do. Arise, let us go hence.

It would make sense, therefore, that if Satan was judged at the time of the cross, then a similar judgment should occur during the replica of 33 A.D. in the year 2015 A.D. This would line up with God removing *the Northern* after this evil entity had done *great things* (magnified). This fits perfectly with the year 2015. It also comes at a time when people are proclaiming: *Where is their God?*

Joel 2:17: Let the priests, the ministers of the LORD, weep between the porch and the altar, and let them say, Spare thy people, O LORD, and give not thine heritage to reproach, that the heathen should rule over them: wherefore should they say among the people, Where *is* their God? 18: <u>Then will the LORD be jealous for his land, and pity his people.</u>

111

When Judgment came at the time of the cross, God was magnified. This was a prayer of Jesus to the Father in which He gave all glory to the Father in Heaven:

> **John 12:27: Now is my soul troubled; and what shall I say? Father, save me from this hour: but for this cause came I unto this hour. 28: Father, glorify thy name. Then came there a voice from heaven, *saying*, I have both glorified *it*, and will glorify *it* again. 29: The people therefore, that stood by, and heard *it*, said that it thundered: others said, An angel spake to him. 30: Jesus answered and said, This voice came not because of me, but for your sakes.**

With the prophecy of Joel 2 proclaiming that God will be magnified soon, it is very possible that the Father's response to Jesus *(I will glorify it again)* was, in fact, pointing us to a time in our distant future. When judgment fell at the time of the cross, men feared, God was glorified, and the salvation of many was the end result. The power of the resurrection of Jesus did secure the resurrection of many as the graves were opened:

> **Matthew 27:51: And, behold, the veil of the temple was rent in twain from the top to the bottom; and the earth did quake, and the rocks rent; 52: And the graves were opened; and many bodies of the saints which slept arose, 53: And came out of the graves after his resurrection, and went into the holy city, and appeared unto many.**

According to the duplication of the Feast of Trumpets to Pentecost (1,335 day duplication), the time of the cross was April 3, 33 A.D. The duplication of this important date would be April 3, 2015 A.D. Will this be the time of the judgment

112

of the *prince of this world*? The similarities between the evil activities at the time of Jesus' 3 ½ years of ministry to the evil activity of today cannot be dismissed.

- Satan came with the Word of God to tempt Jesus and attempt to cause Him to fall down and worship.
- The temple had been overrun with money changers who had turned the house of God into a *house of merchandise.*
- *Perilous times* occur both during the time of Christ and also during the last days.

Note: If the 1,260 days of the *two witnesses* (God's Word) going forth to witness is within the 1,335-day timeframe, then at the anniversary of the cross in 2015 we should see the attack of Satan on God's Word in the churches. If the *two witnesses* (law and the prophets) lay dead in the street for 3 ½ days, then the Word of God is nullified in the fallen houses of God. A desolation for 3 ½ years is possible. What John saw in the book of Revelation was an illustration of how God's Word is "killed" in the houses of God. The two witnesses' dead bodies lying dead in the street of *Jerusalem* (founded by peace) means that the Word of God being "killed" is reserved for the houses of God, not the gospel going forth into all the world. The abomination which makes desolate occurs in the houses of God.

In the next chapter, I want to explore the duplication or similarities with the term *perilous times*, in which the Greek word (*chalepos*-G5467) is only used twice in the New Testament. This, I believe, will be very revealing concerning the days in which we are all living.

Chapter 5—Perilous Times as Defined by the Bible

There are two terms I want to focus on in this chapter. One is the term *last days* and the other is the term *perilous times*. Both terms seem very important in defining the time prior to God being magnified in the year 2015. Let us first look at the term *last days*.

The Last Days

The term *last days* is repeated quite often in both the Old Testament and the New Testament. Micah 4 speaks of the *last days* as a time when the *mountain of the house of the Lord* will be established at *the top of the mountains* and *above the hills*. Many nations shall *flow unto it*. This is very important spiritual language. In Mark 13:14 we read about the command to *flee to the mountains* once the *abomination which makes desolate* is witnessed in the fallen churches. Both verses below, I believe, are speaking of one and the same event. Mark 13:14 is speaking of the abomination as Satan takes his seat of authority; Micah 4 is speaking of the nations being gathered against *the daughter of Zion* saying: *let her be corrupted*:

> **Micah 4:1: But <u>in the last days</u> it shall come to pass, *that* the mountain of the house of the LORD shall be established in the top of the mountains, and it shall be exalted above the hills; and people shall flow unto it. 2: And many nations shall come, and say, Come, and let us go up to the mountain of**

the LORD, and to the house of the God of Jacob; and he will teach us of his ways, and we will walk in his paths: for the law shall go forth of Zion, and the word of the LORD from Jerusalem.

Micah 4:11: Now also many nations are gathered against thee, that say, Let her be defiled, and let our eye look upon Zion.

Mark 13:14: But when ye shall see the abomination of desolation, spoken of by Daniel the prophet, standing where it ought not, (let him that readeth understand,) then let them that be in Judaea flee to the mountains...

It seems that every time God wants us to understand what is being proclaimed there are phrases resembling: *let him that readeth understand*, or *he that has ears to hear, let him hear*. By these statements, God is underscoring the spiritual importance of these verses. That means that we need to compare scripture with scripture to find answers. *Fleeing to the mountains* is another way of God saying that we need to be turning to God instead of where the abomination is taking place:

Psalm 87:1: A Psalm *or* Song for the sons of Korah. His foundation *is* in the holy mountains.

Psalm 72:3: The mountains shall bring peace to the people, and the little hills, by righteousness. 4: He shall judge the poor of the people, he shall save the children of the needy, and shall break in pieces the oppressor.

Psalm 125:2: As the mountains *are* round about Jerusalem, so the LORD *is* round about his people from henceforth even for ever.

The Nations Judged for Coming against God's People

Micah 4 goes on to declare that God will rebuke the *strong nations from afar off*. In Micah 5:15, God promises to *execute vengeance in anger and fury upon the heathen, such as they have not heard*. We also can know that there comes a time in which God will be rebuking Satan, and this should happen midway within the mirror of the *years of Darius* (2015). Satan, who stood accusing Joshua in Zechariah 3, was silenced by the announcement of his impending judgment: *thou shall be rebuked*. Since this was proclaimed in the second year of Darius, we can know that the forecasting of God rebuking Satan of relates to our 2013-2014.

However, this warning seems to be a future *rebuking* by God. The ISA[10] uses the words of *he shall rebuke*. If so, this rebuking of Satan comes not in the second year of Darius (our 2013-2014), but rather, the year 2015 would line up perfectly as the time in which God *removes the Northern*, rebukes Satan, and judges *the prince of this world*. The following points speak of what happens in the last days as mentioned in the New Testament.

The New Testament also Mentions the Last Days

- Acts 2:17 speaks of the first fulfillment of God pouring out His Spirit in the *last days*. The first fulfillment of this was Pentecost 33 A.D. However, the year 2015 lines up with the second fulfillment of God pouring out His Spirit and being magnified.

117

- Hebrews 1:2 speaks of Jesus who as the Son has finished God's Word in the *last days*. This sealing of God's Word includes the book of Revelation given to John on Patmos. Prior to the completion of the Bible, God spoke through the prophets. Once the Word was sealed by Jesus who had become the heir of all things, no further adding to God's Word by anyone should be considered as viable inspired truth. This sealing by God, by His Son in the book of the Revelation of Jesus Christ, enables us to distinguish all other "religions" from the real truth of God's Word- the Bible.

- James 5:3 decrees the warning to the *rich man* who has laid up treasures on earth instead of following Christ's command to lay up treasures in Heaven. Who is the *rich man* spoken of in James? I believe this is speaking to those people who market a "prosperity gospel" instead of the true Gospel of Jesus.

- 2 Peter 3 foretells of the *last days* in which *scoffers, walking after their own lusts* proclaim: *Where is the promise of His coming?* Jude 1 speaks of these same mockers who speak *swelling words* for their own benefit.

- Finally, the words *last days* are associated with *perilous times*. The Greek word for perilous is *chalepos,* and it is only used two times in the New Testament.

2 Timothy 3:1: This know also, that in the last days <u>perilous</u> times shall come.

Matthew 8:28: And when he was come to the other side into the country of the

118

Gergesenes, there met him two possessed with devils, coming out of the tombs, exceeding <u>fierce</u>, so that no man might pass by that way.

One could define the *last days* as from the time of Christ's first coming and onward since the *last days* seem associated to the time in which the activity of devils is significant. However, we are exploring the possibility that the 3 ½ years from 2011 to 2015 are a replication of the 3 ½ years of Christ's ministry. Therefore, the demonic activity may increase during this time prior to God being magnified. Why were the devils apparently aware of *their time of torment*?

Matthew 8:29: And, behold, they cried out, saying, What have we to do with thee, Jesus, thou Son of God? Art thou come hither to torment us <u>before the time?</u>

The question the devils had concerning *the time of their torment* is a curious one. Why would these fallen beings bring this up unless they had some type of understanding of their own torment? This *time of their torment* would, of course, be God's equity for their own activity of tormenting men and women. Mary Magdalene had been tormented with seven devils:

Mark 16:9: Now when *Jesus* was risen early the first *day* of the week, he appeared first to Mary Magdalene, out of whom he had cast seven devils.

I think we can find answers to this question by studying the word *torment*. In 2 Peter 2 we read of the account of Lot being *vexed with the filthy conversation of the wicked*. Lot

119

was *vexed* daily with their *unlawful deeds*. This vexing or torment came to an end when God destroyed Sodom and Gomorrah and two other cities (Duet. 29:23) The end result of this judgment, once it reached a precise time, was that God had been patient long enough and overthrew the wicked cities:

> **2 Peter 2:6: And turning the cities of Sodom and Gomorrha into ashes condemned *them* with an overthrow, making *them* an ensample unto those that after should live ungodly; 7: And delivered just Lot, <u>vexed</u> with the filthy conversation of the wicked: 8: (For that righteous man dwelling among them, in seeing and hearing, vexed his righteous soul from day to day with their unlawful deeds)...**

What is very significant concerning the warnings of 2 Peter 2 is that God lists the following examples for His reason of destruction and overthrow. 2 Peter 2 opens with the following verse that sets the theme and context of the chapter:

> **2 Peter 2:1: But there were <u>false prophets</u> also among the people, even as there shall be <u>false teachers </u> among you, who privily shall bring in damnable <u>heresies</u>, even denying the Lord that bought them, and bring upon themselves swift destruction. 2: And many shall follow their pernicious ways; by reason of whom the way of <u>truth shall be evil spoken of</u>. 3: And <u>through covetousness</u> shall they with feigned words make merchandise of you: whose judgment now of a**

long time lingereth not, and their damnation slumbereth not.

The Lord underscores that *covetousness* is the underlying sin for the false teachers who are proclaiming heresies. Why is God mentioning *heresies* and *false teachers among you*? This is the nature of *great tribulation*. There are people today who are attempting to discredit the Apostle Paul as a *ravening wolf*. If Satan, through others, can undermine the one who called himself the *first example* of God's longsuffering, then Satan may think he has succeeded in thwarting God's salvation plan.

Christ will Overturn, Overturn, Overturn

The next question that needs to be asked is: Does God in His Word, the Bible, make mention of any future prophecies of a similar *overthrow* that happened to Sodom and Gomorrah? The answer is yes, and it may surprise some people that it applies to the fallen houses of God who have fallen into *covetousness* and teaching *heresies* in the midst of the congregations.

The Bible promises that God, who created the heavens and earth, will eventually overthrow the fallen houses of God. In fact, there is one verse which mentions *overturn* not once, but three times. Keep in mind that Jesus also overthrew the fallen temple (moneychangers) in His day. I have seen verses in God's Word where He doubles a word, but when He repeats something three times it is very serious. Let us examine this verse and the triple warning from God's Word.

First, I want to examine the word *wicked* found in Ezekiel 21. I believe that Satan is related to the *wicked prince of Israel* since, as the chief one who rules in the fallen houses of God, his judgment will come swiftly. The congregation of the wicked is mentioned in the following Psalms:

Psalm 26:5: I have hated <u>the congregation of evil doers</u>; and will not <u>sit with the wicked.</u>

Psalm 37:34: Wait on the LORD, and keep his way, and he shall exalt thee to inherit the land: <u>when the wicked are cut off, thou shalt see</u> *<u>it</u>*.

In Ezekiel 21, God proclaims a judgment on Jerusalem and *all the princes*. The *sword* that God draws is to abase the high and exalt the low. It comes as a judgment as Christ will *overturn, overturn, overturn*. There is also a judgment pronounced on the *wicked prince of Israel*. Zedekiah was the last king to reign in the line of the throne of David. He did wickedly and God sent judgment by the way of the King of Babylon. The King of Babylon captured him, slew his sons, put out Zedekiah's eyes, and placed him in brass fetters (2 Kings 25:7). The *sword*, which was sharpened and furbished, was given to the *slayer*. We know from similar language that the slayer was none other than the King of Babylon from the north (Ezekiel 26:7).

However, we also must admit that Satan is also deemed the *slayer* and he is also termed the *Northern* as a spiritual type of the King of Babylon (Joel chapter 2). The exalting of the low and abasing the high is also mentioned in Ezekiel 17:24 where the parabolic language mentions how "all the trees of the field" will know that God is the one who abases the high and exalts the low. Jesus spoke of the *fig tree* and *all the trees* sprouting forth in the context of the kingdom of God being at hand (Luke 21:29). This comes in the final years of history as the Gospel of the Kingdom goes into the entire world. Yet another clue in Ezekiel 21 is found in the following verse:

> **Ezekiel 21:25: And thou, profane wicked prince of Israel, whose day is come, when iniquity *shall have an end*...**

The ISA renders the last section Ezekiel 21:25 as "in era of depravity of end." With the language of abasing the high and exalting the low, plus the mention of the era of the depravity of the end, I believe this *sword* of God which comes upon *all the princes* is related to the judgment upon the houses of God. Ezekiel 21:12 & 13 records how the *sword* comes upon *my people* and it becomes a *trial* or *test*. This trial comes within the *last end of the indignation* (3 ½ years). However, judgment most likely comes around the year 2015 when God and His Word are magnified. Satan is also judged as the *Northern* is removed into a land *barren and desolate*.

God has used the prince of Tyrus, the king of Babylon, the wicked prince of Israel, the pharaoh, and Gog as representations of what Satan performs in the spiritual realm near the end of time. Satan and his kingdom, which are presently exalted, will become low, and this includes the "convert or die" religions who deny the power and authority of Jesus Christ. The following verse declares that it is Jesus' right to sit on the throne of David forever. He is the one who defeated death and He alone has that right. This comes after Satan and his kingdom are judged. No more wickedness will be ruling because Christ alone will have the rule of the spiritual *throne of David* and Jesus' kingdom will have no end:

> **Ezekiel 21:27: I will overturn, overturn, overturn, it: and it shall be no *more*, <u>until he come whose right it is</u>; and I will give it *him*.**

> **Luke 1:32: He shall be great, and shall be called the Son of the Highest: and <u>the Lord God shall give unto him the throne of his father David</u>: 33: And he shall reign over the house of Jacob for ever; and of <u>his kingdom there shall be no end</u>.**

In the year 2011, we were ushered out of the 8,400-day *tribulation* in 2011 and right into the *great tribulation*. Thankfully, God has shortened the days of *great tribulation* so that it is 3 ½ years instead of Jacob's/Joseph's historical 7-year famine. This is what the book of Daniel refers to as the *time, times and half time* and also *the last end of the indignation.* The remaining 3 ½ years of this 7-year period is when salvation will occur in a huge way worldwide.

> **Mark 13:19: For *in* those days shall be affliction, such as was not from the beginning of the creation which God created unto this time, <u>neither shall be</u>. 20: And except that the Lord had shortened those days, no flesh should be saved: but <u>for the elect's sake, whom he hath chosen, he hath shortened the days</u>.**

Salvation must go forth in a huge way once Satan (the *wicked prince of Israel)* is judged by God in 2015. By the way, Israel means: *he will rule with God* or *to prevail with God.* This is seen as God changed Jacob's name to Israel:

> **Genesis 32:28: And he said, Thy name shall be called no more Jacob, but Israel: <u>for as a prince</u>**

<u>hast thou power </u>with God and with men, <u>and hast</u> <u>prevailed.</u>

However, Satan does not want to rule as a created being, but rather, he lifts himself up *as God*. We are living at that time in history where Satan has taken his seat of authority in the fallen houses of God. He seeks to be as God, so that he can be worshipped as God. He does this with prosperity gospels and with *signs and lying wonders* that deceive many people. The Bible informs us of this truth in various verses as Satan has lifted himself up to be *as God:*

> **Ezekiel 28:5: By thy great wisdom *and* by thy traffick hast thou increased thy riches, and thine heart is lifted up because of thy riches:**
> **6: Therefore thus saith the Lord GOD; Because thou hast set thine heart as the heart of God; 7: Behold, therefore I will bring strangers upon thee, the terrible of the nations: and they shall draw their swords against the beauty of thy wisdom, and they shall defile thy brightness.**

> **2 Thessalonians 2:4: Who opposeth and exalteth himself above all that is called God, or that is worshipped; <u>so that he as God sitteth in the temple of God</u>, shewing himself that he is God.**

Of course, Satan's end is destruction and his evil works end in desolation. God has allowed Satan to rule during the final years of history. Then comes a time when *iniquity shall be removed in one day* (Zechariah 3:9). Paul understood the nature of how wickedness works as *fiery darts* are cast forth by evil. We are instructed that the *shield of faith* will *quench* these *fiery darts*. However, we are not to quench the Spirit

125

dwelling within us. We are not to despise the declaration of God's Word but rather prove all things and hold onto that which is good (1 Thessalonians 5:19, 20 & 21). This requires a dedication and focus on the study of God's Word. By the study of God's Word, the Spirit of God will lead us into truth. We will then be able to distinguish truth from deception.

The Bible uses language that once understood can give time clues to when God is about to act in judgment. The overturning of the temple in Jesus day was significant since He promises to *overturn* the fallen houses of God. The *profane wicked prince of Israel* (which title could be a representation of Satan) will be judged and iniquity will have an end at the time of the *era of depravity*. We have learned an important clue in Ezekiel 21. The clue phrase contains the words: *exalt him that is low, and abase him that is high.*

> **Ezekiel 21:25: And thou, <u>profane wicked prince of Israel, whose day is come, when iniquity *shall have* an end,</u>**
> **26: Thus saith the Lord GOD; Remove the diadem, and take off the crown: this *shall* not *be* the same: exalt *him that is* low, and abase *him that is* high.**
> **27: <u>I will overturn, overturn, overturn, it: and it shall be no more, until he come whose right it is; and I will give it him.</u>**

When we study how God *exalts the low* and *abases the high*, we get a real good picture from similar verses in the Bible concerning this action of God. We can also gain understanding when God is going to perform this reversal. In Zephaniah chapter 3, God speaks of a time when He removes the enemy and they shall not see evil (*ra ra-ah* H7451) anymore. This exact Hebrew word is used in Isaiah 47. The *Daughter of Babylon,* due to their trusting in wickedness, experiences the evil (*ra ra-ah*) that comes upon them. Desolation comes instantly upon the fallen houses of God. When God removes the enemy and evil is seen no more, it is at that time God rejoices with joy.

The language in Zephaniah 3 is very similar to the reversal in Joel 2 & 3. It is also similar to the command to work during the years of Darius. This gives us a real good understanding when this reversal by God happens. The year 2015 should be an important marker in the final years of this present world. It could be a time of great reversal:

> **Zephaniah 3:15: <u>The LORD hath taken away thy judgments, he hath cast out thine enemy:</u> the king of Israel, *even* the LORD, *is* in the midst of thee: <u>thou shalt not see evil any more.</u> 16: In that day it shall be said to Jerusalem, Fear thou not: and to Zion, <u>Let not thine hands be slack.</u> 17: The LORD thy God in the midst of thee *is* mighty; he will save, he will rejoice over thee with joy; he will rest in his love, he will joy over thee with singing.**

God will *Overthrow* as He *Overthrew* Sodom

The Bible is full of important phrases that, once understood, can really shed light on God's judgment in the last years. One such phrase is *the daughter of my people*. God is using the judgment which happened to Israel historically, and then He proclaims the future judgment on the fallen houses of God with the phrase *the daughter of my people*:

Lamentations 4:6: For the punishment of the iniquity of the <u>daughter of my people</u> is greater than the punishment of the sin of Sodom, that was overthrown as in a moment, and no hands stayed on her.

As we study the Bible, God has assigned certain phrases to allow us to know who it is that He is referring us to. The term *daughter of my people* is one such phrase. Many people, including some Bible commentators, have erred in thinking that the books of Jeremiah, Lamentations, and Ezekiel are historical books that relate only to the nation of Israel and Israel's historical judgment. The problem with this teaching or belief is that the term *latter days* is sprinkled throughout God's warnings of judgment. This brings us full circle to our time in which we all live. These are the *latter days* in which God judges false worship.

The *works of their hands*—Moses warns the people:

Deuteronomy 31:29: For I know that after my death ye will utterly corrupt *yourselves*, and turn aside from the way which I have commanded you; and <u>evil will befall you in the latter days</u>; because ye will do evil in the sight of the LORD, to provoke him to anger <u>through the work of your hands.</u>

The *works of their hands*—Christ warns the churches:

Revelation 9:20: And the rest of the men which were not killed by these plagues <u>yet repented not of the works of their hands, that they should not worship devils</u>, and idols of gold, and silver, and

brass, and stone, and of wood: which neither can see, nor hear, nor walk:

The Latter Days

During the time of the latter days, God's Word opens up and understanding of His judgment is more perfectly understood:

> **Jeremiah 23:20: The anger of the LORD shall not return, until he have executed, and till he have performed the thoughts of his heart: <u>in the latter days ye shall consider it perfectly.</u> 21: I have not sent these prophets, yet they ran: I have not spoken to them, yet they prophesied.**

Even during the times of *tribulation* God's mercy is available. How important is this message that God's mercy is available even today during a time of *great tribulation*? To understand the scope and depth of God's mercy, look up in the concordance the Hebrew word *chesed* (H2617), the Greek word *eleos* G1656 and see the wonder of God's mercy. Even in the *tribulation* of the latter days God's hand of mercy is reaching out:

> **Deuteronomy 4:28: And there ye shall serve gods, the work of men's hands, wood and stone, which neither see, nor hear, nor eat, nor smell. 29: But <u>if from thence thou shalt seek the LORD thy God, thou shalt find *him*</u>, if thou seek him with all thy heart and with all thy soul. 30: When thou art <u>in tribulation, and all these things are come upon thee, *even* in the latter days, if thou turn to the LORD thy God</u>, and shalt be obedient unto his voice. 31: (For the LORD thy God *is* a merciful God;) he will not forsake thee, neither destroy**

thee, nor forget the covenant of thy fathers which he sware unto them.

Do you notice how God uses similar language in Deuteronomy as He does with the warning to those in the churches from Revelation 9: 20? There is nothing new under the sun; false worship has always existed throughout time. So when God is speaking of the *daughter of my people*, and the *latter days,* we can know the *tribulation* periods of the end (8,400 days and the *time, times and half a time*) are what God has intended for us to understand.

Of course some people will reject this idea until judgment falls, then people will fear. If people do not see change, they assume "all is well." Psalm 55 is an incredible reversal by God as David was crying out to God morning, noon, and evening for God to help him from the persecution of the enemy. Those who persecute will continue to do so until God creates a change:

> **Psalm 55:16: As for me, I will call upon God; and the LORD shall save me. 17: Evening, and morning, and at noon, will I pray, and cry aloud: and he shall hear my voice. 18: He hath delivered my soul in peace from the battle *that was* against me: for there were many with me. 19: <u>God shall hear, and afflict them</u>, even he that abideth of old. Selah. <u>Because they have no changes, therefore they fear not God.</u>**

In my studies of God's Word, I have seen where there is a cut off time when God assures His people that He will intervene and huge changes will take place. Joel 2 speaks of a time when God removes *the Northern* who did *great things* or magnified himself, and then God does *great things* or magnifies Himself. At that time in history the *land* will not fear, and righteousness will go forth. Ezekiel 21:25 also speaks of a time when God judges wickedness. So when is this time that all believers look so foreword to? In all likelihood, the year will be the year 2015.

One Year to a Better Tomorrow?

This book is titled *Seven Years to a Better Tomorrow* because we who are involved with the YouTube channel: *2011studies,* the website: *lettersofpeaceandtruth.com,* and the blog: *1335days.com,* have understood (by God's mercy) that God has set forth two very important timeframes within the final years of history:

1) The first is the 8,400 days of *tribulation* (1988-2011) that was patterned after Israel's 70-year (840 months of *tribulation*).

2) The second is the final 7-year *great tribulation* period (2011-2018) that is cut short at the 3 ½ year mark to allow the Gospel to go forth into the entire world. This is patterned after Joseph's & Jacob's seven years of famine—*great affliction.*

Both *tribulation* periods involve the activity of Satan causing desolation in the houses of God. However, the first half of the last seven years is a period of the *last end of the indignation* or 3 ½ years. This is the period Daniel wanted to know about:

Daniel 8:19: And he said, Behold, I will make thee know what shall be <u>in the last end of the indignation</u>: for at the time appointed the end *shall be.*

I have heard two things being proclaimed by famous leaders in the houses of God. One is that "no man knows the day or hour," and the other is that "Christ can come at any time." Daniel 8 clearly proclaims that there is a *time appointed*. God is never random in His actions. He knows the beginning from the end. He created the sun, moon, and stars for signs, seasons, days, and years. Seasons have everything to do with God's established feast celebrations such as Pentecost and Tabernacles.

One would think that the people declaring such things such as *no man knows the day or hour* would at least study the words *day and hour* or even the word *knoweth* as this Greek word can mean *has seen or perceived*.

It is true that man, in his own feeble sinful mind, cannot see or understand the things of God. How does God reveal things through the study of His Word? The Spirit of God must dwell in a person before they can understand any of the truths of the *last days,* which are proclaimed in God's Word:

> **Matthew 11:27: <u>All things are delivered unto me</u> of my Father: and no man knoweth the Son, but the Father; neither knoweth any man the Father, save the Son, and <u>*he* to whomsoever the Son will reveal *him*.</u>**

To say that *no <u>man</u> knows the day or hour* is one thing. To say that believers in Jesus Christ will know absolutely nothing of His return is quite another. That would be like saying that Jesus, the one who conquered death and is sitting at the right hand of God, knows nothing about the *day and hour* of the judgment which comes upon the fallen houses of God and eventually the nations of the world. I have posted video studies on this topic on the YouTube channel *2011studies* if any reader is interested.

I also wrote in my last book[11] that Isaac Newton really worked hard at understanding the things pertaining to the end. He studied the Bible as a steward of God's Word. The problem was that God was not yet revealing truths concerning the timing of Christ's return on the *last day* during Newton's lifetime.

Although Newton was an intelligent and gifted person who desired to know when Christ would return, he could not know the timing of Christ's return. This is because understanding knowledge from God's Word is not about man's mind, but rather, it is about God revealing truth at the precise time in which He has decreed. God told Daniel, who gained much understanding about our time, *to shut up the word and seal the book even to the time of the end.* It is only at a precise time that God will reveal truth concerning the *last days*. I am dedicating an entire chapter to what Daniel was allowed to know and what was sealed unto the last years of history. The chapter on Daniel will be very revealing.

The Churches Rejection of Knowledge from God

Many churches leaders today really seem to lack the desire to know about the coming of Christ on the *last day*. Daniel was inquisitive; the disciples were also very much in search of answers about Christ's second coming. Why are the people in the churches today who hold the name of Jesus Christ not worried or concerned about the greatest event in human history? I would plead with the leaders in the houses of God worldwide not to limit God's power of revealing truth when the *appointed time* arrives:

> **Daniel 12:4: But thou, O Daniel, shut up the words, and <u>seal the book, *even* to the time of the end</u>: many shall run to and fro, and knowledge shall be increased.**

The Hebrew word for *knowledge* is *daath* (H1847) and is related to understanding God's Word. Job speaks of the *wicked* who reject the knowledge of God (His Word):

> **Job 21:12: They take the timbrel and harp, and rejoice at the sound of the organ. Job 21:13: They spend their days in wealth, and in a moment go down to the grave. 14: Therefore <u>they say unto God, Depart from us; for</u> <u>we desire not the knowledge</u> of thy ways. 15: What *is* the Almighty, that we should serve him? And what profit should we have, if we pray unto him?**

All the while, some pastors, when asked about the coming of Christ in *power and great glory* by members of their congregations, will shut down the conversation with "no man knows the day or hour." Even if the pastors understood *day and hour* to mean a 24-hour period of time and a 60-minute period of time, they could at the very least consider the timeline God has established, which includes the Babylonian captivity of Judah and the post-captivity within the *years of Darius*. By these historical patterns that God has given us, we should all be looking for a possible year of Christ's return and not hiding behind a verse in the Bible that is completely misquoted. Hosea 4:6 speaks of the importance of not rejecting God's knowledge:

> **Hosea 4:6: My people are destroyed for lack of knowledge: because thou hast rejected knowledge,**

I will also reject thee, that thou shalt be no priest to me: seeing thou hast forgotten the law of thy God, I will also forget thy children. 7: As they were increased, so they sinned against me: *therefore* will I change their glory into shame.

One of the saddest things to me is gaining more and more understanding of the coming judgment on the fallen houses of God, yet not being able to convince the leaders that judgment is approaching rapidly. It is very similar to the year 2011 and the grand announcement of the coming of Christ. Some Bible students now fully understand that the mocking of 2 Peter 3 had to come to pass and that this is all part of God's incredible end-time plan:

2Peter 3:3: Knowing this first, that there shall come in the last days scoffers, walking after their own lusts, 4: And saying, Where is the promise of his coming? For since the fathers fell asleep, all things continue as *they were* from the beginning of the creation.

It is one thing if the media and people of this world mocked the announcement of the coming of Christ, but 2 Peter 3 seems to imply that those who believe in creation itself are mocking. The majority of the people in the houses of God wanted nothing to do with the announcement of Christ's coming. Even today, when disturbing activity is going on in the midst of the fallen houses of God, this should be a *red-sky* warning that God's judgment is coming:

Matthew 16:1: The Pharisees also with the Sadducees came, and tempting desired him that he would shew them a sign from heaven. 2: He

> **answered and said unto them, When it is evening,
> ye say, *It will be* fair weather: for the <u>sky is red.</u> 3:
> And in the morning, *It will be* foul weather to day:
> for the sky is red and lowring. O *ye* hypocrites, ye
> can discern the face of the sky; but can ye not
> *discern* the signs of the times?**

This book is not being written to proclaim *peace and safety* and *all is well* in the houses of God, nor to profit financially. Since 2011, I set up the YouTube channel *2011studies* for the purpose of offering free video Bible studies. Now, since we are rapidly approaching 2015 as of this writing, I have a strong conviction of getting this information out before it comes to pass.

With my previous book, I had the same conviction. I wanted to rush the completion of *Countdown* prior to May 21, 2011, so that people could understand that God's mercy will continue. But now, the question is for how long? I originally thought it was 153 days, since that is a significant Biblical number. As of this writing (the year 2014), which lines up with the second year of Darius, God has revealed so much more information, including the final seven years of *great tribulation.* Showing people that God's Word will prove itself to be accurate really takes patience. God is the one revealing bits and pieces of truth at the appropriate time.

Judgment on the Houses of God Must First Come

All is not well in this world, and God's judgment is coming to the fallen houses of God worldwide. There is coming a *better tomorrow,* but we first must be faithful in proclaiming God's truths about the coming judgment upon the fallen houses of God. God will use this judgment in a great way to draw more people to the saving grace of Christ. If God judges His people first, the nations will know that their coming judgment is next. When God *shakes the heavens and the earth*, things will change around the globe:

> **Haggai 2:6: For thus saith the LORD of hosts; Yet once, it *is* a little while, and I will shake the heavens, and the earth, and the sea, and the dry *land*;**
> **7: And I will shake all nations, and the desire of all nations shall come: and I will fill this house with glory, saith the LORD of hosts.**

The year 2011 was a highly significant year for three good reasons:

1) The world was made aware of the coming of Christ on the *last day*. How many people prior to 2011 had bought into the churches propagation of the 1800's John Darby fable that Christ would reign on this sin-cursed earth for 1,000 years? This teaching is not the original teaching of the disciples who walked with Christ and understood how the resurrection of believers would occur on the last day. This announcement made people aware that there is a *last day* and that God is going to recreate *new heavens* and a *new earth* where only righteousness is present:

> **2 Peter 3:12: Looking for and hasting unto the coming of the day of God, wherein the heavens being on fire shall be dissolved, and the elements shall melt with fervent heat? 13: Nevertheless we, according to his promise, look for <u>new heavens and a new earth, wherein dwelleth righteousness.</u>**

John 12:48: He that rejecteth me, and receiveth not my words, hath one that judgeth him: the word that I have spoken, <u>the same shall judge him in the last day.</u>

2) The year 2011 was the 7,000[th] anniversary of the flood in 4990 B.C. Harold Camping's work on the *Biblical Calendar of History*[12] will become more significant as judgment on the houses of God comes in a short time. God had blessed Camping with much understanding of the 8,400 days of *tribulation*, which ended on May 21, 2011. However, what was not understood was how the 8,400 day *tribulation* period would immediately transition into the 7-year *great tribulation* period. We will soon be at the mid-way point of the *great tribulation* period in the year 2015, and the good news, I believe, is that God has shortened the days of the *great tribulation.*

3) The passing of the important dates of 2011, I believe, drove people to study God's Word more. For myself and other believers, we were waiting for God to reveal more information as we were asking Him for further understanding. Prior to May 21, 2011, God gave understanding from the Bible that there would be a post-*tribulation* period. We know this because God spoke about *good and comfortable words* that were to come after Judah's 70-year captivity (840-month *tribulation*). This is why I rushed to finish the book *Countdown to the Last Day.* We knew that the 840-month *tribulation* period that Judah/Jerusalem experienced was the pattern for our 8,400 day *tribulation* period.

Therefore, we can know these *good and comfortable words* (a time of blessing) come after the 23 years (8,400 days) of *tribulation*, which ended May 21, 2011. After the 70-year captivity, God gave the Babylonian kingdom to the Mede (Darius) and Persian (Cyrus), and this became a time of rebuilding that follows the pattern of the *years of Darius* in the Bible. Understanding this was extremely exciting as we continued to study. God has actually followed historical patterns in which we can know the "how and when" prior to Christ's coming on the last day. This book will detail this information and what we believe God has revealed through the study of His Word, the Bible.

I want to re-cap how the Bible defines *perilous times*. The Apostle Paul wrote a letter to Timothy speaking of *perilous times* in the *last days*. The King James translators assigned the Greek word *chalepos* (G5467) to two different English words in the New Testament. In 2 Timothy 3, they translated *chalepos* as *perilous;* in Matthew 8:28, they assigned the word *fierce* to the Greek word *chalepos*. Both verses contain the identical Greek word *chalepos*. So when we are studying for understanding concerning the *perilous times* mentioned by Paul, we must look up G5467 (*chalepos*) to understand the nature of the *last days*. Matthew 8:28 is very revealing since it relates to two men who were truly possessed by devils:

Matthew 8:28: And when he was come to the other side into the country of the Gergesenes, there met him two possessed with devils, coming out of the tombs, <u>exceeding fierce</u>, so that no man might pass by that way. 29: And, behold, they cried out, saying, What have we to do with thee, Jesus, thou

139

Son of God? Art thou come hither to torment us before the time?

I believe we are now mirroring the 3 ½ years of Christ's ministry from the year 2011 to the year 2015. This includes the 1,290 days of desolation and waiting until we reach the 1,335th day at Pentecost in 2015 (May 24, 2015).

Since Paul detailed some of the traits of people during the *perilous times*, I would like to cover these truths in the next chapter. I would like to also present why Satan, the *spirit of antichrist* is working through people to discredit the Apostle Paul's writings during this time of *great tribulation*. Why is Paul, who is the first example of God's longsuffering, coming under attack during the time of God's longsuffering? It is really not that surprising, but it does allow us to know the time we are currently living.

Chapter 6—The Timeline of God's Longsuffering

It is very timely that attacks on the Apostle Paul escalate during this time of the 1,290 days during *great tribulation*. In the past few months, I have seen online videos being made accusing Paul of being a *ravening wolf* and other choice names. As stated in the verses below, we will know the saved of God by the good fruit they bring forth, and we will know the false prophets by their evil fruit.

> **Matthew 7:13 Enter ye in at the strait gate: for wide *is* the gate, and broad *is* the way, that leadeth to destruction, and many there be which go in thereat: 14: Because strait *is* the gate, and narrow *is* the way, which leadeth unto life, and few there be that find it. 15: Beware of false prophets, which come to you in sheep's clothing, but inwardly they are ravening wolves.**

> **Matthew 7: 16: Ye shall know them by their fruits. Do men gather grapes of thorns, or figs of thistles? 17: Even so every good tree bringeth forth good fruit; but a corrupt tree bringeth forth evil fruit. 18: A good tree cannot bring forth evil fruit, neither *can* a corrupt tree bring forth good fruit.**

> **Matthew 7: 19: Every tree that bringeth not forth good fruit is hewn down, and cast into the fire. 20: <u>Wherefore by their fruits ye shall know them</u>. 21: Not every one that saith unto me, Lord, Lord,**

shall enter into the kingdom of heaven; but he that doeth the will of my Father which is in heaven.

The Time of Raving Wolves and Many Antichrists

Jesus' words in Matthew 7 echo the words concerning *many antichrists* coming in the *last days*. Jesus called them *ravening wolves.* This term is also associated with *the princes* inside *Jerusalem*:

> **Ezekiel 22:27: <u>Her princes in the midst thereof *are* like wolves ravening the prey, to shed blood, *and* to destroy souls, to get dishonest gain.</u> 28: And her prophets have daubed them with untempered *morter*, seeing vanity, and divining lies unto them, saying, Thus saith the Lord GOD, when the LORD hath not spoken. 29: The people of the land have used oppression, and exercised robbery, and have vexed the poor and needy: yea, they have oppressed the stranger wrongfully.**

> **Ezekiel 22:30: And I sought for a man among them, that should make up the hedge, and stand in the gap before me for the land, that I should not destroy it: but I found none. 31: Therefore have I poured out mine indignation upon them; I have consumed them with the fire of my wrath: <u>their own way have I recompensed upon their heads,</u> saith the Lord GOD.**

In the past year, I have seen an increasing work of the spirit of antichrist as some people have begun to proclaim that the Apostle Paul was a *ravening wolf* and that Paul was working under the spirit of antichrist. Why is this attack on the Apostle Paul coming today when even the early fellow believers never laid such an outstanding claim? I think the answer is contained in the truth that Paul was actively exposing the *spirit of antichrist*, as was John, and, of course, Jesus Himself:

> **1 John 2:18: Little children, it is the last time: and as ye have heard that antichrist shall come, even now are there many antichrists; whereby we know that it is the last time.**

Peter, when he understood the longsuffering of God pointed every believer in Christ to the Apostle Paul and his epistles. Why would Peter, under the inspiration of the Holy Spirit, point us to Paul's writings if he himself was not defending the truth of what Paul was proclaiming? Let us look at Peter's Words:

> **2 Peter 3:15: <u>And account *that* the longsuffering of our Lord *is* salvation; even as our beloved brother Paul also according to the wisdom given unto him hath written unto you;</u>**
>
> **16: As also in all *his* epistles, speaking in them of these things; in which are some things hard to be understood, which they that are unlearned and unstable wrest, as *they do* also the other scriptures, unto their own destruction.**
>
> **17: Ye therefore, beloved, seeing ye know *these things* before, beware lest ye also, being led away with the error of the wicked, fall from your own stedfastness. 18: But grow in grace, and in the knowledge of our Lord and Saviour Jesus Christ. To him be glory both now and for ever. Amen.**

These words of Peter pointed us to something so key concerning the final years of history. There is no doubt why the *spirit of antichrist* will be working hard to discredit Paul's writings. The Biblical truth remains that the disciples worked together in the *right hand of fellowship*. The verses below are one account of how Paul called out *Elymas* as a *child of the devil* who was seeking to turn away the faith of the deputy:

> **Acts 13:6: And when they had gone through the isle unto Paphos, they found a certain sorcerer, a false prophet, a Jew, whose name *was* Barjesus: 7: Which was with the deputy of the country, Sergius Paulus, a prudent man; who called for Barnabas and Saul, and desired to hear the word of God. 8: But Elymas the sorcerer (for so is his name by interpretation) withstood them, seeking to turn away the deputy from the faith.**
>
> **Acts 13:9: Then Saul, (who also *is called* Paul,) filled with the Holy Ghost, set his eyes on him, 10: And said, <u>O full of all subtilty and all mischief, *thou* child of the devil, *thou* enemy of all righteousness, wilt thou not cease to pervert the right ways of the Lord?</u>**
>
> **Acts 13:11: And now, behold, the hand of the Lord is upon thee, and thou shalt be blind, not seeing the sun for a season. And immediately there fell on him a mist and a darkness; and he went about seeking some to lead him by the hand.**
>
> **Acts 13:12: Then the deputy, when he saw what was done, believed, being astonished at the doctrine of the Lord. 13: Now when Paul and his company loosed from Pathos, they came to Perga in Pamphylia: and John departing from them returned to Jerusalem.**

The accusations today of Paul being a *ravening wolf* or one who was working under the *spirit of antichrist* are coming from the people who are attempting to *turn away many from the faith*. This type of accusation is the *spirit of antichrist* working through men. There is judgment that God will bring about for not only speaking against His chosen elect, but also, for attempting to discredit His Word, the Bible. Darkness came upon *Elymas* for a season as a judgment.

While it is true that Saul (name changed to Paul) persecuted the early church; once the encounter on the road to Damascus with the Lord occurred, things changed. Paul was greatly used by God and even when under the tribulation and pressure of others, his ministry thrived. Paul encouraged other believers to let his life be the example of how God is longsuffering:

> **1 Timothy 1:12: And I thank Christ Jesus our Lord, who hath enabled me, for that he counted me faithful, putting me into the ministry; 13: Who was before a blasphemer, and a persecutor, and injurious: but I obtained mercy, because I did *it* ignorantly in unbelief. 14: And the grace of our Lord was exceeding abundant with faith and love which is in Christ Jesus. 15: This *is* a faithful saying, and worthy of all acceptation, that Christ Jesus came into the world to save sinners; of whom I am chief. 16: Howbeit for this cause I obtained mercy, <u>that in me first Jesus Christ might shew forth all longsuffering, for a pattern to them which should hereafter believe on him to life everlasting.</u> 17: Now unto the King eternal, immortal, invisible, the only wise God, *be* honour and glory for ever and ever. Amen.**

Paul admitted that he blasphemed and persecuted the early church. Since he knew the depths of Satan, he was able to call out those who were doing this same dissuading of the truth. Elymas was a good example, but there are other Biblical examples of those who blaspheme God's people and His Word. There are also examples of people under the spirit of antichrist who falsely accuse true believers of blasphemy. Here are some verses that show the pattern of the *spirit of antichrist* is no different today as it was back then:

Acts 6:7: And the word of God increased; and the number of the disciples multiplied in Jerusalem greatly; and a great company of the priests were obedient to the faith. 8: And Stephen, full of faith and power, did great wonders and miracles among the people. 9: <u>Then there arose certain of the synagogue</u>, which is called *the synagogue* of the Libertines, and Cyrenians, and Alexandrians, and of them of Cilicia and of Asia, <u>disputing with Stephen.</u>

Acts 6:10: And they were not able to resist the wisdom and the spirit by which he spake. 11: Then they suborned men, which said, We have heard him speak blasphemous words against Moses, and *against* God.

Acts 6:12: <u>And they stirred up the people</u>, and the elders, and the scribes, and came upon *him*, and caught *him*, and brought him to the council, 13: And set up false witnesses, which said, This man ceaseth not to speak blasphemous words against this holy place, and the law:

Acts 6:14: For we have heard him say, that this Jesus of Nazareth shall destroy this place, and

146

shall change the customs which Moses delivered us. 15: And all that sat in the council, looking stedfastly on him, saw his face as it had been the face of an angel.

Certain men of the synagogue came accusing Stephen disputing with him. Then when the wisdom by which Stephen spoke put out the flame of the argument, the men of the synagogue *suborned men* (collusion) for the sake of further accusations against Stephen. Why would the Jewish leaders put such an effort into accusing one of God's elect? I believe Acts 6 holds the answer:

Acts 6:7: And the word of God increased; and the number of the disciples multiplied in Jerusalem greatly; and a great company of the priests were obedient to the faith.

It appears that those who were accusing Stephen were afraid of the monetary loss from those who were being converted into the faith of Christ. Stephen must have, by all accounts, known of the judgment coming upon the temple just as Jeremiah knew. Just like today, the believers in Christ know that before Christ returns, judgment must come on the fallen houses of God. When more people begin to obey the command to *come out of her my people*, it is possible that some church leaders who are only concerned with monetary gain will begin very similar accusations. This is what Satan does as the *accuser of the brethren* until we reach that great time in history where God will be magnified:

Revelation 12:10: And I heard a loud voice saying in heaven, Now is come salvation, and strength, and the kingdom of our God, and the power of his Christ: for the accuser of our brethren is cast

147

down, which accused them before our God day and night.

We have learned that Peter called Paul *beloved* and made sure we understood something that Paul understood: *God's longsuffering.* We have also learned how John accompanied Paul in Acts 13 and afterwards departed to Jerusalem. We have further learned that Paul, under the Holy Spirit, called out *Elymus* as a *child of the devil* for his attempts to *turn away the faith* of Sergius Paulus.

The Words of Paul and the Warning of *Perilous Times in the Last Days*

One true test of Paul's words under the guidance of the Holy Spirit concerns his declaration of *perilous times* coming in the *last days*. His understanding of this truth will prove itself to be a continued reality over the next couple of years. The identifiers of *perilous times of the last days* include:

> **2 Timothy 3:1: This know also, that in the last days <u>perilous times shall come</u>. 2: For men shall be lovers of their own selves, covetous, boasters, proud, blasphemers, disobedient to parents, unthankful, unholy, 3: Without natural affection, trucebreakers, false accusers, incontinent, fierce, despisers of those that are good, 4: Traitors, heady, high-minded, lovers of pleasures more than lovers of God; 5: Having a form of godliness, but denying the power thereof: from such turn away.**

Keep in mind that Paul is writing to Timothy (and all believers) concerning those who attempt to resist truth and are reprobate concerning the faith. Paul also in 2 Timothy 10 points out how his manner of life, doctrine, longsuffering, purpose, faith, charity and patience had been made known.

Those who resist truth will proceed no further and their *folly* will be manifest unto all men:

> **2 Timothy 3:8: Now as Jannes and Jambres withstood Moses, so do these also resist the truth: men of corrupt minds, reprobate concerning the faith. 9: <u>But they shall proceed no further: for their folly shall be manifest unto all *men*, as theirs also was.</u> 10: But thou hast fully known my doctrine, manner of life, purpose, faith, longsuffering, charity, patience, 11: Persecutions, afflictions, which came unto me at Antioch, at Iconium, at Lystra; what persecutions I endured: but out of them all the Lord delivered me.**

> **2 Timothy 3:12: Yea, and all that will live godly in Christ Jesus shall suffer persecution. 13: But <u>evil men and seducers shall wax worse and worse, deceiving, and being deceived.</u>**

> **2 Timothy 3:14: But <u>continue thou in the things which thou hast learned</u> and hast been assured of, knowing of whom thou hast learned *them*; 15: And that from a child thou hast known the holy scriptures, which are able to make thee wise unto salvation through faith which is in Christ Jesus.**

> **2 Timothy 3:16: All scripture *is* given by inspiration of God, and *is* profitable for doctrine, for reproof, for correction, for instruction in righteousness: 17: That the man of God may be perfect, thoroughly furnished unto all good works.**

Paul placed an emphasis on judgment for those who *resist the truth*, and he gave the example of two men who withstood Moses by saying, *their folly shall be manifest unto all men.*

149

Paul was the first example of God's longsuffering. It is not surprising that Satan's attacks on the believers in Christ will continue until the day dawns when worldwide salvation will be known by many. Satan (the little horn) wages war on the believers in Christ and also on the holy covenant:

> **Daniel 7:21: I beheld, and the same horn made war with the saints, and prevailed against them…**

> **Daniel 11:30: For the ships of Chittim shall come against him: therefore <u>he shall be grieved, and return, and have indignation against the holy covenant</u>: so shall he do; <u>he shall even return, and have intelligence with them that forsake the holy covenant.</u>**

The good news is that God is going to remove *the Northern* who is Satan, and then judgment will be established. At that time, which I believe we are all rapidly approaching in the year 2015, the believers will *consume and destroy* by the Gospel going forth into all the world prior to Christ's coming on the last day:

> **Daniel 7:25: And he shall speak *great* words against the most High, and <u>shall wear out the saints of the most High</u>, and think to change times and laws: and <u>they shall be given into his hand until a time and times and the dividing of time.</u>**

> **26: But the judgment shall sit, and <u>they shall take away his dominion, to consume and to destroy *it* unto the end.</u>**

We now have a better understanding of the *time, times and half a time*. This 3 ½ years, which mirrors the 3 ½ years of Christ's ministry as evil ramped up and desolation to the temple was seen, is also called the *last end of the indignation.* There will be more on this topic in the chapter concerning what Daniel understood.

False Accusers in the Perilous Times of the Last days

Below are some things that Paul pointed out concerning *perilous times* of the *last days.* These are the traits of people who do not have the Spirit of God:

False Accusers: This Greek word is *diablos* (G1228) and many times it is translated as *devil.* This tells us what spirit is controlling these accusers.

Traitors: This Greek word is *prodotes* (G4273) and it is used in association with Judas being the betrayer. We know that Satan entered into Judas and Judas was called the *son of perdition* as also is Satan. If Satan caused Judas to be a traitor, then in the *perilous times* of today there will also be *traitors or betrayers.*

Unthankful: We see the unthankful attitude of the people who are making accusations against Paul calling him a *ravening wolf* and working under the spirit of Satan. However, we see the opposite from Paul who was very thankful to God. This thankfulness is again showing the spiritual fruits of a real believer in Jesus:

> **Romans 16:3: Greet Priscilla and Aquila my helpers in Christ Jesus: 4: Who have for my life laid down their own necks: <u>unto whom not only I give thanks, but also all the churches of the Gentiles.</u>**

> **Ephesians 1:15: Wherefore I also, after I heard of your faith in the Lord Jesus, and love unto all the**

> **saints, 16: <u>Cease not to give thanks for you,</u> making mention of you in my prayers;**
>
> **2 Thessalonians 2:13: <u>But we are bound to give thanks alway to God for you, brethren beloved of the Lord</u>, because God hath from the beginning chosen you to salvation through sanctification of the Spirit and belief of the truth: 14: Whereunto he called you by our gospel, to the obtaining of the glory of our Lord Jesus Christ. 15: Therefore, brethren, stand fast, and hold the traditions which ye have been taught, whether by word, or our epistle.**

The warning by God's Word in 2 Timothy 3:2 proves the evil nature of the accusers. They will be unthankful. Paul was very thankful as is every believer who has experienced salvation by God's Spirit.

<u>Despisers of those that are good</u>: There is no doubt that the attacks on Paul today are from those that despise those that are good. The Greek word for *good* is *agathos* (G18) and the command to follow that which is good is for every believer in Jesus:

> **3 John 1:11: Beloved, follow not that which is evil, but that which is good. He that doeth good is of God: but he that doeth evil hath not seen God.**

Finally, it is very important that we know the scriptures well enough so that these kinds of attacks that Paul experienced by his accusers (*diablos*) will have no effect on those of us secure in God's Word. Since we are in the *last end of the indignation* (3 ½ years), I suspect these kind of accusations will continue but not for too long. Also, at this time there will be people that bear good fruit and other people who as servants of sin bear no good fruit. Paul's life was an example of bearing good fruit:

> **Romans 6:20: For when ye were the servants of sin, ye were free from righteousness. 21: <u>What fruit had ye then in those things whereof ye are now ashamed?</u> For the end of those things *is* death. 22: But now being made free from sin, and become servants to God, ye have your fruit unto holiness, and the end everlasting life. 23: For the wages of sin *is* death; but the gift of God *is* eternal life through Jesus Christ our Lord.**

Which of the accusers of Paul and his writings are concerned with *fruit unto holiness, and everlasting life*? I would argue that none have this concern and love. Which of the accusers of fellow believers are speaking about their thankfulness to God? Again, I would argue that I have heard no such thankfulness coming from these people attacking Paul. We will know them by their fruits. Their evil works will bare them out.

There is one final truth I want to point out concerning this time in which we are living. Since 2011, I became aware through the study of 2 Peter 3 that we are living in a time which can be called: *the time of God's longsuffering.* 2 Peter 3 is very significant in declaring that the flood of Noah's day was very much related to the coming of Christ on the last day.

Since 2011 was the 7,000[th] year anniversary of the Noachian Flood, many did believe that the year 2011 had incredible potential for Jesus' coming (*parousia*). However, the information concerning God's longsuffering was always there in 2 Peter 3. In fact, Peter wanted us all to know the importance of the wisdom given to the beloved brother Paul.

For me, that began my close investigation into Paul's epistles. Looking up the word *longsuffering* brought forth many truths.

Paul's Teachings from the Book of Isaiah

Paul understood that God would *endure with much longsuffering* the vessels of wrath in order to show mercy on the vessels of grace. God will make His power and mercy known. Paul, many times was drawing from the book of Isaiah and teaching these principles based on the understanding God had given him:

> **Isaiah 64:7: And there is none that calleth upon thy name, that stirreth up himself to take hold of thee: for thou hast hid thy face from us, and hast consumed us, because of our iniquities. 8: But now, O LORD, thou *art* our father; we *are* the clay, and <u>thou our potter; and we all *are* the work of thy hand.</u> 9: Be not wroth very sore, O LORD, neither remember iniquity for ever: behold, see, we beseech thee, we *are* all thy people.**

> **Romans 9:21: <u>Hath not the potter power over the clay</u>, of the same lump to make one vessel unto honour, and another unto dishonour? 22: *What* if <u>God, willing to shew *his* wrath, and to make his power known, endured with much longsuffering</u> the vessels of wrath fitted to destruction:**

> **Romans 9:23: And <u>that he might make known the riches of his glory on the vessels of mercy,</u> which he had afore prepared unto glory.**

In the context of the promise of His coming and the flood of Noah's day, Peter understood what Paul understood. There is a reason why the world would not perish as it did with the worldwide flood in 4990 B.C. Peter laid forth that *one thing* that we were not to misunderstand:

2 Peter 3:8: But, beloved, be not ignorant of this one thing, that one day *is* with the Lord as a thousand years, and a thousand years as one day.

We had arrived at the 7,000^(th) anniversary of the flood in the year 2011. Surely, Peter did not want us to be ignorant of this major time clue. Instead, Peter was alerting us to another important truth:

2 Peter 3:9: <u>The Lord is not slack concerning his promise</u>, as some men count slackness; <u>but is longsuffering to us-ward</u>, not willing that any should perish, but that all should come to repentance.

What Bible Truths Were Missed Prior to 2011?

We missed something very important and that is how God is longsuffering. Perhaps it was not the time for God to reveal this grand truth, since the mocking of 2 Peter 3 had to come to pass. God's patience is the reason 2011 came and went. He was not done revealing truth concerning the years of Darius, or the 3 ½ years of the *last end of the indignation*, or Elijah's prayer that it not rain for 3 ½ years where false worship was taking place. The Lord is not slack concerning His promise, but rather He is enduring with great patience so we can arrive at the *blessed is he that waits and comes to the 1,335^(th) day*. He is enduring so that from Pentecost 2015, the *Gospel of the kingdom* will go forth into all the world as a witness to the nations; then the end will come. Salvation is governing these final seven years from 2011 to 2018:

> **Matthew 24:14: And this gospel of the kingdom shall be preached in all the world for a witness unto all nations; and then shall the end come.**

The *Gospel of the kingdom* is received when God's Spirit causes people think different and believe the good news. Salvation will continue to the *last day*. This is the longsuffering and mercy of the most high God who created all things. Can you hear the command of Jesus as He proclaimed: *the kingdom of God is at hand: repent and believe the Gospel?*

> **Mark 1:14: Now after that John was put in prison, Jesus came into Galilee, preaching the gospel of the kingdom of God, 15: And saying, The time is fulfilled, and the kingdom of God is at hand: repent ye, and believe the gospel.**

Since Matthew 24:14 is proclaiming that the *Gospel of the kingdom* will be preached in all the world prior to the end, then we can know that people will *repent and believe* the good news. We are all going to be entering into such an incredible time of salvation once we reach Pentecost 2015, and after that time, that any other teaching of "no more salvation" will simply fall by the wayside.

Paul the First Example of God's Longsuffering

Once we grasp the importance of Peter pointing us to what Paul understood concerning God's longsuffering, then we can understand why the *spirit of antichrist* is attempting to discredit and turn many away from a huge portion of God's Word. Paul's writings speak much about God's longsuffering. He was the first example for those who would believe unto eternal life. God's longsuffering is such a critical issue regarding the final seven years of history. That

156

is why it is no surprise when we see Satan's emissaries waging war on Paul's writings and his character. Paul obtaining mercy from God allowed him to be an example of God's longsuffering:

> **1Timothy 1:15: This *is* a faithful saying, and worthy of all acceptation, that Christ Jesus came into the world to save sinners; of whom I am chief. 16: Howbeit <u>for this cause I obtained mercy, that in me first Jesus Christ might shew forth all longsuffering, for a pattern to them which should hereafter believe on him to life everlasting.</u>**

What an incredible statement from Paul. Jesus showed Paul all longsuffering for a pattern to the people who, from Paul's life and onward, would believe on Him to life everlasting. Now let us take this a step further. Since 2011, we have entered into a period of God's longsuffering. This means that salvation will be at the forefront of the final years of history. Keep this important truth of Pentecost 2015 in mind because we are rapidly approaching that time of great worldwide blessing and salvation. Once again, look at the arrival time of the second fulfillment of the 1,335th day, which is Pentecost in the year 2015:

The Pattern of the 1,335 Days Repeats from 2011 to 2015!		
9-28-0029 Feast of Trumpets (Jesus is Baptized)	←1,335 Days→	5-24-0033 Pentecost
9-28-2011 Feast of Trumpets	←1,335 Days→	5-24-2015 Pentecost

It is good news that God is longsuffering as we rapidly approach the 1335th day in the year 2015. Another significant truth about this time prior to Christ's glorious return is that similarities to the time of Daniel's captivity. God is giving wisdom and understanding to His people in these last days like He gave to Daniel. This is the topic of the next chapter. What important information was Daniel given, and what remaining information was reserved for the time of the end? Let's look at this exciting information.

Chapter 7—Wisdom & Understanding-Daniel's Captivity

When we study the account of Daniel during the 70-year captivity of Judah/Jerusalem, we cannot escape the truth that Daniel was given understanding by God about the *tribulation* periods. It took 21 days for Daniel to begin to have an answer from God, but it did come. Then as we look back and understand how much understanding was given during the 8,400 days ending on May 21, 2011, which is 4 x 2,100, we shake our heads in amazement knowing that God is the same yesterday, today, and forever.

Therefore, Daniel, Jeremiah, Amos and other men that God used to proclaim His Word are no different than any believer in Christ today. The key in Daniel's life was that he sought out God for understanding. Amos humbly admitted that he was not a prophet or a prophet's son, but rather, a herdsman and a fig farmer. Then God changed things for him and He commanded Amos to go and prophesy unto His people Israel:

> **Amos 7:14: Then answered Amos, and said to Amaziah, I *was* no prophet, neither *was* I a prophet's son; but I *was* an herdman, and a gatherer of sycamore fruit:**
>
> **Amos 7:15: And the LORD took me as I followed the flock, and the LORD said unto me, <u>Go, prophesy unto my people Israel.</u>**

God can use anyone He chooses to proclaim His truths. As we approach the year 2015 and this great time of salvation, I hope more people will understand the importance of asking for wisdom from God and desiring to serve Him. As we serve God and teach His truths from the Bible, more people will then also understand and teach others about the coming of Christ on the *last day*. So what understanding did Daniel receive from God? What limitations were set on him in understanding the things of the end?

<u>Daniel was Given Understanding</u>

In the past couple of years, I have found Daniel 11 to be one of the most difficult books in the Bible. Yet, I still will continue to study it. We wait upon God for understanding. Daniel was studying the book of Jeremiah, and through his study he understood important truths during the first year of Darius:

> **Daniel 9:2: In the first year of his reign I Daniel understood by books the number of the years, whereof the word of the LORD came to Jeremiah the prophet, that he would accomplish seventy years in the desolations of Jerusalem.**

> **Daniel 9:3: And I set my face unto the Lord God, to seek by prayer and supplications, with fasting, and sackcloth, and ashes...**

We know also that Daniel really sought understanding from God concerning the things of the end of time. In Daniel chapter 10, we learn how Daniel set his heart to understand:

> **Daniel 10:11: And he said unto me, O Daniel, a man greatly beloved, understand the words that I speak unto thee, and stand upright: for unto thee**

am I now sent. And when he had spoken this word unto me, I stood trembling.

Daniel 10:12: Then said he unto me, Fear not, Daniel: <u>for from the first day that thou didst set thine heart to understand</u>, and to chasten thyself before thy God, thy words were heard, and I am come for thy words.

Daniel 10:13: But the prince of the kingdom of Persia withstood me <u>one and twenty days</u>: but, lo, Michael, one of the chief princes, came to help me; and I remained there with the kings of Persia.

Daniel 10:14: Now I am come to make thee understand what shall <u>befall thy people in the latter days</u>: for yet the vision *is* for *many* days.

For those who wish to argue that Daniel's people in *the latter days* are the people of the Jewish nation, we must remember who was in the midst of the furnace with Daniel's companions in *tribulation*. The Son of God was there protecting them in the fire. Daniel's *people in the latter days* are those that believe in the Son of God, Jesus Christ. God's salvation plan is for Jew and Gentile:

Daniel 3:25: He answered and said, Lo, I see four men loose, walking in the midst of the fire, and they have no hurt; and the form of the fourth is like the Son of God.

I make this point because some church leaders are focusing way too much on the nation Israel in prophecy when the *Israel of God* are the ones who have been saved by God's Spirit, both Jew and Gentile:

Galatians 6:15: For in Christ Jesus neither circumcision availeth any thing, nor uncircumcision, <u>but a new creature.</u> 16: And as many as walk according to this rule, peace *be* on them, and mercy, <u>and upon the Israel of God.</u>

The Lord Jesus, in the book of Revelation, gave the understanding that the *New Jerusalem* is, in fact, the believers worldwide who have been saved by His Spirit. A very similar error made by some church leaders is that they are teaching that the temple in Jerusalem must be built first in order to fulfill prophecy. This teaching is based on the wrong doctrine of Christ reigning out of Jerusalem for 1,000 years. The Hebrew word for *Jerusalem* is *yru-shalaime* and means *founded peaceful*. The Hebrew word *shalem* (H7999) means *safe* or *restored*, and there is nothing greater in which the believer in Jesus Christ possesses. We are safe and at peace with His free gift of salvation and eternal life:

John 14:27: <u>Peace I leave with you, my peace I give unto you</u>: not as the world giveth, give I unto you. Let not your heart be troubled, neither let it be afraid.

Revelation 21:1: And I saw a new heaven and a new earth: for the first heaven and the first earth were passed away; and there was no more sea. 2: And I John saw the holy city, <u>new Jerusalem</u>, coming down from God out of heaven, prepared as a bride adorned for her husband.

Paul understood this peace and love of Christ. Nothing can separate us from the love of God, not powers, angels, things present or things to come. Not even death can separate the believer in Christ from God's love:

Romans 8:38: For I am persuaded, that neither death, nor life, nor angels, nor principalities, nor powers, nor things present, nor things to come, 39: Nor height, nor depth, nor any other creature, shall be able to separate us from the love of God, which is in Christ Jesus our Lord.

God is concerned with the salvation of both Jew and Gentile. The *circumcision of the heart* is what is important for believers worldwide. God's saving Spirit is what identifies the true *Israel of God*. Once a person experiences salvation by God's Spirit then nothing can separate them from the love of God.

Go Thy Way Daniel

The year 2011, which was the end of the 8,400 days of *tribulation* (4 x 21 x 100), was an important year of further understanding coming forth from God's Word. It became apparent that Daniel was given understanding about the things of the end, but how much information was Daniel given? I like the persistence of Daniel as well as the disciples when they were on the Mount of Olives. There on the mount, the disciple's asked Jesus: *What shall be the sign of thy coming and the end of the world* (age)?

Matthew 24:3: And as he sat upon the mount of Olives, the disciples came unto him privately, saying, Tell us, when shall these things be? And what *shall be* the sign of thy coming, and of the end of the world?

Daniel also posed a similar question about the last years but the question he posed was: *what shall be the hereafter of these?* Daniel's question was so very intriguing that I really wanted to understand why this particular question was denied an answer. Did Daniel receive an answer to his question? No, he was told twice to *go thy way*. He was also told that this information will be sealed until the time of the end.

Therefore, there would be an answer contained in God's completed Word but revealed only at a precise time in history. We are now living in that time in which God is unsealing this information. For Daniel, this must have been heartbreaking because it seemed that he was very concerned about fellow believers after hearing what would happen to them during this present time of *great tribulation*.

I have placed a reference chart in the back of this book to distinguish between the 8,400-day *tribulation* period and the 7-year *great tribulation* period. The good news concerning the 7-year *great tribulation* is the possibility that the Lord of heaven and earth has shortened the days to 3 ½ years—2011 to 2015. Then following is the 3 ½ years of rain as the Gospel goes into *all the world as a witness unto the nations*. Finally, the powerful coming of Christ on the last day will occur. This 3 ½ year period also relates to Daniel's question because the time clue he was given concerning the time of *great tribulation* was: *a time, times and half time* or 3 ½ years. He was concerned about what would happen after the 3 ½ years. Let us look at these verses from Daniel 12 and discuss each one:

Daniel 12:1 declares that *there will be a time of trouble (tribulation) such as never was since there was a nation*. Michael, the great prince, whose name means *who is like God,* shall stand up for *the children of thy people*. This verse also mentions that *thy people* whose names are written in the book *shall be delivered*. The people delivered are the believers in Jesus whose names are written in the Lamb's book of life (Revelation 21:27). This is again evidence of what group of people the book of Daniel is referring to as God calls them *thy people* or in other words Daniel's people. The believers in Jesus are the ones delivered in the time of trouble (*tribulation*) as Psalm 37:39-40 declares:

> **Psalm 37:39: But the salvation of the righteous is of the LORD: <u>he is their strength in the time of trouble</u>. 40: And <u>the LORD shall help them, and deliver them</u>: he shall deliver them from the wicked, and save them, because they trust in him.**

The Hebrew word for delivered is *mawlat* (H4422) and many times in God's Word this word means *to escape*. Below are two verses that show the use of *mawlat* or *to escape*. The first one is from Jeremiah 51 where the command to flee out of Babylon is given, which according to the book of Revelation is a prophecy against the fallen houses of God.

The second verse is from Genesis in which Lot was told to escape out of Sodom. We also know from the book of Revelation how God calls the fallen houses of God: *Sodom and Egypt*. Both verses are a strong warning to flee out of the fallen houses of God during this time of *great tribulation:*

> **Jeremiah 51:6: Flee out of the midst of Babylon, and <u>deliver</u> every man his soul: be not cut off in her iniquity; for this *is* the time of the LORD'S vengeance; he will render unto her a recompence.**

> **Genesis 19:17: And it came to pass, when they had brought them forth abroad, that he said, <u>Escape for thy life</u>; look not behind thee, neither stay thou in all the plain; escape to the mountain, lest thou be consumed.**

Understanding Christ's Command to Escape Out

In order to show why this escaping out of the fallen houses of God must occur, let us establish this truth from the Bible:

> **Revelation 18:2: And he cried mightily with a strong voice, saying, Babylon the great is fallen, is fallen, and <u>is become the habitation of devils, and the hold of every foul spirit, and a cage of every unclean and hateful bird</u>.**

> **Revelation 18:3: For all nations have drunk of the wine of the wrath of her fornication, and the kings of the earth have committed fornication with her, and the merchants of the earth are waxed rich through the abundance of her delicacies.**

> **Revelation 18:4: And I heard another voice from heaven, saying, <u>Come out of her, my people, that ye be not partakers of her sins, and that ye receive not of her plagues.</u> 5: For her sins have reached unto heaven, and God hath remembered her iniquities.**

The overthrowing of Sodom was the historical example of Christ overturning where *idleness, fullness of bread* and not strengthening the *poor and the needy* (Ezekiel 16:49). The historical account of Jesus' zeal when He overthrew the moneychangers also forecasts the overthrowing of the fallen houses of worship during the *great tribulation* period:

> **Amos 4:11: <u>I have overthrown *some* of you</u>, as God overthrew Sodom and Gomorrah, and ye were as a firebrand plucked out of the burning: yet have ye not returned unto me, saith the LORD.**

For the believers in Christ, escaping out where God commands us to escape to is critical. We are to flee to God whose righteousness is as the mountains. Daniel 12:1 is encouraging for believers because we know God is allowing us to escape so that we do not fall into the snare of the fowler:

> **Psalm 124:6: Blessed *be* the LORD, who hath not given us *as* a prey to their teeth. 7: <u>Our soul is escaped as a bird out of the snare of the fowlers</u>: the snare is broken, and we are escaped. 8: Our help *is* in the name of the LORD, who made heaven and earth.**

> **Psalm 125:2: As the mountains are round about Jerusalem, <u>so the LORD is round about his people from henceforth even for ever</u>.**

There is yet another verse which underscores how the believers will escape out of *great tribulation*. This verse really places an emphasis on where this *great tribulation* takes place; it occurs where Satan has taken his seat of authority. If any pastor believes that Satan is not interested in the houses of God, then any such pastor is underestimating the power of the enemy. Another verse which underscores how believers will escape this *great pressure* is Jeremiah 30:7. Jacob, who represents all of *the Israel of God,* shall be saved out of *great tribulation:*

> **Jeremiah 30:7: Alas! For that day *is* great, so that none *is* like it: <u>it *is* even the time of Jacob's trouble</u>; but he shall be saved out of it.**

Daniel 12:1 and also Matthew 24:21 speak of the *time of trouble* that has never been before. This could be because of the worldwide scope of *great tribulation* or pressure. If anyone wants to get an example of this pressure or tribulation, review Paul's life. In Macedonia the flesh did not have rest; they had *fightings without* and *fears within*. God sent comfort to Paul as he endured the pressure. He joyed in that comfort of fellow believers coming to him. With all three accounts below of the *time of trouble*, there is also salvation/deliverance mentioned in the midst of this *time of trouble*. We have read Jeremiah 30:7 and the declaration that *Jacob* will be *saved out of* the time of trouble. Let's review each *time of trouble*:

- Jeremiah 30:7- A time of trouble and there is none like it. The time of Jacob's trouble is a 7-year period (famine in the land), but he will be saved out of it. Historically, Jacob was saved out of it as he came to dwell in the land of Goshen. The greater picture today is all about Christ saving His people out of this present *time of trouble*.

- Daniel 12:1- A time of trouble such as there never was since there was a nation. *Michael*, whose name means *who is like God*, stands up for God's people. God's people who are found written in the book are delivered. It appears when Michael (*Myka-el*) *stands up,* Satan comes to his end. This comes at the time in which tidings from *the north* and *the east* trouble Satan and he goes with great fury/haste to take away a great many.

  Remember also how Satan comes against the *Prince of Princes* (Christ Himself) and is broken without power (Daniel 8:25). The language of Satan coming to his *end* lines up with Joel 2 as the *Northern* is removed. I believe the *end* mentioned in Daniel 11: 45 relates to the finishing of the 3 ½ years in 2015. This is what the *wonders* mentioned in the book of

Daniel was all about-*a time, times and half time.* Daniel was not given the hereafter of the 3 ½ years; he was only given information concerning the 3 ½ years.

- Matthew 24:21- A time of *great tribulation* such as never has been since the world began. Unless those days are shortened no flesh would be saved. Again, we have God rescuing His people and salvation going forth worldwide.

I believe all three accounts are speaking of the same time period of 3 ½ years, and then comes the huge change. The year 2015 qualifies as the most likely year for God's interception of Satan's evil activity. Since Daniel was told to seal up the Word and go his way, it is up to the believers in Christ to proclaim the truth of this timeframe of 3 ½ years, and also the final 3 ½ years of the gospel going forth into all the world.

God Uses His Creation to Represent His People

Daniel 12:3 mentions the time in which we are living now as those who are *wise shall shine as the brightness of the firmament* of the heavens. One thing that is extremely important in Bible study is to look closely at all the places a word is found in the Bible. The word *shine* really should have been translated as *warn* or *teach*.

Therefore, the wise (the believers to whom God has given wisdom), will be warning/teaching others of God's coming judgment. This transpires before God creates *new heavens and a new earth*. This time to *shine* (warn) is now! The lights in the firmament were established to separate the night from the day. In times of *tribulation* or darkness the believers are to warn.

God uses representations of His creation to demonstrate a believer's role of announcing Christ's glorious return on the *last day*. He uses trees to represent His planting of believers. Only a masterful creator can construct His Word in such a way that it reflects His masterful creation of life:

> **Jeremiah 17:7: Blessed *is* the man that trusteth in the LORD, and whose hope the LORD is. 8: For <u>he shall be as a tree planted by the waters</u>, and *that* spreadeth out her roots by the river, and shall not see when heat cometh, but her leaf shall be green; and shall not be careful in the year of drought, neither shall cease from yielding fruit.**

Daniel 12:4 informs us that Daniel was instructed to shut (*sasham* H5640) up the words and seal the book unto the time of the end when many *shall run to and fro* and knowledge will be increased. The first time Daniel was instructed to *shut up the words* was regarding the vision of the *evening morning*.

The beginning of the 2,300 *evening mornings* was the start of the 8,400-day *tribulation* period. Both the 2,300 *evening mornings* and the *time, times and half time* is when Satan is allowed to desolate. The latter *time, times and half time* is a literal 3 ½ years and also called *the last end of the indignation.* I do believe this time period is from 2011 to 2015 because this pattern was established during Christ's 3 ½ year ministry.

In other words, the 1,290/1,335 prophecy repeats twice in history. After a time of desolation (temple overrun), there comes a time of judgment (the cross). Then there comes a time of great worldwide salvation (Pentecost). The pattern of the 3 ½ years is seen again from the Feast of Trumpets in 2011 to Pentecost in 2015. The difference this time is how the judgment comes on the fallen houses of God for departing from God's Word. Now let's go back to Daniel 12.

Daniel was told that *knowledge will be increased*. If we use the original Hebrew word for knowledge (*daath* H1847), we will understand how this word relates to the knowledge of God's Word:

> **Psalm 119:66: <u>Teach me good judgment and knowledge:</u> for I have believed thy commandments. 67: Before I was afflicted I went astray: but now have I kept thy word.**

God uses the language of many running *to and fro* in Amos 8:12. God sends a famine in the land and many go *to and fro* seeking God's Word but cannot find it. It truly is God's mercy that He eventually releases knowledge of His Word and many people will understand His Word after a time of *famine* during the *great tribulation*.

Remember also that the *great affliction* of Joseph's time was when Jacob (Israel) had to go into Egypt because they found no sustenance in Canaan. His son, Joseph, set them up in the fruitful land of Goshen at Pharaoh's decree. This time of famine of hearing God's Word is the last seven years called the *great affliction* or *great tribulation*. The good news is that Jesus promises that these days will be shortened so that salvation will go forth in a huge way:

> **Mark 13:19: For <u>*in* those days shall be affliction, such as was not from the beginning of the creation</u> which God created unto this time, <u>neither shall be.</u> 20: And except that the Lord had shortened those days, no flesh should be saved: but for the elect's sake, whom he hath chosen, he hath shortened the days.**

Acts 7:11: Now there came a dearth over all the land of Egypt and Chanaan, and <u>great affliction: and our fathers found no sustenance.</u>

As we live in this time of *great affliction (tribulation)*, it is important that we seek God for understanding and mercy. This world is heading for a huge change. Christian persecution or pressure coming upon Christians is on the rise worldwide. There are lands where Christians are told to "covert or die," they have a choice to move, pay an extreme tax or face persecution. The *spirit of antichrist* is working everywhere in these final years. In 1 John 2:18, God's Word proclaims that we can know it's the *last time* due to *many antichrists*. The *Great Tribulation* mentioned in Matthew 24 places more of the focus on false Christ's and false prophets:

Matthew 24:11: And <u>many false prophets</u> shall rise, and <u>shall deceive many</u>. 12: And because iniquity shall abound, the love of many shall wax cold. 13: But he that shall endure unto the end, the same shall be saved. 14: And this gospel of the kingdom shall be preached in all the world for a witness unto all nations; and then shall the end come.

The rejection of Jesus being the anointed one, the Son of God, is also a sign of the spirit of Antichrist. Many religions of the world do the very thing that 1 John is warning us about. World religions place Jesus on the level of "a prophet" and ignore how the Bible proclaims that He is the Son of God. The good news is that God is going to *shake the heavens and the earth*. The kingdoms of the world will become *of the Lord* and *of Christ; He shall be reigning into the eons of the eons* (Revelation 11:15- ISA). Changes are soon coming!

<u>Daniel 12 Reveals an Important Time Clue</u>

Daniel 12:5 mentions how Daniel looked and beheld two others, one who stood on one side of the river and one who stood on the other side. In Daniel 10, there is mention of the river which was also one of the four rivers mentioned in Genesis 2:14 (*hiddekel*) as it is called the third river flowing out of Eden:

> **Daniel 10:5: Then I lifted up mine eyes, and looked, and behold a certain man clothed in linen, whose loins *were* girded with fine gold of Uphaz:**
>
> **6: His body also *was* like the beryl, and his face as the appearance of lightning, and <u>his eyes as lamps of fire</u>, and his arms and his feet like in colour to polished brass, and the voice of his words like the voice of a multitude.**

Who is the one clothed *in linen girded with fine gold* whose voice was *like the voice of a multitude* and eyes like flames of fire? It is none other than the Lord Jesus Himself. We know this from similar language from the book of Revelation:

> **Revelation 1:13: And in the midst of the seven candlesticks *one* like unto the Son of man, clothed with <u>a garment</u> down to the foot, and <u>girt about the paps with a golden girdle</u>. 14: His head and *his* hairs *were* white like wool, as white as snow; and <u>his eyes *were* as a flame of fire</u>; 15: And his feet like unto fine brass, as if they burned in a furnace; and <u>his voice as the sound of many waters.</u> 16: And he had in his right hand seven stars: and out of his mouth went a sharp twoedged sword: and**

his countenance *was* as the sun shineth in his strength.

The Lord was above the waters, and one other stood on one side of the bank of the river, and yet another stood on the other side. Then we read of the big question by one or both of the two beings standing by the bank of the river Hiddekel. It is not clear who asked this question or whether it was asked in unison. The King James translators injected *one said* but the question may have been asked in unison by both beings on both sides of the river. What was that big question for the Lord, who was above the waters, clothed in fine linen and whose eyes were a flame of fire? The question was about the time in which we are all currently living. It is exciting to know that what Daniel heard applies to this very time in history, the *time, times and half time* or 3 ½ years. Let's review the question that was asked by Daniel.

How Long Shall it be to the End of These Wonders?

Daniel 12:6: And *one* said to the man clothed in linen, which *was* upon the waters of the river, How long *shall it be to* the end of these wonders?

In searching out the Hebrew word *pele* (H6382) which has properly been translated as *wonders*, I find these *wonders* are truly an amazing thing performed by God. From Biblical times in the past until right up to the final years of history, God is performing great wonders. Grace, mercy and salvation will be the end result. To get a glimpse of the word *wonders* or *pele* below are a few examples of God's power.

Isaiah 29 mentions the *wonders* that God performs to those people whose lips honor Him, but their hearts are far from Him. God causes a spirit of deep sleep and closes the eyes of the prophets and rulers. It is no wonder why the rulers in the houses of God do not know the time of their judgment:

> **Isaiah 29:11: And the vision of all is become unto you as the words of a book that is sealed, which *men* deliver to one that *is* learned, saying, Read this, I pray thee: and he saith, I cannot; for it is sealed:**
>
> **12: And the book is delivered to him that is not learned, saying, Read this, I pray thee: and he saith, I am not learned.**
>
> **13: Wherefore the Lord said, Forasmuch as this people draw near *me* with their mouth, and with their lips do honour me, but have removed their heart far from me, and <u>their fear toward me is taught by the precept of men</u>:**
>
> **14: Therefore, behold, I will proceed to do a <u>marvelous work</u> among this people, <u>*even a* marvelous work and a wonder</u>: for the wisdom of their wise *men* shall perish, and the understanding of their prudent *men* shall be hid.**

This marvelous work God performs is to bring down the lofty and to exalt the lowly. Satan working in the midst of the fallen houses of God has caused a great pride to be seen just as Moab was full of pride in his land. The chapter entitled: *Within Three Years the Glory of Moab Will be Despised* will show how the timing of God lowering the glory of the fallen houses of worship relates to the timeframe around the year 2015. With Moab, God once again is using an historical account to show how judgment will come on the fallen houses of worship.

While speaking about the wonder God performs, the book of Lamentations also addresses *the daughter of Zion* or the fallen houses of God. In Lamentations, God said that *she came down wonderfully*:

> **Lamentations 1:9: Her filthiness *is* in her skirts; she remembereth not her last end; therefore she came down wonderfully: she had no comforter. O LORD, behold my affliction: for <u>the enemy hath magnified *himself*</u>.**
>
> **10: The adversary hath spread out his hand upon all her pleasant things: for she hath seen *that* <u>the heathen entered into her sanctuary</u>, whom thou didst command *that* they should not enter into thy congregation.**

After Daniel asked the question: *How long until the end of these wonders?* he was given the time reference of 3 ½ years. However, Daniel did not seem to understand past the time reference of 3 ½ years because it was to be sealed until the time of the end. That is what makes this so exciting and does a great service to confirm God's Word as truth:

> **Daniel 12:7: And I heard the man clothed in linen, which *was* upon the waters of the river, when he held up his right hand and his left hand unto heaven, and sware by him that liveth for ever that <u>*it shall be* for a time, times, and an half</u>; and when he shall have accomplished to scatter the power of the holy people, all these *things* shall be finished.**

When Satan shall have accomplished to *break the hand* or *scatter the power* of the people of holiness, this ends the reign of Satan. Then, according to Joel 2, Satan is removed by God. While looking at the Hebrew word *qodesh* (H6944), we see Satan's acts against the holiness of God's salvation plan and His covenant:

- Satan's heart shall be against the *covenant of holiness* or God's salvation (Daniel 11:28)
- Satan shall have intelligence with those who *forsake the covenant of holiness*. He has great indignation and the 3 ½ years is called *the last end of the indignation*.
- Satan is the king of fierce countenance who understands God's parables (translated as *dark sayings*). By his craft (deceit/deceiving) he prospers and practices to destroy the *power of the holy people* until he stands up against the *Prince of Princes* (the Lord Jesus Christ), and he is *broken without hand* (power). This truth is found in Daniel 8:23-25:

Daniel 8:23: And in the latter time of their kingdom, when the transgressors are come to the full, a king of fierce countenance, and understanding dark sentences, shall stand up. 24: And his power shall be mighty, but not by his own power: and he shall destroy wonderfully, and <u>shall prosper, and practise, and shall destroy the mighty and the holy people</u>. 25: And through his policy also he shall cause craft to prosper in his hand; and he shall magnify *himself* in his heart, and by peace shall destroy many: <u>he shall also stand up against the Prince of princes; but he shall be broken without hand.</u>

I believe the timing of Satan being *broken without power* is the year 2015. This is based on Joel 2 as God removes *the Northern* after a time of Satan magnifying himself. It is also based on Daniel 7 where the believers in Christ will *consume and destroy* the kingdom of Satan once *judgment sits:*

> **Daniel 7:25: And he shall speak *great* words against the most High, and shall wear out the saints of the most High, and think to change times and laws: and <u>they shall be given into his hand until a time and times and the dividing of time</u>.**

> **26: But the judgment shall sit, and they shall take away his dominion, <u>to consume and to destroy *it* unto the end</u>.**

> **27: And the kingdom and dominion, and the greatness of the kingdom under the whole heaven, shall be given to the people of the saints of the most High, whose kingdom *is* an everlasting kingdom, and all dominions shall serve and obey him.**

While studying Daniel 12, it was difficult to find another verse which uses the phrase or words *wear out the saints of the most High*. The Hebrew word *wear* is *b'la* (H1080), and it is used once in Daniel 7:25. However, a similar word *balah* (H1086) is used in 1 Chronicles 17 in which God promises that *neither shall the children of wickedness waste them anymore*. This is precisely how Satan operates. The *children of wickedness* are used of Satan to ware down the believers and accusations are one method of attack. Satan desired *to sift* Peter *like wheat*. While Peter was warming himself by the fire, the accusations began as he was accused of being one of Jesus' disciples. What Satan may not know is that this creates strength in the believer and in time, Peter was able to strengthen fellow believers in Christ:

178

Luke 22:31: And the Lord said, Simon, Simon, behold, Satan hath desired *to have* you, that he may sift *you* as wheat: 32: But I have prayed for thee, that thy faith fail not: and <u>when thou art converted, strengthen thy brethren.</u>

No More Wearing Down of God's People

The incredibly good news of this present time coming to a rapid close it that God eventually performs a powerful reversal:

1 Chronicles 17:9: Also I will ordain a place for my people Israel, and will plant them, and they shall dwell in their place, and shall be moved no more; <u>neither shall the children of wickedness waste them any more, as at the beginning</u>...

According to Daniel 12, once the believers are given into the hand of the enemy for a period of 3 ½ years, there may be an exhaustion felt by believers in Christ. This happens until Christ *rises up to the prey* and things begin to turn around.

Daniel has a great concern about this and asks: *What shall be the end of these?* This question could relate to the end of all the things mentioned in Daniel 12 or he could be asking what shall be the end of *these* meaning God's people. Daniel was told that for a *time, times and half of time* the people of God would be given into the hand of the enemy. At the end of the 3 ½ years, *all these shall be finished* (*exhausted*). The Hebrew word for *finished* is *kalah* (H3615), which has also been translated as *exhausted*. I do believe Daniel's concern was for the believers of the end. His question shows that while he did get a time reference, he did not quite understand:

179

> **Daniel 12:8: And I heard, but I understood not: then said I, O my Lord, what** *shall be* **the end of these** *things***? 9: And he said, Go thy way, Daniel: for the words are closed up and sealed till the time of the end.**

Daniel became a similitude of what would occur at the time of the end. He experienced illness and felt desolated (*astonished*):

> **Daniel 8:27: And I Daniel fainted, and was sick** *certain* **days; afterward I rose up, and did the king's business; and I was** <u>astonished</u> **at the vision, but none understood** *it.*

Perhaps this is why he was inquiring about *the end of these.* The Hebrew word *end* in which Daniel asked about is very different from the other uses of the word *end* in Daniel 12. To paraphrase what Daniel was asking, we could say: *What shall be the hereafter of these?* or *What shall be the future of these?* The Hebrew word for *end* is *achariyth* (H319), and the following verse uses this same word:

> **Proverbs 19:20: Hear counsel, and receive instruction, that thou mayest be wise** <u>in thy latter end.</u>

Daniel was asking about *after* the period of a *time, times and half a time.* He was asking the question directed at the *hereafter of these.* What shall be the future for God's people who live during this time after the 3 ½ years? I think the book of Jeremiah says it best:

> **Jeremiah 29:11: For I know the thoughts that I think toward you, saith the LORD,** <u>thoughts of peace, and not of evil, to give you an expected end.</u>

> **12: Then shall ye call upon me, and ye shall go and pray unto me, and I will hearken unto you. 13: And ye shall seek me, and find *me*, when ye shall search for me with all your heart. 14: And I will be found of you, saith the LORD: and I will turn away your captivity, and I will gather you from all the nations, and from all the places whither I have driven you, saith the LORD; and I will bring you again into the place whence I caused you to be carried away captive.**

Job, who also had to endure the attack of Satan, was blessed double at the *latter end.*

> **Job 42:12: So the LORD blessed the latter end of Job more than his beginning: for he had fourteen thousand sheep, and six thousand camels, and a thousand yoke of oxen, and a thousand she asses.**

Daniel was given the period of 3 ½ years, which is the last end of the defiance or indignation. Then we arrive at God's reversal, which is great for His people as we will all rejoice but His indignation at that time comes upon His enemies:

> **Isaiah 66:14: And when ye see this, your heart shall rejoice, and your bones shall flourish like an herb: and the hand of the LORD shall be known toward his servants, and his indignation toward his enemies.**

There were 23 years of *tribulation* from 1988 to 2011, and then there is a period of 7 years which is patterned after the time of Jacob's trouble. These 7 years of *great tribulation* are significant since God has shortened this time to 3 ½ years for the sake of salvation going forth unto the *last day.* Yet, the entire period is still 7 final years. I believe 2015 to 2018 are

God's final years of history where the Gospel will go forth worldwide.

> **Matthew 24:14: And this gospel of the kingdom shall be preached in all the world for a witness unto all nations; and <u>then shall the end come</u>.**

I know for the reader of this book, you may have seen repeated verses in different chapters. The reason I am doing this is because so much of this information fits perfectly in the final 7 years. Let us review the final verses of Daniel 12:

> **Daniel 12:9: And he said, Go thy way, Daniel: for the words *are* closed up and sealed till the time of the end. 10: Many shall be purified, and made white, and tried; but the wicked shall do wickedly: and none of the wicked shall understand; but <u>the wise shall understand</u>. 11: And from the time *that* the daily *sacrifice* shall be taken away, and the abomination that maketh desolate set up, *there shall* be a thousand two hundred and ninety days. 12: <u>Blessed *is* he that waiteth, and cometh to the thousand three hundred and five and thirty days</u>. 13: But go thou thy way till the end *be*<u>: for thou shalt rest, and stand in thy lot at the end of the days.</u>**

The 1,335 days, which includes the 1,290 days, has been shown to be from the time John the Baptist baptized Christ to finally arriving at the time of Pentecost in 33 A.D. Harold Camping did some pronounced work on this prophecy and showed how it related to Jesus' 3 ½ year ministry. We have seen already how this precise pattern repeats from the year 2011 to the year 2015 when we finally arrive at the 1,335[th] day. I believe Daniel wanted to know what would happen to God's people after the 3 ½ years or *time, times and half a time* of *great tribulation.* He wanted to know the *hereafter* of *these.* He was told twice to *go thy way.* The last time he was told to *go thy way till the end be,* and then he was promised that he would *rest* and stand in his inheritance or *lot at the end of the days.*

> **Psalm 16:5: The LORD *is* the portion of mine inheritance and of my cup: <u>thou maintainest my lot.</u>**

The word *end* in Daniel 12:8 is different than the word *end* in Daniel 12:13. The first means *hereafter* and second means *extremity.* Daniel was allowed to know about the 3 ½ years but he was not given understanding to the *hereafter* or past the 3 ½ years. At the very end or extremity of the days, the very *last day,* Daniel will be resurrected to stand in his inheritance. The following verse, which mentions the warning of the flood, shows how the Hebrew word *qets* (H7093) means *final extremity*:

> **Genesis 6:13: And God said unto Noah, <u>The end of all flesh</u> is come before me; for the earth is filled with violence through them; and, behold, I will destroy them with the earth.**

I want to close this chapter with a Psalm. God has truly blessed His people with wisdom and understanding. When God mentions *that none of the wicked shall understand* but the *wise shall understand,* we know that it is only by God giving wisdom that anyone can become wise. The wicked are too busy doing wickedly, but if one is humble and asks God for wisdom, God will honor His promise. We then must be patient for God to take action and keep His way:

> **Psalm 37:32: The wicked watcheth the righteous, and seeketh to slay him. 33: The LORD will not**

leave him in his hand, nor condemn him when he is judged. 34: <u>Wait on the LORD, and keep his way, and he shall exalt thee to inherit the land: when the wicked are cut off, thou shalt see *it*.</u>

In assembling the topics for this book, I wanted to make sure that a discussion of *unto the coming of the Lord* was addressed. James chapter five holds some incredible time clues concerning *the coming of the Lord* on the *last day*. This is great information to explore.

Chapter 8—Unto the Coming of the Lord-
Elijah & Job

Have you ever read a section of God's Word and wondered why God placed that particular bit of information in His Word, only to understand at a later time that there is colossal reason why the information is there? The book of James has been one of my favorite books of the Bible, especially in my earlier studies.

I remember reading in James 5:1 the words: *if any of you lack wisdom* and how that got my attention. It was like I was raising my hand in a classroom and saying: "uh yeah, I could use some over here." The more I read that verse, the more that promise becomes significant.

After all, this is a promise from the God who created this world with His spoken word. Who would not want wisdom from the One who can create such an incredible universe? I did ask God and continue to ask Him for wisdom. I am not one who passes up such a great promise:

> **James 1:5: If any of you lack wisdom, let him ask of God, that giveth to all *men* liberally, and upbraideth not; and it shall be given him. 6: But let him ask in faith, nothing wavering. For he that wavereth is like a wave of the sea driven with the wind and tossed.**

Here we all are living in the time in which Daniel was so inquisitive, and, once again, the book of James holds some incredible truths. I love God's Word and thank Him for the truths of hope it contains. One such hope is the coming of the Lord on the *last day*. The hope of every believer in Christ is that we see Him coming in *power and great glory* as the light shines from the east to the west. *Every eye shall see Him* and no longer will the name of God be taken for granted by a world which has attempted to remove His truths from daily life.

In James 5, in the context of *unto the coming of the Lord*, God brings to the forefront Elijah and Job. Why are Elijah and Job mentioned and not any other men of God that the Lord has directed in the past?

Concerning Job:

> **James 5:10: Take, my brethren, the prophets, who have spoken in the name of the Lord, for an example of suffering affliction, and of patience. 11: Behold, we count them happy which endure. Ye have heard of the patience of Job, and have seen the end of the Lord; that the Lord is very pitiful, and of tender mercy.**

Concerning Elijah (*Helias* in Greek):

> **James 5:17: Elias was a man subject to like passions as we are, and he prayed earnestly that it might not rain: and <u>it rained not on the earth by the space of three years and six months</u>. 18: And he prayed again, and the heaven gave rain, and the earth brought forth her fruit.**

Before I get into these verses concerning Job and Elijah, I wanted to present some important verses mentioned earlier in James 5:

James 5:7: <u>Be patient therefore, brethren, unto the coming of the Lord</u>. Behold, the husbandman waiteth for the precious fruit of the earth, and hath long patience for it, until he receive the early and latter rain. 8: Be ye also patient; stablish your hearts: for the coming of the Lord draweth nigh.

In James 5:7, God is alerting us to the fact that He is being patient for the sake of salvation. The *precious fruit of the earth* are those people who are saved by the Spirit of God, which Christ equated to the wind that blows:

John 3:7: Marvel not that I said unto thee, Ye must be born again. 8: The wind bloweth where it listeth, and thou hearest the sound thereof, but canst not tell whence it cometh, and whither it goeth: so is every one that is born of the Spirit.

Knowing how God's Spirit saves people and cleanses them from sin is exciting since we are now rapidly approaching the year 2015. Will Pentecost 2015 match or surpass Pentecost 33 A.D. where about 3,000 were saved by God's Spirit in one day? Since Pentecost in 2015 will be worldwide, I believe it will surpass the historical Pentecost in 33 A.D. The pattern of the 1,335 days repeats from the year 2011 to the year 2015! This means that a good possibility of a second fulfillment of Pentecost will come at Pentecost 2015! From the year 2015 onward it is Gospel time worldwide.

The Pattern of the 1,335 Days Repeats from 2011 to 2015!		
9-28-0029 Feast of Trumpets (Jesus is Baptized)	←1,335 Days→	5-24-0033 Pentecost
9-28-2011 Feast of Trumpets	←1,335 Days→	5-24-2015 Pentecost
From Cross to Pentecost 33 A.D.	50 Days of Waiting	About 3,000 saved by God's Spirit in one day.
From Anniversary of Cross in 2015	50 Days of Waiting	Worldwide Salvation by God's Spirit.
2015 to 2018	*2 Witnesses Arise*	Gospel proclaimed

The aspect of patience is completely understandable. If God is waiting for the *precious fruit of the earth*, which is the salvation of people worldwide, then we also need to exercise patience so that people can become saved by God's Spirit. Job was a good example of patience during a period of attack by Satan. Since Satan was active during Job's time and also the final *last end of the indignation*, then we can understand why God wants us to learn from Job's experience. Some very relevant language is found in the book of Job such as *the time of trouble.*

God has Reserved Treasures of Hail

> **Job 38:22: Hast thou entered into the treasures of the snow? Or hast thou seen the treasures of the hail, 23: <u>Which I have reserved against the time of trouble</u>, against the day of battle and war? 24: By**

188

what way is the light parted, *which* scattereth the east wind upon the earth?

The *time of trouble* can be translated as the *time of tribulation*. In the final years of history God has expanded on the historical patterns of *tribulation*; both Judah's 70-year *tribulation* and Jacob's 7-year *great tribulation*. A few times in the Bible God uses snow as a reference to His Word and also as a spiritual reference of the cleansing of His salvation:

Psalm 148:8: Fire, and hail; snow, and vapour; stormy wind fulfilling his word...

Isaiah 1:18: Come now, and let us reason together, saith the LORD: <u>though your sins be as scarlet, they shall be as white as snow</u>; though they be red like crimson, they shall be as wool.

Isaiah 55:9: For *as* the heavens are higher than the earth, so are my ways higher than your ways, and my thoughts than your thoughts. 10: For as the rain cometh down, <u>and the snow from heaven</u>, and returneth not thither, but watereth the earth, and maketh it bring forth and bud, that it may give seed to the sower, and bread to the eater: 11: <u>So shall my word be that goeth forth out of my mouth: it shall not return unto me void, but it shall accomplish that which I please, and it shall prosper *in the thing* whereto I sent it.</u>

Assuredly, God has reserved the *treasures of snow* as an illustration of His Word which goes forth out of His mouth and it will *not return void*. It will prosper during the time of *trouble/tribulation* and especially after the 3 ½ years. God also uses similar analogies with the *dew of heaven* and *rain* to show the power of His Word:

> **Deuteronomy 32:1: Give ear, O ye heavens, and I will speak; and hear, O earth, the words of my mouth. 2: <u>My doctrine shall drop as the rain, my speech shall distil as the dew, as the small rain upon the tender herb, and as the showers upon the grass</u>: 3: Because <u>I will publish the name of the LORD</u>: ascribe ye greatness unto our God.**

There is much to learn from the book of Job, including the fact that Satan brought about destruction to Job's seven sons and three daughters which totaled ten (a number of tribulation). The youths were *eating and drinking wine* in the eldest son's house when a strong wind, from the wilderness, touched the *four corners* of the house and they were killed. Job's concern for his children was that if while sinning, they were blessing God.

The Hebrew word for *blessed* is *barak* (H1288). While certain Hebrew words can have two meanings, further study of what Satan was requesting of God really explains this time of tribulation for Job. The King James translators used the translation of *cursed God* instead of the translation of *blessed God*: *it may be that my sons have sinned and cursed God*. In other words, if someone is sinning and then thanking or blessing God for sin, that would bring about a judgment. This activity is seen in the book of Zechariah:

> **Zechariah 11:4: Thus saith the LORD my God; Feed the flock of the slaughter; 5: Whose possessors slay them, and hold themselves not guilty: and <u>they that sell them say, Blessed be the LORD; for I am rich: and their own shepherds pity them not.</u>**

I believe this is why Job was so concerned for his sons and offered burnt sacrifices in case his sons were sinning and then *blessing God.* This kind of thing is also seen today in the houses of God as some pastors profit from the teaching of prosperity gospels, and then bless God for their ill gained prosperity. God is a God of equity who cares for the *poor and needy,* yet His judgment comes on those who forsake the *poor and needy* who are representing God's people:

> **Ezekiel 22:29: The people of the land have used oppression, and <u>exercised robbery</u>, and have <u>vexed the poor and needy</u>: yea, they have oppressed the stranger wrongfully.**

God, when He finds not one man who will stand in the gap before Him, He then sends *recompense upon their own heads* as seen in Ezekiel 22:31:

> **Ezekiel 22:31: Therefore have I poured out mine indignation upon them; I have consumed them with the fire of my wrath: <u>their own way have I recompensed upon their heads</u>, saith the Lord GOD.**

The number ten is seen a few times in the book of Job. Ten can be a number related to *tribulation;* the book of Job can really reflect times of *tribulation:*

> **Revelation 2:9: I know thy works, and tribulation, and poverty, (but thou art rich) and *I know* the blasphemy of them which say they *are* Jews, and are not, but are the synagogue of Satan. 10: Fear none of those things which thou shalt suffer: behold, <u>the devil shall cast *some* of you into prison, that ye may be tried; and ye shall have tribulation ten days</u>: be thou faithful unto death, and I will give thee a crown of life.**

Job 19:1: Then Job answered and said, 2: How long will ye vex my soul, and break me in pieces with words? 3: <u>These ten times have ye reproached me</u>: ye are not ashamed *that* ye make yourselves strange to me.

Satan's request to God was that if the hedge of protection around Job was removed and all that Job possessed was *touched*, then he would not bless God to His face:

Job 1:11: But put forth thine hand now, and touch all that he hath, and he will curse thee to thy face.

In the ISA there is the negative word of *not* that is not seen in the King James translation. Satan, with evil intent, was declaring that all blessing was due to God not hiding His face from Job. If all that Job had was *touched* (removed) would Job still bless God? Here is one Psalm that underscores God's blessing by God not hiding His face:

Psalm 27:8: *When thou saidst*, <u>Seek ye my face</u>; my heart said unto thee, <u>Thy face, LORD, will I seek</u>. 9: Hide not thy face *far* from me; put not thy servant away in anger: thou hast been my help; leave me not, neither forsake me, O God of my salvation.

After Satan, by the edge of the sword of the Sabeans (Sheba), the edge of the sword of the Chaldeans, a destroying wind, fire, and harm to his flesh takes almost everything in Job's life; what is Job's reaction?

Job 1:20: Then Job arose, and rent his mantle, and shaved his head, and fell down upon the ground, and worshipped, 21: And said, Naked came I out of my mother's womb, and naked shall I return

thither: the LORD gave, and the LORD hath taken away; <u>blessed be the name of the LORD</u>.

I believe Job's wife was not harmed because of the Biblical principle of the husband and wife becoming *one flesh*. God told Satan: *only upon himself put not forth thy hand*. That command by God to Satan would include Job's wife. The only other ones that *escaped* were the messengers who brought Job the bad news.

The book of Job is full of language of tribulation. Job was enduring tribulation, at the hands of Satan, as an illustration of the final years of tribulation. Riddled throughout Job's words are evidences of this truth. Job's words of *anguish of my spirit* can be translated as *tribulation of my spirit*. I counted eight times were the Hebrew word for tribulation/adversary is seen in the book of Job. *Tribulation of my spirit* is one of the eight times that this Hebrew word *Tsar* (H6862) is used in the book of Job:

Job 7:11: Therefore I will not refrain my mouth; I will speak in the <u>anguish of my spirit</u>; I will complain in the bitterness of my soul.

<u>The Major Time Clue of Elijah's Prayer- 3 ½ years</u>

James 5:17: Elias was a man subject to like passions as we are, and he prayed earnestly that it might not rain: and it rained not on the earth by the space of three years and six months. 18: And he prayed again, and the heaven gave rain, and the earth brought forth her fruit.

God sprinkles time clues within His Word to be discovered by those who are studying the Bible. I had wondered before why God would mention the 3 ½ years of Elijah praying for no rain and no rain from heaven was given. Why was Elijah praying for no rain? The answer is found in the Bible.

The Sin of Samaria- The Sin of Jezebel and Ahab

We need to go back to the Old Testament to find out the reason for Elijah telling Ahab that no rain would come for a period of 3 ½ years. In the Old Testament, we find that the people of Samaria were involved with false worship. Ahab and Jezebel, his wife, brought Samaria into evil practices by erecting false worship there.

Elijah prayer for no rain would encompass a period of 3 ½ years. A number like *three years and six months* seems like an odd number unless there is a real truth to be discovered and then applied to the final seven years of *great tribulation*. We must remember how James 5 is speaking of *unto the coming of the Lord*. We are to look to Job and Elijah for a very good reason. History is repeating and false worship is happening in the fallen houses of God worldwide. There is also the aspect of how Jesus' warning to the seven churches included casting some people into a bed of *great tribulation* with Jezebel:

> **Revelation 2:21: And I gave her space to repent of her fornication; and she repented not. 22: Behold, I will cast her into a bed, and them that commit adultery with her into <u>great tribulation</u>, except they repent of their deeds.**

Ahab and Jezebel- Leaders of False Worship

When Jesus references *great tribulation* and also the historical name of Jezebel, we must look at everything concerning the period of *great tribulation*. We must also study what Jezebel and Ahab did historically:

194

> **1Kings 16:30: And Ahab the son of Omri did evil in the sight of the LORD above all that *were* before him. 31: And it came to pass, as if it had been a light thing for him to walk in the sins of Jeroboam the son of Nebat, that he took to wife Jezebel the daughter of Ethbaal king of the Zidonians, and went and served Baal, and worshipped him. 32: And <u>he reared up an altar for Baal in the house of Baal, which he had built in Samaria.</u>**

Elijah gives Ahab the warning concerning the withholding of *dew* and *rain:*

> **1Kings 17:1: And Elijah the Tishbite, *who was* of the inhabitants of Gilead, said unto Ahab, As the LORD God of Israel liveth, before whom I stand, <u>there shall not be dew nor rain these years,</u> but according to my word.**

Of course there is a real spiritual application in God's Word to *dew and rain* representing His Word. There is a judgment aspect to the withholding of *dew or rain* also, due to false worship. God sends a famine of hearing His Word. In Luke 4:25, Jesus addressed the time of famine during Elijah's 3 ½ years. He was addressing the men of the synagogue. The leaders in the synagogue did not like what Jesus was saying. Luke 4 declares they became *filled with wrath:*

> **Luke 4:25: But I tell you of a truth, many widows were in Israel in the days of Elias, when the heaven was shut up three years and six months, <u>when great famine was throughout all the land;</u> 26: But unto none of them was Elias sent, save unto Sarepta, *a city* of Sidon, unto a woman *that was* a widow. 27: And many lepers were in Israel in the time of Eliseus the prophet; and none of**

> **them was cleansed, saving Naaman the Syrian. 28:
> And all they in the synagogue, when they heard
> these things, were filled with wrath, 29: And rose
> up, and thrust him out of the city, and led him
> unto the brow of the hill whereon their city was
> built, that they might cast him down headlong. 30:
> But he passing through the midst of them went his
> way…**

This great *famine* also applies to the fallen houses of God as the leaders have lulled to sleep the congregation, not at all concerned for their own coming judgment.

In James 5 we have seen how God is the husbandman who waits for the *precious fruit of the earth* until He receives the *early and latter rain*. We know the first section of the *great tribulation* period is 3 ½ years. We learned this from the book of Daniel (*time, times and half a time*) and also from how 3 ½ years relates to Elijah's prayer of *no rain or dew* for 3 ½ years. However, Elijah prayed again and the earth brought forth fruit. In the last half of the final seven years, we will see an explosion of the Gospel message and people will be very willing to listen. God shutting up heaven comes from His people serving other gods:

> **Deuteronomy 11:14: That I will give *you* the rain
> of your land in his due season, the first rain and
> the latter rain, that thou mayest gather in thy
> corn, and thy wine, and thine oil. 15: And I will
> send grass in thy fields for thy cattle, that thou
> mayest eat and be full. 16: Take heed to
> yourselves, that your heart be not deceived, and ye
> turn aside, and serve other gods, and worship
> them; 17: <u>And *then* the LORD'S wrath be kindled
> against you, and he shut up the heaven, that there</u>**

196

be no rain, and that the land yield not her fruit; and *lest* ye perish quickly from off the good land which the LORD giveth you.

The Day for a Year Principle

There have been ways in which God has written His Word which some may argue: "Why would He write things so complicated." I believe God wants us to study His Word. I expect that His Word, which established the foundations of this world, would be complex. There are no short cuts when it comes to the study of God's Word. The way God uses time intervals is most fascinating. In the book of Ezekiel, God establishes the *day for a year* principle in which Ezekiel lays on His side for so many days to represent the years of the sin of both Israel and Judah.

> **Ezekiel 4:5: For I have laid upon thee the years of their iniquity, according to the number of the days, three hundred and ninety days: so shalt thou bear the iniquity of the house of Israel. 6: And when thou hast accomplished them, lie again on thy right side, and thou shalt bear the iniquity of the house of Judah forty days: I have appointed thee each day for a year.**

This demonstration by Ezekiel established the *day for a year* principle. In light of this truth, there are verses in the Bible which speak of the time of *great tribulation*, yet the verses use days instead of what the days represent, i.e., 3 ½ days where the two witnesses lay dead in the street seems to be the first 3 ½ years of the final seven years. Then they arise and stand once again before the God of the earth. What John witnesses as a vision represents God's Word. The Word of God has power once again, especially when judgment comes upon the fallen houses of God. There is yet one more Bible verse which may indicate that the *day for a year* principle is being employed.

In the *Third Day* "We Shall Live in His Sight"

There are a few verses in Hosea which relate so much to God as the husbandman who is waiting for *the early and latter rain* as found in James 5. These verses are special because they are qualified by the words *if we follow on to know the Lord*. The following verses from Hosea 6 detail a healing process by God:

> **Hosea 6:1: Come, and let us return unto the LORD: for he hath torn, and he will heal us; he hath smitten, and he will bind us up. 2: After two days will he revive us: in the third day he will raise us up, and we shall live in his sight. 3: Then shall we know, _if we follow on to know the LORD_: his going forth is prepared as the morning; and he shall come unto us as the rain, as the <u>latter _and_ former rain</u> unto the earth.**

Hosea 6 is speaking to God's people who went through the first *tribulation* period of 8,400 days. Then the mirror of the years of Darius begins to unfold. After *two days* (two years) *he will revive us*. The anniversary of the flood in the year 2011 was not insignificant. God related this time to *the waters of Noah* in Isaiah 54. There the Lord also speaks about *hiding His face* for a period of time. Even with the years of Darius, the command to *work for I am with you* did not come until the second year of Darius. There was a delay in repairing the destruction for a two-year space of time. There was also great opposition from the enemies who opposed the building of the house of God at Jerusalem:

> **Ezra 4:23: Now when the copy of king Artaxerxes'
> letter *was* read before Rehum, and Shimshai the
> scribe, and their companions, they went up in
> haste to Jerusalem unto the Jews, <u>and made them
> to cease by force and power.</u> 24: Then ceased the
> work of the house of God which *is* at Jerusalem.
> So it ceased unto the second year of the reign of
> Darius king of Persia.**

After two days God promises that He will revive His people
who understand His Word, and in the third day we will live
in His sight. The ISA renders *we shall live in His sight* as: *we
shall live to faces of Him.* This is not a foreign idea while we
live on this present earth. Both Elijah and Elisha spoke of *the
Lord God of Israel before whom I stand.* Elijah at that time
was proclaiming his *no dew/rain* warning to Ahab while still
working for God on this earth:

> **1 Kings 17:1: And Elijah the Tishbite, *who was* of
> the inhabitants of Gilead, said unto Ahab, *As* the
> <u>LORD God of Israel liveth, before whom I stand,</u>
> there shall not be dew nor rain these years, but
> according to my word.**

Living in God's sight is a good thing. When He hides His
face from us due to our sin, then that is not a good thing.
However, God's mercy is seen greatly once we pass the time
of God hiding His face. He promises that it will only be for a
short while. When we begin to see what happens in the
second year of Darius (our 2013-2014 Nisan to Nisan), it
starts to get really exciting for the believers in Jesus Christ.
Those who have obeyed His command to depart out of the
fallen houses of God are still commanded to work for He is
with us. God promises that with *everlasting kindness* He will
show mercy on His people:

> **Isaiah 54:7: For a small moment have I forsaken thee; but with great mercies will I gather thee. 8: In a little wrath I hid my face from thee for a moment; but with everlasting kindness will I have mercy on thee, saith the LORD thy Redeemer. 9: For this *is as* the waters of Noah unto me: for *as* I have sworn that the waters of Noah should no more go over the earth; so have I sworn that I would not be wroth with thee, nor rebuke thee.**

Studies were presented on the *2011studies* channel showing how God *hid His face* from May 21, 2011 to May 2012. This lined up so perfectly with May 21, 2011 being the 7,000[th] year anniversary of the flood. Historically, when Noah and his family stepped off the ark onto a cleansed earth, they were instructed to be *fruitful and multiply.* To be *fruitful and multiply* is an important Biblical phrase, not only for the eight people who came off the ark to replenish the earth, but also for the increasing of worldwide salvation as God saves people across the globe in our day.

Believers Will be *Fruitful & Multiply*-Post 2012 A.D.

> **Leviticus 26:9: For I will have respect unto you, and make you fruitful, and multiply you, and establish my covenant with you. 10: And ye shall eat old store, and bring forth the old because of the new.**

> **Jeremiah 23:3: And I will gather the remnant of my flock out of all countries whither I have driven them, and will bring them again to their folds; and they shall be fruitful and increase. 4: And I will set up shepherds over them which shall feed them:**

and they shall fear no more, nor be dismayed, neither shall they be lacking, saith the LORD.

Hosea 6:1-3 has truly incredible promises. Believers in Christ turn to the Lord and then begin to know and understand what God will be performing in the final years of history. This understanding is established as sure as the dawn comes up every day. The rain periods in Hosea 6 are similar to Joel 2 when God commands the land to *fear not* for He will do *great things*. This is after God removes *the Northern* (Satan) who did *great things*. This is precisely why the "day for a year principle" seems to apply to Hosea 6. There is a word used in Hosea 6 that has the meaning of *directing* or *teaching*.

The Hebrew language is really incredible because God has used certain words such as *former rain* with an origin of *directing* or *teaching*. This is why I believe there is a real spiritual application to God *waiting for the early and latter rain*, which brings forth fruit. James chapter 5 is really saying the same thing as Hosea 6 and Joel 2. God's Word will be magnified in a great way and <u>understanding</u> will be known by His people.

The Hebrew word for *former rain* is *yoreh* (H3138) and is an active participle of *yarah* (H3384) which is underlined in the following verses:

> **Genesis 46:28: And he sent Judah before him unto Joseph, <u>to direct</u> his face unto Goshen; and they came into the land of Goshen.**
>
> **Exodus 4:10: And Moses said unto the LORD, O my Lord, I *am* not eloquent, neither heretofore, nor since thou hast spoken unto thy servant: but I *am* slow of speech, and of a slow tongue. 11: And**

> the LORD said unto him, Who hath made man's
> mouth? Or who maketh the dumb, or deaf, or the
> seeing, or the blind? Have not I the LORD? 12:
> Now therefore go, and I will be with thy mouth,
> and <u>teach thee</u> what thou shalt say.

Therefore, the rain which God mentions in Joel 2, James 5,
and Hosea 6 is related to God showing us, teaching us and
enlarging our understanding of the Word so that many will
experience salvation. The rains of *understanding* and
directing would fit the definition for *former rain* perfectly.
There is, however, a warning to those people in the houses of
God who do not seek God's understanding. Jeremiah
prophesied and insisted that Jerusalem would *become heaps.*
Jeremiah 5 declares that wicked men are among God's
people. As *a cage full of birds* so their houses are full of
deceit; they have become *great and rich.* There is something
that God says in the midst of this language that really shows
how the leaders in the fallen houses of God are not focused
on the understanding of God's *rain and harvest* period:

> Jeremiah 5:23: But this people hath a revolting
> and a rebellious heart; they are revolted and gone.
> 24: <u>Neither say they in their heart, Let us now fear
> the LORD our God, that giveth rain, both the
> former and the latter</u>, in his season: he reserveth
> unto us the appointed weeks of the harvest. 25:
> Your iniquities have turned away these *things*, and
> your sins have withholden good *things* from you.

<u>The Fair Warning to the Houses of God</u>

The book of Revelation is the warning to the seven churches,
which are a representation of <u>all churches worldwide</u>. Some
of the teachings coming forth from the fallen houses of God

are so Biblically inaccurate that it makes it a true reality for believers to obey the command of Christ to *flee out*. Some of the teachings were not the original teachings of the disciples but rather came many years later in the late 1800's.

While the Bible is teaching a last day resurrection of believers, many churches are propagating the "silent rapture" doctrine of John Nelson Darby[13] (November 18, 1800-April 29, 1882), followed by a seven-year *tribulation* period on earth. The main problem with this teaching is that the Bible indicates how the believers will go through the time of *tribulation* and *great tribulation* (Matthew chapter 24, Revelation 17:4). The believers will also be here when Christ comes in *power and great glory* on the last day:

> **1 Corinthians 15:50: Now this I say, brethren, that <u>flesh and blood cannot inherit the kingdom of God</u>; neither doth corruption inherit incorruption. 51: Behold, I shew you a mystery; We shall not all sleep, but we shall all be changed, 52: In a moment, in the twinkling of an eye, <u>at the last trump: for the trumpet shall sound, and the dead shall be raised incorruptible, and we shall be changed</u>.**

The above verses should prompt a red-flag concerning the *silent rapture*. The teaching that other people will be left behind is being propagated in many of the houses of God in our time. The suggestion that flesh and blood ruling on this earth with Christ during the proposed *millennium reign* is foreign to the Bible:

> **1Thessalonians 4:14: For if we believe that Jesus died and rose again, even so them also which sleep in Jesus will God bring with him. 15: For <u>this we say unto you by the word of the Lord</u>, that we**

which are alive and remain unto the coming of the Lord shall not prevent them which are asleep. 16: For the Lord himself shall descend from heaven with a shout, with the voice of the archangel, and with the trump of God: and the dead in Christ shall rise first: 17: Then <u>we which are alive and remain shall be caught up together with them in the clouds, to meet the Lord in the air: and so shall we ever be with the Lord.</u> 18: Wherefore comfort one another with these words.

What complicates the wrong doctrines of the late 1800's further is that Cyrus Ingerson Scofield (August 19, 1843-July 24, 1921)[14], who published the Scofield reference Bible, had placed reference notes in the margins of his particular translation of the Bible. These reference notes are dangerous in that the reader will be influenced by the adopted teachings of Darby. What believers in Christ should do is compare Scripture with Scripture and not reply on reference notes placed in the margins of such error-filled translations.

<u>Fallen Babylon- A Habitation of Devils</u>

In the midst of the warnings of the book of Revelation, there are verses which indicate that fallen Babylon has become a *habitation of devils*. Before anyone begins to argue that *fallen Babylon* is something else besides the fallen houses of God, let us address the language which proves that fallen Babylon is the fallen houses of God. The fallen houses of God have become part of the world with *lying signs and wonders*, strangers in the midst, and the "ministers" who are proclaiming that prosperity and gain is Godliness:

1Timothy 6:5: Perverse disputings of men of corrupt minds, and <u>destitute of the truth,</u>

supposing that gain is godliness: from such withdraw thyself. 6: But godliness with contentment is great gain. 7: For we brought nothing into this world, and it is certain we can carry nothing out.

Purple, Scarlet, Gold and Precious Stones

Many years ago when the temple was erected as a house for God on earth, there were certain materials which were needed to build this grand house on earth. God gave very precise details and measurements. The colors, the gold, and the precious stones listed in the Revelation 17 are identical to the materials in which God's house was built:

> **Exodus 26:1: Moreover thou shalt make the tabernacle *with* ten curtains *of* fine twined linen, and blue, and purple, and scarlet: *with* cherubims of cunning work shalt thou make them.**

> **Exodus 39:8: And he made the breastplate *of* cunning work, like the work of the ephod; *of* gold, blue, and purple, and scarlet, and fine twined linen.**

The Woman Clad in Purple-*Mystery Babylon*

The great thing about God's Word is that when verse by verse comparisons are made, truth does come forth. If one proclaims that fallen Babylon is the fallen houses of God worldwide, then that person should be able to prove it by God's Word alone. We don't need to reply on our minds to guess that it may be America or Rome. God's Word gives answered when properly studied. Let us look at the language of fallen Babylon:

> **Revelation 17:3: So he carried me away in the spirit into the wilderness: and I saw a woman sit upon a scarlet coloured beast, full of names of blasphemy, having seven heads and ten horns. 4: And <u>the woman was arrayed in purple and scarlet colour, and decked with gold and precious stones</u> and pearls, having a golden cup in her hand full of abominations and filthiness of her fornication: 5: And upon her forehead *was* a name written, MYSTERY, BABYLON THE GREAT, THE MOTHER OF HARLOTS AND ABOMINATIONS OF THE EARTH.**

Gold and Precious Stones: Solomon Instructed with Precise Details to Build the House of God

The gold and also the precious stones were an incredible aspect of the garnishing of the house of God:

> **2 Chronicles 3:5: And the greater house he ceiled with fir tree, which he overlaid with fine gold, and set thereon palm trees and chains. 6: And he garnished the house with <u>precious stones for beauty: and the gold *was* gold of Parvaim.</u>**

> **2 Chronicles 3:9: And the weight of the nails *was* fifty shekels of gold. And he overlaid the upper chambers with gold. 10: And in the most holy house he made two cherubims of image work, and overlaid them with gold.**

By God giving Solomon such precise measurements and materials for His house, we can understand who the woman named *Mystery Babylon* represents. The fallen houses of God worldwide have become *Mystery Babylon*.

The command of Christ is that when we see the abomination which makes desolate take place, then it is time to *flee to the mountains*, which is God Himself:

> **Mark 13:14: But when ye shall see the abomination of desolation, spoken of by Daniel the prophet, standing where it ought not, (let him that readeth understand,) then let them that be in Judaea flee to the mountains...**

Jesus spoke in parables and Judaea (Judea) represents where God has placed the believers. Judea is a grand representation of where the house of God was and also where the worshipping of God took place. Jesus was proclaiming in the language of His Word that when we who are in the houses of God (Judea) observe the abomination that makes desolate then we are to flee out. Ezra 5:8 speaks of the province of Judea where the house of the great God was:

> **Ezra 5:8: Be it known unto the king, that <u>we went into the province of Judea, to the house of the great God</u>, which is builded with great stones, and timber is laid in the walls, and this work goeth fast on, and prospereth in their hands.**

Fleeing to the mountains is another way of saying flee to God for protection:

> **Psalm 36:5: Thy mercy, O LORD, *is* in the heavens; *and* thy faithfulness *reacheth* unto the clouds. 6: <u>Thy righteousness is like the great mountains</u>; thy judgments are a great deep...**

> **Micah 4:1: But in the last days it shall come to pass, *that* <u>the mountain of the house of the LORD shall be established in the top of the mountains,</u>**

and it shall be exalted above the hills; and people shall flow unto it. 2: And many nations shall come, and say, <u>Come, and let us go up to the mountain of the LORD, and to the house of the God of Jacob;</u> and he will teach us of his ways, and we will walk in his paths: for the law shall go forth of Zion, and the word of the LORD from Jerusalem.

The command to *come out of her my people* was for the *tribulation* of the 8,400 days which ended on May 21, 2011, but it is also for this time during the *great tribulation* of 3 ½ years. God is not gently asking us to come out. He is commanding us to come out due to the plagues coming upon the fallen houses of God, which have become a *habitation of devils*:

Revelation 18:2: And he cried mightily with a strong voice, saying, Babylon the great is fallen, is fallen, and is become the habitation of devils, and the hold of every foul spirit, and a cage of every unclean and hateful bird. 3: <u>For all nations have drunk of the wine of the wrath of her fornication,</u> and the kings of the earth have committed fornication with her, and the merchants of the earth are waxed rich through the abundance of her delicacies. 4: And I heard another voice from heaven, saying, <u>Come out of her, my people, that ye be not partakers of her sins, and that ye receive not of her plagues.</u> 5: For her sins have reached unto heaven, and God hath remembered her iniquities.

God is waiting for the *precious fruit of the earth*, and we can know that once this period of 3 ½ years has come to a close in the year 2015, we will see that God will be lifted up in a great way:

> **James 5:18: <u>And he prayed again, and the heaven gave rain, and the earth brought forth her fruit.</u> 19: Brethren, if any of you do err from the truth, and one convert him; 20: Let him know, that he which converteth the sinner from the error of his way shall save a soul from death, and shall hide a multitude of sins.**

Since passing May 21, 2011 (the 7,000th anniversary of the flood and the worldwide announcement of Judgment Day), there has been *err from the truth*. Announcing to the world that *a spiritual* Judgment Day has arrived and salvation is no longer available was/is a grievous error from the truth. The world and the churches did not need an immediate answer as to why we passed 2011. The mocking had to come according to 2 Peter 3. For those fellow believers who proclaimed a message of *no more salvation*, now is the time to think different and begin bringing the Gospel of Jesus Christ once again.

I really hope the information in this book will show God's longsuffering and how He is *not willing than any would perish.* God is showing us that many people will come to repentance and the knowledge of Christ. God's power will be known very shortly, and the world will know who controls the *heavens and earth*. In the next chapter, I want to address something that we began discussing post 2011. God has detailed Biblical history so closely that even the *years of Darius* fit precisely into the final seven years. God *sets up kings* and *removes kings* for a good reason. This change of power by the hand of God will be explored in the next chapter.

Chapter 9—Patterns of Tribulation & Post Tribulation

Almost everyone is familiar with the phrase the *writing on the wall*. I am not sure, though, that most people are aware how that one event recorded in the Bible was so significant for our day. The Bible already has established that God is the one who *removes kings* and *sets up kings*.

> **Daniel 2:20: Daniel answered and said, Blessed be the name of God for ever and ever: for wisdom and might are his: 21: And he changeth the times and the seasons: <u>he removeth kings, and setteth up kings:</u> he giveth wisdom unto the wise, and knowledge to them that know understanding...**

When God removed Belshazzar from Babylon and gave the kingdom to the Mede and Persian (Darius and Cyrus), He set forth implications that are being realized at this time in history. Why are the years of Darius important in these final years of history? It is because the years of Darius became a time of rebuilding that which had been destroyed. Likewise, the rebuilding of God's eternal house happens in the final seven years of history; the years of Darius just so happen to fit perfectly within these seven years. Remember that just as God has established patterns for the times of *tribulation*, including the current *great tribulation*, He also has a pattern of rebuilding or *post tribulation events*. Let us explore this idea further.

The Patterns of Tribulation

Judah's 70-year or 840 months of captivity is the pattern for our 23-year *tribulation* period or 8,400 days which ended May 21, 2011.

Jacobs's time of trouble or *great affliction* was during the seven years (84 months) of famine in Canaan. This pattern fits the final seven years of *great tribulation,* which, by God's hand and mercy, has been shortened to 3 ½ years. Then it is followed by 3 ½ years where God is magnified in a great way and salvation continues unto the *last day.*

We are well into the 3 ½ years of *great tribulation* and rapidly approaching the time of great salvation worldwide starting at Pentecost 2015 (yet, another duplication of an original Biblical event in 33 A.D.). At the time of this writing, there are approximately twelve months until we reach the $1,335^{th}$ day where there will be that great time of great salvation worldwide.

There is still another pattern of rebuilding, which was originally set forth by God with the rebuilding of Jerusalem and the temple. In order for the establishing of this pattern, God historically had to remove Belshazzar and set-up the Mede and the Persian to accomplish this task.

When studying the Bible, I noticed how the *years of Darius* were fairly detailed. Why would God be outlining the years of Darius with such great detail? Since knowing previously about the *good and comfortable words* which came after Judah's 70-year *tribulation,* it makes sense that *good and comfortable words* would also come after the 23-year *tribulation* period (8,400 days) which ended May 21, 2011. In other words, we must not only look at the patterns of *tribulation* which God has established, but also what comes

<u>after</u> the time of *tribulation* such as *good and comfortable words*. Also, we need to understand what comes after the time of *great tribulation* of 3 ½ years.

God's Blessing After Tribulation

In both cases, God's plan was to prosper His people and to rebuild after a time of desolation. In our day after the 3 ½ years of *great tribulation* comes the period of time in which we will see a double fulfillment of the 1,335-day prophecy.

This is why the years of Darius are so very important to understand. Let us begin with the time when God was giving the kingdom into the hands of Darius and Cyrus:

> **Daniel 5:25: And this *is* the writing that was written, MENE, MENE, TEKEL, UPHARSIN. 26: This *is* the interpretation of the thing: MENE; God hath numbered thy kingdom, and finished it. 27: TEKEL; Thou art weighed in the balances, and art found wanting. 28: PERES; Thy kingdom is divided, and given to the Medes and Persians.**

Belshazzar sees the writing on the wall and dies that very night; then the *years of Darius* begin:

> **Daniel 5:30: In that night was Belshazzar the king of the Chaldeans slain. 31: And <u>Darius the Median took the kingdom,</u> *being* about threescore and two years old.**

Probably the best way to look at the years of Darius is to list them with the events that take place in each year. First, though, we must establish when Darius took the kingdom. In my last book, I mentioned the Cyrus Cylinder which is held in the British Museum. This historical artifact shows how in October of 539 B.C. Cyrus came into Babylon and conquered it peacefully. Thus, 539 B.C. was the end of Judah's captivity and the beginning of the *years of Darius* after the death of Belshazzar. The following statements concerning the Cylinder's writings and the year Cyrus peacefully conquered Babylon are as follows:

"On October 12 (Julian calendar; October 7 by the Gregorian calendar) 539 BC, Achaemanid army without any conflict entered the city of Babylon. Cyrus the Great himself, on October 29, entered the city, assuming the titles of "King of Babylon, king of Sumer and Akkad, king of the four corners of the world." Cyrus the Great, on this cylinder describes how he conquers the old city of Babylon and how his mighty army in peace marched into the city.[15]

The passages in the Bible which speak of Cyrus are important because we know they relate to our present time. The reason being is that God gave the kingdom of Babylon to Cyrus and Darius after the 70-year *tribulation* of Judah. God controlled everything, even the stirring up of the spirit of Cyrus to proclaim the following:

> **2 Chronicles 36:22: Now in the first year of Cyrus king of Persia, that the word of the LORD *spoken* by the mouth of Jeremiah might be accomplished, the LORD stirred up the spirit of Cyrus king of Persia, that he made a proclamation throughout all his kingdom, and *put it* also in writing, saying,**

> **2 Chronicles 36:23: Thus saith Cyrus king of Persia, <u>All the kingdoms of the earth hath the LORD God of heaven given me; and he hath charged me to build him an house in Jerusalem,</u> which is in Judah. Who *is there* among you of all his people? The LORD his God *be* with him, and let him go up.**

214

In order to accomplish God's task of building the house in Jerusalem, the Lord had to place in power Cyrus and Darius. Now that we are living in the mirror of the years of Darius we know this work of building His eternal house is the task at hand. The Gospel of Jesus Christ must go forth into all the world before the end comes. From the initial edict of Cyrus' proclamation to build the temple, to the opposition which came, to eventually God waking the people up to work in the second year of Darius, the house was eventually built. The completion of the house of God was in the sixth year of Darius. The sixth year of Darius lines up with our year 2018. It seems that the beautification of the temple once completed, lines up with the final seven months prior to the last day of the Feast of Tabernacles. The beautification relates to the salvation of God's final elect worldwide.

The Gates of Brass and Iron

We also have a verse regarding Cyrus (God calls Cyrus *my shepherd*) that mentions the two leaved gates which are made of brass and iron. This is a most fascinating verse since there is a connection with brass and iron to *tribulation*. There is even a Psalm which indicates that God *breaks the gates of brass and bars of iron*. When we read this verse we can know that God is reversing the times of *tribulation* worldwide:

> **Psalm 107:13: Then <u>they cried unto the LORD in their trouble</u>, and he saved them out of their distresses. 14: He brought them out of darkness and the shadow of death, and brake their bands in sunder. 15: Oh that *men* would praise the LORD *for* his goodness, and *for* his wonderful works to the children of men! 16: For <u>he hath broken the gates of brass, and cut the bars of iron in sunder</u>.**

How can we be sure that brass and iron relates to *tribulation?* I will list some verses below for your further study. These verses all relate to brass and iron:

- Psalm 107:13- The Hebrew word trouble (*Tsar Tsar* H6862) means tribulation/adversary (compare to Hosea 5:15). *Trouble and distress* is also mention in Zephaniah 1:15- The context is the *Day of the Lord* (judgment on the fallen houses of God).

- Leviticus 26:19 uses language of how God will make the *heaven as brass and earth as iron* for not keeping His statutes. This is a punishment for sin which results in laboring in vain and sorrow of heart. The land does not produce fruit.

- Deuteronomy 28:23 speaks of what happens when we keep and do the statutes and commandments of God, but also when we refuse to do His statues and commandments. Again, *the heaven shall be as brass and the earth shall be as iron.* This judgment equates a definite harsh time for not obeying God's commands. Note: Read Deuteronomy 28 in its entirety.

- Jeremiah 6:26 mentions how the spoiler comes upon the *daughter of my people. Grievous revolters* who work slanderously are compared to brass and iron.

- The forth beast of Daniel 7:19 whose *teeth were of iron and nails of brass* devoured, brake, and stamped the residue. The kingdom of Satan coming against the believers show how the language of brass and iron relates to *tribulation.* It also relates to *great tribulation* until *judgment sits* and the believers are given back the kingdom by God to *consume and destroy* Satan's dominion.

This is why Psalm 107 speaks of praising God for His goodness. When He *breaks the gates of brass*, and *cuts the bars of iron asunder*, it will become a time of praising God for His great reversal. Now when we look again at the verses related to Cyrus, we can know how this reversal relates to our time (the final seven years). It becomes a time of making the *crooked places straight* which is also related to the 3 ½ years of Christ's ministry and especially Pentecost 33 A.D. and Pentecost 2015.

> **Isaiah 45:1: Thus saith the LORD to his anointed, to Cyrus, whose right hand I have holden, to subdue nations before him; and I will loose the loins of kings, to open before him the two leaved gates; and the gates shall not be shut; 2: I will go before thee, and make the crooked places straight: I will break in pieces the gates of brass, and cut in sunder the bars of iron...**

> **Isaiah 40:3: The voice of him that crieth in the wilderness, Prepare ye the way of the LORD, make straight in the desert a highway for our God. 4: Every valley shall be exalted, and every mountain and hill shall be made low: and the crooked shall be made straight, and the rough places plain: 5: And the glory of the LORD shall be revealed, and all flesh shall see *it* together: for the mouth of the LORD hath spoken *it*.**

Many times when I read a verse I ask *when will this happen?* The glory of the Lord being revealed relates to when God *shakes the heavens and the earth.* Since the forecasting of God *shaking the heavens and earth* occurred in the second year of Darius, we will shortly see how the glory of the Lord

217

will be revealed as we are now in the mirror of the third year of Darius:

> **Haggai 2:6: For thus saith the LORD of hosts; Yet once, it *is* <u>a little while, and I will shake the heavens, and the earth, and the sea, and the dry land</u>; 7: And I will shake all nations, and the desire of all nations shall come: and <u>I will fill this house with glory, saith the LORD of hosts.</u>**

<u>The Times of Brass & Iron- Tribulation and After</u>

Judah's 70-year captivity (840 months) was a pattern for our 8,400-day *tribulation* period. Therefore, we can follow the pattern of 539 B.C. and know how our year 2011 would have been the replica of the start point as the kingdom of Babylon was given to Cyrus and Darius.

However, the very first official year of Darius would have been the start of the next year-Nisan 538 B.C. (Note: see the *All-Important Accession Year System* on the following page). Remember that we are not only considering the patterns of *tribulation* but also what comes <u>after</u> the *tribulation* period. Darius' reign came after the 70-year *tribulation*/captivity of Judah. Therefore, it would make perfect sense that what God commanded in each year of Darius the Mede, these commands would relate to our 2011 and onward. However, is this correct? What qualifies as the official first year of King Darius the Mede? Let's look carefully at this most important timeline of these final seven years.

The Bible only mentions up to the sixth year of Darius. It was in the sixth year in which the temple was completed. Wait a minute, six years added to 2011 is the year 2017 right? Yes, this presented a problem since the other time paths showed a 7-year pattern to the year 2018, but after

218

more study and book review[16] the accession year system must be considered. This became an extremely important discovery. The accession year system allows us to fit the six years of Darius within the final seven years of history and arrive within the year 2018. Thus, giving us a time when the eternal house of God (salvation) will be complete. God has performed and dictated all of history in such an incredible way that only a powerful and mighty God can bring this all to pass.

The All-Important Accession Year System

It took me a while to understand the *Accession Year System* so please be patient with me as I give a brief description of the historical kingships and when a king's official first year began.

Even though Darius took the Babylonian kingdom that very night Belshazzar was slain (539 B.C.), Darius's official year (in which records were kept) would have been the start of the following new year. This would have been in Nisan of the year 538 B.C. With this information we can see how the six years of Darius and the commands by God in those certain years would line up with the 7-year *great tribulation* period (2011-2018).

In 539 B.C., Darius took the kingdom the very night Belshazzar died. In October of that same year Cyrus enters into Babylon peacefully. The Medes and the Persians now rule but Darius's first official year of reign begins in Nisan 538 B.C.

Darius' official first year- Nisan 538 B.C. to Nisan 537 B.C.

Darius' second year- Nisan 537 B.C. to Nisan 536 B.C.

Darius' third year- Nisan 536 B.C. to Nisan 535 B.C.

Darius' forth year- Nisan 535 B.C. to Nisan 534 B.C.

Darius' fifth year- Nisan 534 B.C. to Nisan 533 B.C.

Darius' sixth year- Nisan 533 B.C. to Nisan 532 B.C.

The Replica of Darius' Years Past the 8,400-day *Tribulation* Ending May 21, 2011

October of 2011 would have lined up with Cyrus taking Babylon peacefully. Darius's first *official year* in 538 B.C. would have lined up with <u>our Nisan 2012</u>.

Nisan 2012 to Nisan 2013- Darius' first year

Nisan 2013 to Nisan 2014- Darius' second year

Nisan 2014 to Nisan 2015- Darius' third year

Nisan 2015 to Nisan 2016- Darius' fourth year

Nisan 2016 to Nisan 2017- Darius' fifth year

Nisan 2017 to Nisan 2018- Darius' sixth year

The *accession year system* which was used back in Darius' time allows for a perfect lining up of Darius' sixth year, when the temple was completed, to our year 2018. This confirms that the years of Darius fit within the 7-year pattern of the final years (2011 to 2018) perfectly. Understanding comes first and then the command to work.

The First Year of Darius the Mede

This year was very important since it was the year in which Daniel received an answer to his prayer requesting understanding of the things of the end.

Daniel 9:1: <u>In the first year of Darius</u> the son of Ahasuerus, of the seed of the Medes, which was made king over the realm of the Chaldeans; 2: In the first year of his reign I Daniel understood by books the number of the years, whereof the word of the LORD came to Jeremiah the prophet, that he would accomplish seventy years in the desolations of Jerusalem.

Daniel 10:21: But I will shew thee that <u>which is noted in the scripture of truth</u>: and *there is* none that holdeth with me in these things, but Michael your prince.

Daniel 11:1: Also I in <u>the first year of Darius the Mede</u>, *even* I, stood to confirm and to strengthen him. 2: And now will I shew thee the truth.

The first year of Darius is related to our year 2012-2013 (Nisan to Nisan). At the start time of this writing, January 2014, we are in the pattern of second year of Darius. However, at the completion of this book in a few months and we will be in the third year of Darius. Even though the third year of Darius is not mentioned in the Bible, the command to work and build still is extremely important. Let's look at the commands that God gives in the second year of Darius.

The Second Year of Darius

Haggai 1:1: In the second year of Darius the king, in the sixth month, in the first day of the month, came the word of the LORD by Haggai the prophet unto Zerubbabel the son of Shealtiel, governor of Judah, and to Joshua the son of Josedech, the high priest, saying, 2: Thus speaketh the LORD of hosts, saying, <u>This people say, The</u>

**time is not come, the time that the LORD'S house
should be built.**

Is Salvation Over? - Is it Really not Time to Build God's Eternal House?

It is always an amazing thing to see how yesterday of times past is so much like today. In 539 B.C. some of the Hebrew people came out of the Babylonian captivity. This time relates to the end of our 8,400-day *tribulation* period. After the Hebrew people came out of captivity, they were saying that the time has not come that the LORD'S house should be built. After both May 21, 2011 and October 21, 2011 came and went, some people who brought the message of "Judgment Day is coming," started to proclaim "Judgment Day has come and salvation is over." We know from scriptures that this is impossible since God has a covenant with day and night. This covenant with day and night includes God multiplying the *seed of David*. This is language of those who become saved through the work of Christ by the Spirit of God. Jeremiah 33 proclaims this truth:

> **Jeremiah 33:20: Thus saith the LORD; <u>If ye can
> break my covenant of the day, and my covenant of
> the night, and that there should not be day and
> night in their season</u>; 21:** *Then* **may also my
> covenant be broken with David my servant, that
> he should not have a son to reign upon his throne;
> and with the Levites the priests, my ministers. 22:
> As the host of heaven cannot be numbered, neither
> the sand of the sea measured: <u>so will I multiply the
> seed of David my servant</u>, and the Levites that
> minister unto me.**

The New Testament declares that Christ came from *the seed of David*. The *multiplying of the seed of David* is language to indicate that many will become saved in accordance with God's covenant with day and night.

> **John 7:42: Hath not the scripture said, That <u>Christ cometh of the seed of David</u>, and out of the town of Bethlehem, where David was?**

> **Romans 1:1: Paul, a servant of Jesus Christ, called *to be* an apostle, separated unto the gospel of God, 2: (Which he had promised afore by his prophets in the holy scriptures,) 3: <u>Concerning his Son Jesus Christ our Lord, which was made of the seed of David according to the flesh</u>; 4: And declared *to be* the Son of God with power, according to the spirit of holiness, by the resurrection from the dead...**

What about the multiplying of the *Levites* that minister unto God? Is not this talking about the descendants of national Israel? When we read Isaiah 66, we see how God there proclaims that he will make of the isles and nations *Levites* and *priests*. In Malachi 2, God promises a curse to the priests who do not hear, nor lay it to heart to give glory unto His name. God chooses people from the nations to make them *priests* and *Levites*, which is one way of saying God will set things straight and choose His people in the final years of history. The duty of a priest is to keep the knowledge of God and teach it:

> **Malachi 2:7: For the priest's lips should keep knowledge, and they should seek the law at his mouth: for *he* is the messenger of the LORD of hosts.**

Isaiah 66:21: And I will also take of them for priests *and* for Levites, saith the LORD. 22: For as the new heavens and the new earth, which I will make, shall remain before me, saith the LORD, so shall your seed and your name remain.

Isaiah chapter 66 and Malachi chapter 2 should be fully read to grasp what God is going to do. How God uses *priests* and *Levites* is very similar to how God carries over the name *Jerusalem*. He will finish the completion of *the New Jerusalem* by saving many from all nations. The new peaceful city will be made up of believers worldwide. He will also make some *Levites* and *priests* who minister and keep the knowledge of His law. Newly saved people will be become the *messengers of truth* while those in charge of His Word who previously did not give glory to His name will be judged. God defines His own language and *workers of iniquity* is a phrase that relates to the people who are related to wickedness (Luke 13:27, Psalm 28:3). The illustrations of judgment upon Israel and later the fallen houses of God show that God is Holy and His judgments are righteous.

My hope is that by the year 2015, when we arrive at the *blessed he is that waits and comes to the 1,335th day* believers who have been proclaiming "salvation is over" will think differently and begin bringing the Gospel. The mocking of *where is the promise of His coming?* had to come to pass. That, however, does not mean that we had to provide an incorrect answer to the people who were mocking. We learn by prayer and patience that God is longsuffering for the reason of salvation. God's salvation by His Spirit will eventually cover the globe.

Though it Tarry (Linger)-*Wait for it*

In the year 2011, I began reading Habakkuk 2 because of the language of standing upon *the watch* and also the words *what shall I answer when I am reproved?* God gave me a song at that time and I posted it on the YouTube channel *2011studies*. I called the song "What shall I tell them?" The answer to the question in the song is "I'll tell them be ready." The lyrics were built around Habakkuk 2. The idea is we are to wait, though the vision of the end tarries, it will surely come. The just will live by HIS faith:

> **Habakkuk 2:1: I will stand upon my watch, and set me upon the tower, and will watch to see what he will say unto me, and what I shall answer when I am reproved. 2: And the LORD answered me, and said, Write the vision, and make *it* plain upon tables, that he may run that readeth it. 3: For the vision *is* yet for an appointed time, but <u>at the end it shall speak, and not lie: though it tarry, wait for it; because it will surely come, it will not tarry</u>. 4: Behold, his soul *which* is lifted up is not upright in him: but the just shall live by his faith.**

The verses above use two different Hebrew words for tarry. It is like saying: *though it linger wait for it, for it will come and not tarry long or be deferred.* Lot *lingered* until the angels took him, his wife and two daughters by the hand and set them forth outside the city. Judgment was about to come upon the city (Genesis 19:16).

There is one thing about the prayer of Elijah that really stands out. The 3 ½ years of no rain seems like a halfway mark of the final seven years. Since he prays again and rain comes that would suggest a good last half of the seven years. I have looked for other verses that would confirm this truth and Habakkuk chapter 3 has one verse that seems to relate to God reviving the work in *the midst of the years:*

> **Habakkuk 3:1: A prayer of Habakkuk the prophet upon Shigionoth. 2: O LORD, I have heard thy speech, *and* was afraid: O LORD, <u>revive thy work in the midst of the years</u>, in the midst of the years make known; in wrath remember mercy. 3: God came from Teman, and the Holy One from mount Paran. Selah. His glory covered the heavens, and the earth was full of his praise.**

God points us to Job and Elijah in James 5 as examples for us all *unto the coming of the Lord.* In this chapter, I have only scratched the surface of the information in the book of Job and concerning Elijah. God willing, I will be able to present more in video studies on the *2011studies* channel. The topics I will address on the *2011studies* channel will most likely include (but not be limited to) the following:

- The *great rains* of Elijah, Joel 2, and James 5
- Why the body of Moses was disputed by Satan
- Why Elijah was taken up to Heaven
- Why Moses and Elijah were at the mount of transfiguration

The Two Witnesses of Revelation 11

I need to squeeze one more topic in this chapter because I believe it relates to God turning things around in the year 2015. The two witnesses in Revelation 11 stand on their feet after 3 ½ days and the people who behold them fear. They are called up to stand before the God of the earth. Keep in mind that when Elijah was warning Ahab, he stated that he *stands before the Lord* and then continued to warn Ahab. When John saw incredible things while on the Island of

Patmos, he saw things that represent a certain truth. The woman clothed in purple, as we have seen, was a representation of the fallen houses of God, which God names *fallen Babylon*. Therefore, the two witnesses represent something very important.

The two witnesses, I believe, represent the very Word of God (the law and the prophets) as seen by Moses and Elijah on the mount of transfiguration. For 3 ½ days the bodies of the two witnesses lay in the street dead. Then at that crucial halfway mark, the breath of life enters into them and they stand. God has previously used the "day for a year principle." So the 3 ½ days can be the period from 2011 to 2015. God's Word will no doubt have power, and when judgment comes to pass, this can cause a great fear in people:

> **Revelation 11:11: And <u>after three days and an half the Spirit of life from God entered into them</u>, and they stood upon their feet; and great fear fell upon them which saw them. 12: And they heard a great voice from heaven saying unto them, Come up hither. And they ascended up to heaven in a cloud; and their enemies beheld them.**

There have been attempts to relate the above account in Revelation 11 to the rapture or resurrection of the believers. However, we have an outline of the two witnesses in the Old Testament. How is that possible? It is possible because God calls the two witnesses *the two olive branches*, which brings us to the book of Zechariah where the *two olive branches* are mentioned. The two witnesses, who are the olive branches, at one time in the future are made alive and called to *come up hither*. The focus in Zechariah 4 is the *two anointed ones*:

> **Zechariah 4:12: And I answered again, and said unto him, What *be these* two olive branches which through the two golden pipes empty the golden *oil* out of themselves? 13: And he answered me and said, Knowest thou not what these *be*? And I said, No, my lord. 14: Then said he, <u>These *are* the two anointed ones, that stand by the Lord of the whole earth.</u>**

In Zechariah 4:14, the King James Bible says *stand by the Lord,* and the ISA says *stand on the Lord.* The Hebrew word for *by* is *al (H5921),* and it is also used as *over,* so even *stand over the Lord* could apply as the meaning. Revelation 11:14 says that the two olive branches and two candlesticks are *standing before the God of the earth.*

> **Revelation 11:4: These are the two olive trees, and the two candlesticks standing <u>before</u> the God of the earth.**

The important thing is that blessing from God is present at certain times when the Hebrew word for anointing is found in the Bible. This really underscores the importance of Joel 2 as God is being magnified once *the Northern* is removed. In Joel 2, that same word for oil (*clarified/anointed*) is found when God begins to bless His people. The focus of *anointed* or *clarified oil* really stands out in Zechariah 4:14. Below, I will list times of when God withholds blessing and then times of when he blesses where the Hebrew word for *anointed* or *clarified/oil* is used. Notice the time references in each of the verses. I am very convinced that this relates to salvation. The very Word of God having real power once the 3 ½ years is complete and also the Spirit of God blessing lives after the 3 ½ years is complete. It is very likely that both will be true. I am also convinced that 2015 is one important year in God's timeline of salvation to usher this time of blessing in.

The Times When God Withholds Blessing

The focus on these verses will be on *anointed ones* or *clarified oil,* which is related to the two olive branches.

- God sends the *nation of fierce countenance* as a judgment which destroys the oil among other things:

  Deuteronomy 28:50: A nation of fierce countenance, which shall not regard the person of the old, nor shew favour to the young: 51: And he shall eat the fruit of thy cattle, and the fruit of thy land, until thou be destroyed: which *also* shall not leave thee *either* corn, wine, *or* oil, or the increase of thy kine, or flocks of thy sheep, until he have destroyed thee.

- Joel 2 has very similar language as Deuteronomy 28. It is a time of wasting by evil. The *Northern* is a name for Satan who sets forth destruction upon the houses of God:

  Joel 1:9: The meat offering and the drink offering is cut off from the house of the LORD; the priests, the LORD'S ministers, mourn. 10: The field is wasted, the land mourneth; for the corn is wasted: the new wine is dried up, the oil languisheth.

Times of Blessing by God

- Remember this time of destruction in Joel 1 is prior to God being magnified in Joel 2. Then we see the result of God being magnified with the verses in Joel 2 as God gives back the blessing of *corn, wine and oil*:

> **Joel 2:18: Then will the LORD be jealous for his land, and pity his people. 19: Yea, the LORD will answer and say unto his people, Behold, I will send you corn, and wine, <u>and oil</u>, and ye shall be satisfied therewith: and <u>I will no more make you a reproach among the heathen</u>...**

- Then there are some verses in Hosea chapter 2 which really underscores the corn (increase), wine and oil as a blessing for those who become part of the eternal inheritance. It is there where God proclaims that people will no longer call Him *Baali* (possessor of) but rather *Ishi* (similar to husband or joined to).

> **Hosea 2:20: <u>I will even betroth thee unto me in faithfulness</u>: and thou shalt know the LORD. 21: And it shall come to pass in that day, I will hear, saith the LORD, I will hear the heavens, and they shall hear the earth; 22: And <u>the earth shall hear the corn, and the wine, and the oil</u>; and they shall hear Jezreel. 23: And I will sow her unto me in the earth; and I will have mercy upon her that had not obtained mercy; and I will say to *them which were* not my people, Thou *art* my people; and they shall say, *Thou art* my God.**

Why does God mention Jezreel? The word Jezreel means *God will sow*. Elijah ran ahead of Ahab to the entrance of Jezreel when the heavy rain began. Jezebel, the instigator, was also killed in the valley of Jezreel signifying a judgment on those who are involved in false worship and teach others to do the same. God also uses a term called *the day of Jezreel*.

Hosea 1:11: Then shall the children of Judah and the children of Israel be gathered together, and appoint themselves one head, and they shall come up out of the land: for great *shall be* the day of Jezreel.

We touched a bit on the years of Darius in this chapter but I only got up to the second year of Darius. There are so many important topics to cover in this book, and the years of Darius need a separate chapter. So let us study the years of Darius and how his reign was so important in the rebuilding of the temple. We have six *years of Darius* to cover as the sixth year was when the temple was completed. God has performed a *reliving of history* very perfectly.

Chapter 10—The Years of Darius Repeated 2011-2018

In the last chapter we looked at the first two years of Darius, but the Bible mentions up to the sixth year of Darius. We also saw how the years of Darius line up with our 2011 to 2018. I will copy the outline of these years again to start this chapter off in the right direction:

Darius' official first year- Nisan 538 BC to Nisan 537 BC

Darius' official second year- Nisan 537 BC to Nisan 536 BC

Darius' official third year- Nisan 536 BC to Nisan 535 BC

Darius' official forth year- Nisan 535 BC to Nisan 534 BC

Darius' official fifth year- Nisan 534 BC to Nisan 533 BC

Darius' official sixth year- Nisan 533 BC to Nisan 532 BC

The Replica of Darius' Years Past the 8,400 Days Ending May 21, 2011

October of 2011 would have lined up with Cyrus taking Babylon peacefully. Darius's first official year in 538 B.C. would have lined up with our Nisan 2012.

Nisan 2012 to Nisan 2013- Darius' first year

Nisan 2013 to Nisan 2014- Darius' second year

Nisan 2014 to Nisan 2015- Darius' third year

Nisan 2015 to Nisan 2016- Darius' fourth year

Nisan 2016 to Nisan 2017- Darius' fifth year

Nisan 2017 to Nisan 2018- Darius' sixth year

- The first year of Darius- knowledge was given to Daniel concerning the things of the end. Daniel also prospered in the reign of Cyrus and Darius:

   Daniel 6:28: So this Daniel prospered in the reign of Darius, and in the reign of Cyrus the Persian.

- The second year of Darius- God is not pleased with Israel as they lived in their *ceiled houses* while His house lies in waste. He commands them to work for He will be with them in the re-building of the temple. God forecasts a shaking of the heavens and earth in the second year of Darius. He also forecasts the rebuking of Satan in this important year of Darius (Zechariah 3:2). Due to previous opposition, the temple building was halted by enemies until the edict to construct the temple by Cyrus was found at Achmetha, in the palace of the Medes:

   Ezra 6:1: Then Darius the king made a decree, and <u>search was made in the house of the rolls</u>, where the treasures were laid up in Babylon. 2: And there was found at Achmetha, in the palace that *is* in the province of the Medes, <u>a roll, and therein *was* a record thus written</u>: 3: In the first year of Cyrus the king *the same* Cyrus the king made a decree *concerning* the house of God at Jerusalem, Let the house be builded...

- The third year of Darius- This year is not mentioned in the Bible. The command to work, for God is with us, is still carried over into the years following including the sixth year of Darius.

- The fourth year of Darius- The fourth year of Darius is mentioned in the book of Zechariah. God is addressing the priests and those declaring God's Word in the house of the Lord. God is pleading with them through the prophet Zechariah not to repeat the actions of the 70-years of captivity. He demands that they execute true judgment, and *show mercy* and *compassions every man to his brother*. He also commands them to oppress not the widow, the fatherless, the stranger, nor the poor, and *let none of you imagine evil against his brother in your heart*. However, they refused to listen and God's judgment came:

Zechariah 7:13: Therefore it is come to pass, *that* as he cried, and they would not hear; so they cried, and I would not hear, saith the LORD of hosts: 14: But I scattered them with a whirlwind among all the nations whom they knew not. Thus the land was desolate after them, that no man passed through nor returned: for they laid the pleasant land desolate.

Nisan 2015 to Nisan 2016 is the fourth year of Darius. This is why the warning to the leaders of the houses of God must go forth now. Even though they may not listen to God's Word, once judgment comes, they will know the reason why judgment has come.

- The fifth year of Darius- The fifth year of Darius, like the third year of Darius, is not mentioned in the Bible. However, the effects of the judgment which comes in the mirror of the fourth year of Darius will carry over. Nisan 2016 to Nisan 2017 is the mirror of Darius' fifth year.

- The sixth year of Darius- This is the last mention of the years of Darius in the Bible. This is the year in which historically the temple was completed. Nisan 2017 to Nisan 2018 is the mirror of Darius' sixth year. Will the year 2018 be the year in which the eternal temple of God made up of believers worldwide will be complete, which is seven years from the 7,000[th] anniversary of the flood? I believe God is going to be revealing more in the coming years concerning the year 2018. I am going to speak in a later chapter concerning the possibilities within the final seven months leading up to the last day of the Feast of Tabernacles-2018. The topic will be *the beautification of the temple.* For now, here are the verses in Ezra 6 which show that the temple was completed in the sixth year of Darius in which there was joy:

Ezra 6:14: And the elders of the Jews builded, and they prospered through the prophesying of Haggai the prophet and Zechariah the son of Iddo. And they builded, and finished *it*, according to the commandment of the God of Israel, and according to the commandment of Cyrus, and Darius, and Artaxerxes king of Persia. 15: <u>And this house was finished on the third day of the month Adar, which was in the sixth year of the reign of Darius the king</u>. 16: And the children of Israel, the priests, and the Levites, and the rest of the children of the captivity, <u>kept the dedication of this house of God with joy,</u>

The second year of Darius was a pivotal marker in the rebuilding process. The enemies had made their attempts to halt the rebuilding of both Jerusalem and the temple. Until the proof of the Cyrus roll to rebuild the temple was found, there were certain enemies who caused problems with the rebuilding. I remember back in 2011 when the mocking was really strong. After that year, there seemed to be a shying away from really presenting the complete Word of God. If one brings the good news of forgiveness of sins and the free gift of eternal life through the work of Christ, the rest of the story must also be told: judgment is coming on the fallen houses of God first, and then the world will also experience judgment on the *last day.*

As we lined up the years of Darius with our current years, we know that the <u>second year of Darius</u> is important because God commands us to *consider our ways* and then to *work*:

> **Haggai 1:3: Then came the word of the LORD by Haggai the prophet, saying, 4:** *Is it* **time for you, O ye, to dwell in your cieled houses, and this house** *lie* **waste? 5: Now therefore thus saith the LORD of hosts; Consider your ways. 6: Ye have sown much, and bring in little; ye eat, but ye have not enough; ye drink, but ye are not filled with drink; ye clothe you, but there is none warm; and he that earneth wages earneth wages** *to put it* **into a bag with holes.**

God underscores how we should consider our ways. The heaven over us has been *stayed from the dew*, and the earth has been *stayed from her fruit*. Again, this fits with James chapter 5 very well. The earth will bring forth its fruit, but the work must be done first, and the *early* and *latter rain* of understanding must also occur. God promises that He is with us, so there should not be any fear that will keep believers from accomplishing this task of bringing the Gospel worldwide.

> **Haggai 1:13: Then spake Haggai the LORD'S messenger in the <u>LORD'S message unto the people, saying, I</u>** *am* **<u>with you, saith the LORD.</u> 14:**

> **And the LORD stirred up the spirit of Zerubbabel the son of Shealtiel, governor of Judah, and the spirit of Joshua the son of Josedech, the high priest, and the spirit of all the remnant of the people; and <u>they came and did work in the house of the LORD of hosts, their God</u>, 15: In the four and twentieth day of the sixth month, <u>in the second year of Darius the king.</u>**

The Second Year of Darius- *Be Strong and Work for I am With You*

The command to *work* and *be strong* for God is with us begins in the second year of Darius, which mirrors our 2013-2014. However, that is only the beginning since the temple will not be completed until the sixth year of Darius. Will the eternal house of God in which believers are living stones be completed in 2018? This sure does line up with the sixth year of Darius. The following verses express the reality that now is the time to be working:

> **Haggai 2:4: Yet now be strong, O Zerubbabel, saith the LORD; and be strong, O Joshua, son of Josedech, the high priest; and <u>be strong, all ye people of the land, saith the LORD, and work: for I *am* with you, saith the LORD</u> of hosts: 5: *According to* the word that I covenanted with you when ye came out of Egypt, so my spirit remaineth among you: <u>fear ye not</u>.**

Nisan 2013 to Nisan 2014- A Mirror of Darius' Second Year

There is yet even more God wants His people to know in the mirror of the second year of Darius. He will bless past a certain point of the second year of Darius. This makes perfect sense due to the historical opposition which came after the return from captivity. After the 8,400 days in the year 2011 there was a delay of accomplishing work as people seemed disillusioned concerning May 21, 2011 and October 21, 2011. Now that we are in the mirror of the second year of Darius there should be no excuses. We are commanded by God to work for He is with us. We are commanded by God to work also since <u>He will bless the work</u>.

<u>God Blesses From This Day Upward- Which Day?</u>

The Biblical Calendar in Haggai 2 mentions that God will begin blessing starting on the 24th day of the ninth month in the second year of Darius. This would equal our calendar date of November 27, 2013. Since we just completed the second year of Darius as of April 1, 2014, this promise of blessing is still very new.

Therefore, getting this information out as soon as possible is critical. There really will not be much time for proper checks on grammar or typos. I will go back over the first publication of *Seven Years to a Better Tomorrow* and make appropriate checks at a later date. Please be patient with us on this matter. Here is the verse which mentions how God will bless past our calendar date of November 27, 2013:

> **Haggai 2:18: Consider now from this day and upward, from the four and twentieth day of the ninth *month*, *even* from the day that the foundation of the LORD'S temple was laid, consider *it.* 19: <u>Is the seed yet in the barn?</u> Yea, as yet the vine, and the fig tree, and the pomegranate, and the olive tree, hath not brought forth: <u>from this day will I bless *you.*</u>**

The reason God smote their crops with *blasting, mildew, and hail* was that the *works of their hands were unclean*.

239

> **Haggai 2:17: I smote you with blasting and with mildew and with hail in all the labours of your hands; <u>yet ye *turned* not to me</u>, saith the LORD.**

From this example in Haggai, we can know where blessings come from. If we serve God and the works of our hands are not unclean or our motivation is correct, then God will honor that. In the book of Revelation, God brings past history right up to the present as He speaks of the *works of their hands* being evil. Why would the book of Revelation be speaking of *idols of gold* and *worshipping devils*? God is drawing from past history and equating these actions to what is happening in the fallen houses of God:

> **Revelation 9:20: And the rest of the men which were not killed by these plagues <u>yet repented not of the works of their hands</u>, <u>that they should not worship devils</u>, and idols of gold, and silver, and brass, and stone, and of wood: which neither can see, nor hear, nor walk: 21: Neither repented they of their murders, nor of their sorceries, nor of their fornication, nor of their thefts.**

> **Jeremiah 1:16: And I will utter my judgments against them touching all their wickedness, who have forsaken me, and have <u>burned incense unto other gods</u>, and <u>worshipped the works of their own hands.</u>**

The Corn (increase), Wine, and Oil

In God's Word of truth, there are times in which He uses a type of an original earthly blessing to represent something much larger. The words *corn, wine, and oil* are grouped together as a blessing. I believe God does this to show His increase or blessing especially regarding salvation.

240

Deuteronomy speaks of God's blessing <u>if</u> the commandments, statutes, and judgments are kept. Part of the blessing mentioned in Deuteronomy includes the *corn, wine, and oil.*

> **Deuteronomy 7:12: Wherefore it shall come to pass, if ye hearken to these judgments, and keep, and do them, that the LORD thy God shall keep unto thee the covenant and the mercy which he sware unto thy fathers...**

The *corn, wine, and oil* are significant in our time because in the book of Joel, after God removes the *Northern,* these precise words are used. One effect of this blessing is God removes the *reproach* of His people and they are blessed. This is recognized in the *eyes of the nations:*

God Removes the Reproach of His People

> **Joel 2:18: Then will the LORD be jealous for his land, and pity his people. 19: Yea, the LORD will answer and say unto his people, Behold, I will send you corn, and wine, and oil, and ye shall be satisfied therewith: and <u>I will no more make you a reproach among the heathen</u>...**

The good news about the second half of these final years is that God will remove the shame or reproach of His people. God, who is mighty, will perform a great reversal with His people. We will no longer be a reproach, but rather, we will be known by God being with us. This is why we do not need to refrain from bringing the good news of salvation through Christ. Read the following verses from Zephaniah 3 and know that God will perform this mighty work:

> **Zephaniah 3:18: I will gather *them that are* sorrowful for the solemn assembly, *who* are of thee, *to whom* the reproach of it *was* a burden. 19: Behold, at that time I will undo all that afflict thee: and I will save her that halteth, and gather her that was driven out; and I will get them praise and fame in every land where they have been put to shame. 20: At that time will I bring you *again*, even in the time that I gather you: for I will make you a name and a praise among all people of the earth, when I turn back your captivity before your eyes, saith the LORD.**

The year 2015 should turn out to be a very significant year. There is one last thing mentioned in the second year of Darius that really needs careful study. God mentions something not only once but twice in Haggai in the context of the second year of Darius. The Lord seems to be forecasting an event that will soon change things worldwide. The phrase that God uses is *I will shake the heavens and earth*. What does this phrase mean?

God Promises to Shake the Heavens and Earth

The book of Haggai has been the focus in this chapter. There God desires His people to return back to Him and then blessing will follow. Where once was loss of crops due to the *works of their hands*, from a certain point in the *second year of Darius* there will be God's blessing. In this setting of Haggai 2, God mentions that He is going to *shake the heavens and the earth*. With the way God has written His Word, we can suspect this kind of phrase to mean major changes. A phrase with a similar expression of power is when the Lord rebukes Satan. This is no small thing since a prior rebuking by the Lord of Heaven caused the Red (Reed) sea to dry up:

> **Psalm 106:9: <u>He rebuked the Red sea also, and it was dried up</u>: so he led them through the depths, as through the wilderness. 10: And he saved them from the hand of him that hated *them*, and redeemed them from the hand of the enemy.**

> **Isaiah 17:13: The nations shall rush like the rushing of many waters: but <u>*God* shall rebuke them, and they shall flee far off</u>, and shall be chased as the chaff of the mountains before the wind, and like a rolling thing before the whirlwind.**

Finally, when God rebukes Satan it will end a time of desolation and God will create great blessings for His people:

> **Malachi 3:11: And <u>I will rebuke the devourer for your sakes</u>, and he shall not destroy the fruits of your ground; neither shall your vine cast her fruit before the time in the field, saith the LORD of hosts. 12: And all nations shall call you blessed: for ye shall be a delightsome land, saith the LORD of hosts.**

Just as circumstances change when God rebukes, the shaking of *the heavens and earth* will produce a substantial change in this world. In Haggai 2, God mentions the *shaking* twice. Let us look at these important verses:

> **Haggai 2:20: And again the word of the LORD came unto Haggai in the four and twentieth *day* of the month, saying, 21: Speak to Zerubbabel, governor of Judah, saying, <u>I will shake the</u>**

> **heavens and the earth; Haggai 2:22: And I will
> overthrow the throne of kingdoms, and I will
> destroy the strength of the kingdoms of the
> heathen; and I will overthrow the chariots, and
> those that ride in them; and the horses and their
> riders shall come down, every one by the sword of
> his brother. Haggai 2:23: In that day, saith the
> LORD of hosts, will I take thee, O Zerubbabel, my
> servant, the son of Shealtiel, saith the LORD, and
> will make thee as a signet: for I have chosen thee,
> saith the LORD of hosts.**

There are some really good clues in these verses. Not only is
the phrase of God shaking the *heavens and earth* found in
these verses, but God also says that He will *overthrow the
throne of kingdoms and He will destroy the strength of the
kingdoms of the heathen (*also translated as *nations).* There
also seems to be a real connection with the historical account
of the Exodus out of Egypt. The Hebrew word for strength is
chozeq (H2392), and it is found in connection with God's
hand of power bringing the Israelites out of Egypt:

> **Exodus 13:3: And Moses said unto the people,
> Remember this day, in which ye came out from
> Egypt, out of the house of bondage; for by
> strength of hand the LORD brought you out from
> this *place*: there shall no leavened bread be eaten.**

God underscores this Egyptian theme in one of the verses of
Haggai where He reminds us of the covenant or promise. The
Lord does this in the context of *work for I am with you*:

> **Haggai 2:5: *According to* the word that I
> covenanted with you when ye came out of Egypt,
> so my spirit remaineth among you: fear ye not.**

The pursuit of the Israelites by Pharaoh and his armies saw a grand overthrow by God's hand. God calls the fallen houses of God *Sodom and Egypt* in the book of Revelation, so the *houses of bondage* also seem to fit this judgment of God. Overthrowing the *strength of the nations* is going to be something to behold. David also spoke of the *hand of his enemies* and how God saved him from them. Again, a pursuit by the power or hand of the enemy is overthrown by God's *power* or *hand*. How God does all of this is going to be something incredible to observe. In Haggai 2, God brings up the aspect of judgment by saying that the *horses and their riders shall come down by the sword of his brother.*

This kind of a judgment is not a new idea in the Bible. God can create an atmosphere of *infighting* even in the fallen houses of God.

- In Judges 7:22, 300 men of Gideon's army blew the trumpet and *the LORD set every man against his brother.*
- In 1 Samuel 14:20, when Saul and the people with him came to the battle, *every man's sword was against his brother* and there was *great confusion.*
- In Ezekiel 38:21, God calls for a sword against Gog throughout all of God's mountains and proclaims how *every man's sword shall be against his brother.*

When God comes against Satan, all nations will know and God will be magnified:

Ezekiel 38:23: Thus will I magnify myself, and sanctify myself; and I will be known in the eyes of many nations, and they shall know that I *am* the LORD.

Any type of *pursuing* of the believers in Christ during the times of *tribulation* will be met by God's hand. There does come a time of recompense. Isaiah 34:8 speaks of a specific year for recompenses:

> **Isaiah 34:8: For *it is* the day of the LORD'S vengeance, *and* the year of recompences for the controversy of Zion.**

In Isaiah 34:16 God commands that we search the book of the Lord. I believe the judgment on Satan and the fallen houses of God is so masked in the Bible with various language of past history, such as *the glory of Moab shall be contemned*, that most of this is overlooked as being strictly historical. This, however, is how God has written His Word. God has an overview and scope of all of history. Therefore, He not only controlled history, but He now is using the past to demonstrate His judgments during the culmination of these final years.

> **Isaiah 34:16: Seek ye out of the book of the LORD, and read: no one of these shall fail, none shall want her mate: for my mouth it hath commanded, and his spirit it hath gathered them.**

Prior to the above verse, which states *none shall want her mate*, God is painting a picture of complete <u>desolation in the palaces</u>. The owl is there; the vulture and her mate are there; the raven shall dwell there, and the cormorant and the bittern shall possess it. God is using unclean birds as a picture of what the book of Revelation calls *a cage of every unclean and hateful bird* and *a habitation of devils:*

> **Jeremiah 5:26: For among my people are found wicked *men*: they lay wait, as he that setteth snares; they set a trap, they catch men. 27: As a cage is full of birds, so *are* their houses full of deceit: therefore they are become great, and waxen rich.**

> **Revelation 18:2: And he cried mightily with a strong voice, saying, <u>Babylon the great is fallen</u>, is fallen, and is become the habitation of devils, and <u>the hold of every foul spirit, and a cage of every unclean and hateful bird</u>. 3: For all nations have drunk of the wine of the wrath of her fornication, and the kings of the earth have committed fornication with her, and the merchants of the earth are waxed rich through the abundance of her delicacies. 4: And I heard another voice from heaven, saying, <u>Come out of her, my people, that ye be not partakers of her sins, and that ye receive not of her plagues.</u>**

<u>God Created the Heavens and Earth- God will Shake the Heavens and Earth</u>

> **Genesis 2:1: Thus the heavens and the earth were finished, and all the host of them. 2: And on the seventh day God ended his work which he had made; and he rested on the seventh day from all his work which he had made.**

Yes, God created the heavens and earth and all creation in seven days, not seven years, not seven thousand years. We know this from the phrase: *the <u>evening and the morning</u> were the first day.* We then come all the way to the final seven years of history where, in the mirror of the second year of

Darius, God promises that He will *shake the heavens and earth*. The first time God mentions this truth, He also says *a little while*. That should tell us why the *shaking* was not within the second year of Darius. Instead, it is a short forecasting of the fact that God will be *shaking the heavens and the earth*. When will God *shake the heavens and the earth?*

There is one verse mentioned in the book of Joel which also mentions Christ roaring out of Zion and uttering His voice out of Jerusalem. In the context of His *voice roaring,* do the *heavens and earth shake?* Joel 2 mentions *fear not O land* because God will be magnified. The language found in Joel 3:16, concerning Christ roaring and *shaking the heavens and earth,* seems to be approximately the same time frame as the *shaking* in Haggai. I suspect that the year 2015 would be the timing of God *shaking the heavens and earth*:

> **Joel 3:16: The LORD also shall roar out of Zion, and utter his voice from Jerusalem; and the heavens and the earth shall shake: but the LORD *will be* the hope of his people, and the strength of the children of Israel.**

The Sun and the Moon Shall be Darkened

What about Joel 3:15 where it talks about the sun and the moon being darkened and the stars withdrawing their shining? Unfortunately, there are times in which the King James translators may have taken liberty to make a verse sound different than what the original words are actually saying. I will present the King James translation of Joel 3:15 and then below that verse will be the ISA rendering of that same verse:

Joel 3:15: The sun and the moon shall be darkened, and the stars shall withdraw their shining.

ISA: sun and moon they are somber and stars they gather brightness of them.

The Hebrew word for somber is *qdru (H6937)* and this word is also found in another verse that mentions mourning. I really believe that when there are times of God's judgment going forth, He will use the time keepers as a reflection of the light of this world being spiritually somber. In the verses below, David is somber *qdr* (H6937) or *mourning*:

Psalm 38:4: For mine iniquities are gone over mine head: as an heavy burden they are too heavy for me. 5: My wounds stink and are corrupt because of my foolishness. 6: I am troubled; I am bowed down greatly; <u>I go mourning</u> all the day long.

The same truth goes for *the stars shall withdraw their shining*. It actually says that *the stars shall gather brightness of them*. This may be a reference to what we understood in the book of Daniel where we read: *they that be wise shall shine as the brightness of the firmament.* The word *shine* means to *teach or warn*. The Hebrew word incorrectly translated as *withdraw* actually means *to gather*.

ISA: sun and moon they are somber and stars they gather brightness of them.

The impact between Christ and His creation during the time of judgment can cause a reaction of somberness or mourning.

Will there be any physical showing or change in the sun, moon, and stars during the time of God's judgment when we reach the halfway mark in the year 2015? The mirror of the original 3 ½ years are the years 2011 to 2015. When Christ hung on the cross, the earth became dark, the sun was darkened, and God was glorified:

> **Luke 23:44: And it was about the sixth hour, and there was a darkness over all the earth until the ninth hour. 45: And the sun was darkened, and the veil of the temple was rent in the midst.**
> **46: And when Jesus had cried with a loud voice, he said, Father, into thy hands I commend my spirit: and having said thus, he gave up the ghost. 47: Now when the centurion saw what was done, he glorified God, saying, certainly this was a righteous man.**

The years 2014 and 2015 are significant in God's timeline of history. In the next chapter, I want to explore something that is really quite amazing. There is going to be a blood moon tetrad in the years 2014 and 2015. What is really amazing is that these eclipses occur during precise feast celebrations that God established long ago. While the language of the sun and moon being *somber* may be spiritual language, there may be an outward warning from these great lights during this blood moon tetrad. What impact will this have on the fallen houses of God once we reach the blood moon eclipses in the year 2015? Is this tetrad representing the *signs and seasons* that Genesis chapter one mentions?

> **Genesis 1:14: And God said, Let there be lights in the firmament of the heaven to divide the day from the night; and let them be for signs, and for**

seasons, and for days, and years: 15: And let them be for lights in the firmament of the heaven to give light upon the earth: and it was so. 16: And God made two great lights; the greater light to rule the day, and the lesser light to rule the night: *he made* **the stars also. 17: And God set them in the firmament of the heaven to give light upon the earth...**

The timekeepers that give light upon the earth may also be warning us that God is preparing to judge the fallen houses of God. In the next chapter, we are going to look at the blood moon tetrads (four eclipses) which occur in the years 2014 and 2015. These eclipses land on the first day of the Feast of Passover in both years and also the first day of the Feast of Tabernacles in both years. Is this all just a coincidence? Let us explore what is going to happen with God's timekeepers in 2014 and 2015. The year 2015 should be a time of great significance as the final eclipses occur on these precise feast days.

Chapter 11—The Blood Moon Tetrad of 2014 & 2015 - Pre-Warning to the Houses of God?

When I first heard of the blood moon tetrad that will be occurring in the years 2014 and 2015, I was thinking this may just be a four-time eclipsing of the moon. Then when I saw how these eclipses fall on God's precise feast celebrations, I became very interested. Some pastors believe that these blood moons relate to the nation of Israel. Instead, I became interested in these red moon eclipses as a warning to the fallen houses of God. There is however always a possibility of a parallel between Jerusalem and the houses of God.

In Zechariah 14:2 God promises to gather all nations against *Jerusalem*. At that time God pours out His indignation upon the nations. Since judgment upon the fallen houses of God is something that will take place prior to Jesus coming on the last day; it is hard to know which *Jerusalem* God is referring to. The fallen houses of God must be the first choice due much Biblical proclamations against the *daughter of my people*.

However, we can't rule out a parallel between Jerusalem as Israel's pronounced capital and the houses of God. The international community does not recognize Jerusalem as Israel's capital. Therefore, the nations coming against Jerusalem is very viable in the near future. We also must recognize how God defines Jerusalem. The *New Jerusalem* mentioned in the book of Revelation is the eternal peaceful city of God. This establishes the connection between *Jerusalem* and Christianity. The *New Jerusalem* will be comprised of believers in Christ from many nations. The timing of the bride (believers) and bridegroom (Christ) meeting up would signify God's completion of His salvation:

> **Revelation 21:2: And I John saw the holy city, <u>new Jerusalem</u>, coming down from God out of heaven, prepared as a bride adorned for her husband. 3: And I heard a great voice out of heaven saying, Behold, the tabernacle of God is with men, and he will dwell with them, and they shall be his people, and God himself shall be with them, and be their God. 4: And God shall wipe away all tears from their eyes; and there shall be no more death, neither sorrow, nor crying, neither shall there be any more pain: for the former things are passed away.**

Does this blood moon tetrad line up with God's judgment upon *fallen Babylon* which is a spiritual name for the fallen houses of God? The years 2014 and 2015 are not only significant in accordance with the years of Darius, but they are significant with something else that I will cover in the next chapter (Moab and Kedar). I am lining up these two chapters back to back to show the significance of the timing of God's judgment on *Jerusalem* or God's houses worldwide.

It is ironic that the leaders in the houses of God are pointing elsewhere for God's judgment to fall? Like historical Jerusalem ignoring Jeremiah's warnings, the houses of God do not know the timing of their own judgment:

> **Jeremiah 8:5: Why *then* is this people of Jerusalem slidden back by a perpetual**

254

backsliding? They hold fast deceit, they refuse to return. 6: I hearkened and heard, *but* they spake not aright: no man repented him of his wickedness, saying, What have I done? Every one turned to his course, as the horse rusheth into the battle. 7: Yea, the stork in the heaven knoweth her appointed times; and the turtle and the crane and the swallow observe the time of their coming; <u>but my people know not the judgment of the LORD</u>.

I am sure the leaders in the fallen houses of God will not like this message of soon coming judgment. However, it is written in God's Word, so it will come to pass. God's Word even proclaims there will be an attitude of *we will see no sorrow*:

> **Revelation 18:7: How much she hath glorified herself, and lived deliciously, so much torment and sorrow give her: for she saith in her heart, <u>I sit a queen, and am no widow, and shall see no sorrow</u>.**

In the book of Genesis, God sets the lights in the heavens and declares that these are for *signs, seasons, days and years*. God also mentions that they *rule* the day and night. The Hebrew word for *rule* has also been translated as *dominion*. Thus, the sun has dominion over the day, and the moon and stars have dominion over the night. During the Exodus out of Egypt, Judah was God's sanctuary and Israel was His dominion (rule):

> **Psalm 114:1: When Israel went out of Egypt, the house of Jacob from a people of strange language; 2: <u>Judah was his sanctuary, *and* Israel his dominion.</u> 3: The sea saw it, and fled: Jordan was driven back.**

When God is warning believers to *come out of her my people* so that they do not experience the plagues, is it possible that God will send a warning by the timekeepers becoming *somber*? Perhaps the eclipses are a pre-warning to flee out before the coming judgment. The last of the four total eclipses may be a final warning to signify judgment on the fallen houses of God worldwide in the year 2015. The first eclipse in the year 2015 occurs on the first day of the Feast of Passover and the last one occurs on the first day of the Feast of Tabernacles. Passover as recorded in Exodus 12:12 states the judgment upon false worship and *all the gods of Egypt*: *against all the gods of Egypt I will execute judgment: I am the LORD.*

Flee out of Spiritual *Sodom and Egypt*

The 2015 blood moon eclipses may indeed be signifying the judgment on false worship and the *coming out of Egypt.* The first blood moon in the year 2015 falls precisely on the first day of Passover (April 4, 2015). The second blood moon eclipse falls on the first day of Tabernacles (September 28, 2015). These Old Testament feasts have everything to do with fleeing out before judgment comes (especially Passover). Tabernacles signifies the process after coming out of Egypt and dwelling in booths/tabernacles. Since the book of Revelation names the fallen houses of God *Sodom and Egypt,* the idea of fleeing out of the fallen houses of God is very similar to Passover and also the Exodus out of Egypt. When God's Word and the anointed *olive branches* (two witnesses) lay dead in the street, this is a representation of how God's commands and Word (the law and the prophets) are disregarded (lay dead) in the churches (*Sodom and Egypt*):

Revelation 11:8: And their dead bodies *shall lie* in the street of the great city, which spiritually is called Sodom and Egypt, where also our Lord was crucified.

The reason Jesus was not crucified inside the city of Jerusalem was because the sacrifice offering by the high priest (for sin) was done outside of the great city. Jesus being the high priest and also the sacrifice fulfilled the requirements that He may sanctify His people with His own blood:

Hebrews 13:11: For the bodies of those beasts, whose blood is brought into the sanctuary by the high priest for sin, are burned without the camp. 12: Wherefore Jesus also, <u>that he might sanctify the people with his own blood, suffered without the gate.</u> 13: <u>Let us go forth therefore unto him without the camp, bearing his reproach.</u> 14: <u>For here have we no continuing city, but we seek one to come.</u>

One could assert that the first to bear Jesus' reproach was Simon the Cyrenian who was compelled to bear Jesus' cross. Simon became the example of every believer to bear Jesus' reproach in this world:

Mark 15:21: And they compel one Simon a Cyrenian, who passed by, coming out of the country, the father of Alexander and Rufus, to bear his cross.

Simon was behind Jesus bearing His cross and this fulfills the command of Jesus in order to become a learner or disciple of the Lord from Heaven. In the following verse the words *come after me* can be translated as *come behind me*. This is

257

exactly what Simon the Cyrenian did. Simon picked up His cross and followed behind Jesus, thus illustrating what a believer does in this life as a follower/learner of the Lord:

> **Luke 14:27: And whosoever doth not bear his cross, and come <u>after me</u>, cannot be my disciple.**

> **Luke 23:26: And as they led him away, they laid hold upon one Simon, a Cyrenian, coming out of the country, and on him they laid the cross, that he might bear *it* <u>after Jesus</u>.**

The timing of the judgment of the cross and the Passover eclipse in 2015 is very significant. For God to forewarn of a coming judgment through His Word shows mercy. To forewarn also through the great lights becoming *somber* and syncing up with the Feast of Passover and the Feast of Tabernacles shows incredible mercy:

> **Psalm 136:7: To him that made great lights: for his mercy *endureth* for ever: 8: The sun to rule by day: for his mercy *endureth* for ever: 9: The moon and stars to rule by night: for his mercy *endureth* for ever.**

The entire context of Psalm 136 is God bringing His people out of Egypt. He also shows the larger picture of the believers in Christ coming out of *Sodom and Egypt*:

> **Psalm 136:13: To him which divided the Red sea into parts: for his mercy *endureth* for ever: 14: And made Israel to pass through the midst of it: for his mercy *endureth* for ever: 15: But overthrew Pharaoh and his host in the Red sea: for his mercy *endureth* for ever.**

Within Psalm 136 there is a reversal mentioned where God rescues His people from the hands of the enemy. There is also language of God remembering our *low estate* (*shephel-*H8213). Since there comes a time when God exalts the low and abases the high (Ezekiel 17:24 & Ezekiel 21:26), the year 2015 seems to be the timing of this event.

Let Them be for Signs and Seasons

The following chart shows where the four blood moon tetrad (eclipses) land in the years 2014 and 2015. The two feasts (Feast of Passover and the Feast of Tabernacles) signify judgment on historical Egypt (Pharaoh and his armies) and the coming out of Egypt. The chart below shows the dates of the four blood moon eclipses. These eclipses are important because they land on precise feast days that God has established. The eclipses in 2015 should be significant:

The Four Blood Moon Eclipses

April 15, 2014	Blood Moon	First Day of Passover- 2014
October 8, 2014	Blood Moon	First Day of Tabernacles-2014
April 4, 2015	Blood Moon	First Day of Passover-2015
Sept. 28, 2015	Blood Moon	First Day of Tabernacles-2015

All four eclipses occur on a full moon, and Psalm 81 declares that the trumpet be blown in the month (*new*) on the full moon.

The Importance of the Blowing of the Trumpet (*Shophar*)

Psalm 81:3: Blow up the trumpet in the new moon, in the time appointed, on our solemn feast day.

While the King James translators use *new moon* to represent the word *month,* we can know from studying the Hebrew word *chodesh (H2320)* how the trumpet (*shophar*) was to be blown on the full moon of the month. These four eclipses occur at the time of the full moon. Psalm 81 is all about God *removing the burden* and God's people calling upon Him in the time of trouble (tribulation). God delivers in the time of trouble:

Psalm 81:6: I removed his shoulder from the burden: his hands were delivered from the pots. 7: <u>Thou calledst in trouble, and I delivered thee</u>; I answered thee in the secret place of thunder: I proved thee at the waters of Meribah. Selah.

The trumpet (*shophar*) has been blown at a few historical places and times in the Bible including the fall of Jericho where the *mighty men of valor* were defeated. The phrase *mighty men of valor* is also associated with the *spoiling of Moab* (Jeremiah 48:14), which relates to the *glory of Moab* being contemned. In the next chapter we will explore how this relates to the fallen houses of God.

There is yet another Psalm which really underscores the power of the blowing of the trumpet (*shophar*). I want to present Psalm 47 in full. Read this Psalm carefully focusing on how at the sound of the trumpet (*shophar*) God is exalted. I believe there are very real implications regarding this Psalm and the year 2015:

Psalm 47:1: To the chief Musician, A Psalm for the sons of Korah. O clap your hands, all ye people; shout unto God with the voice of triumph. 2: For the LORD most high *is* terrible; *he is* a great King over all the earth. 3: He shall subdue the people under us, and the nations under our feet. 4: He shall choose our inheritance for us, the excellency of Jacob whom he loved. Selah. 5: <u>God is gone up with a shout, the LORD with the sound of a trumpet.</u> 6: Sing praises to God, sing praises: sing praises unto our King, sing praises. 7: For God *is* the King of all the earth: sing ye praises with understanding. 8: God reigneth over the heathen: God sitteth upon the throne of his holiness. 9: The princes of the people are gathered together, *even* the people of the God of Abraham: for the shields of the earth *belong* unto God: he is greatly exalted.

Did you notice how God is *gone up with a shout with <u>the sound of the trumpet</u>* (*shophar*)? God is King of all the earth and He will subdue the people and the nations! God being *greatly exalted* relates very well with Joel 2 once God removes the *Northern* (Satan) and He is magnified. The *shields of the earth* relate to battle. King Solomon made shields of gold. Rehoboam made shields of brass (2 Chronicles 12:10). Gog's great company (a picture of Satan's forces), all come with *bucklers, shields and swords* (Ezekiel 38:4). In addition to the *shields of the earth* belonging to God, God Himself is the shield for every believer in Christ:

2 Samuel 22:3: The God of my rock; in him will I trust: <u>he is my shield, and the horn of my salvation, my high tower, and my refuge, my saviour;</u> thou savest me from violence. 4: I will call

on the LORD, who is worthy to be praised: <u>so</u> <u>shall I be saved from mine enemies.</u>

We are approaching that critical time in history where with the sound of the trumpet, at the time of the full moon, the Lord begins the great reversal. All roads lead to the year 2015 as the beginning of God's judgment process.

While researching the historical blood moon tetrads, I found that some people, including some church leaders, suggest a pattern of how these tetrads involve the Jewish people. Here is a chart that shows the *possible* Jewish connection with the past three historical blood moon tetrads. This is not a complete listing of the historical tetrads (note: see NASA's site[17]). Again, the eclipses of 2014-2015 are showing a time of judgment upon the houses of worship, since this lines up with the midway part of the seven years in 2015.

1493-1494 A.D. •4-2-1493 •9-25-1493 •3-22-1494 •9-15-1494	Blood Moon Tetrad- Catalog:1401-1500 (NASA)	Jews expelled from Spain (edict of 1492) prior to Blood Moons of 1493-1494
1949-1950 A.D. •4-13-1949 •10-7-1949 •4-2-1950 •9-26-1950	Blood Moon Tetrad Catalog:1901-2000 (NASA)	Israel declared a nation in 1948 (5-14-1948) prior to the blood moons of 1949-1950
1967-1968 A.D. •4-24-1967 •10-18-1967 •4-13-1968 •10-6-1968	Blood Moon Tetrad Catalog:1901-2000 (NASA)	Near the time of Israel's Six-Day War (June 5-10, 1967)

I find it significant that from 1948, when Israel was declared a nation, to the year 2018 there are a total of 70 years. The number 70 which is 7x10 has always been a complete time (7) of *tribulation* (10). The year 2018 is also 7,007 years past the time of the flood in 4990 B.C. The prime factors of 7,007 are 7x7x11x13. All these factors are important Biblical numbers. The number 7 is completeness and rest and can also show 49 (7x7). The number 11 relates to the coming of Christ and 13 relates to the end of the world. The number 13 can also represent the gospel going to the gentile nations since Paul was the 13th apostle. Paul was made an ambassador to the gentiles by the Lord Jesus Christ. I covered Biblical numbers and factors in my last book and I have also included some of the main Bible numbers in the back of the book.

Two men of the Biblical history that God wants us to focus on are Elijah and Job. In James chapter 5, this focus on Elijah and Job is in the context of *unto the coming of the Lord*. The number seven is understood with Elijah since his prayer was for 3 ½ years of no rain, which is half of 7. With Job the number 7 shows up in the following ways:

- Job had seven sons.
- Job had seven thousand sheep (doubled to 14 thousand after the trial by Satan).
- For seven days and seven nights Job's friends sat in quietness due to Job's grief.
- Job 5:19: He shall deliver thee in six troubles: yea, in seven there shall no evil touch thee.
- God commands Eliphaz the Temanite to offer up seven bullocks and seven rams as Job was to pray for all three of his friends.

I do not think we can fully eliminate a parallel between the nation of Israel and the houses of God. However, God focuses on Satan taking his seat where he should not be. The coming judgment on Satan is observed with various types and figures in the Bible such as Gog (Ezekiel 38), Pharaoh (Ezekiel 32:2) and even the King of Babylon (Isaiah 14:4).

People involved in the falling away, which includes *signs and lying wonders,* are also awaiting judgment according to God's Word. Jesus said a wicked and adulterous generation seeks after a sign (Matthew 16:4). False worship under the guise of *the power of God* should never be taken lightly. 2 Thessalonians chapter 2 teaches plainly that Satan has sought worship in the houses of God. This delusion can be so powerful that if possible it would deceive the elect of God.

This deception, however, thanks to God's Word and His Spirit warning us, will not overtake the believers. The believers in Christ who have understanding become beacons or stars as we warn the churches and the world of the coming judgment.

The *Parousia* (Coming) of Christ and the *Falling Away*

The first verse below is focused on the *coming* (*parousia*-G3952) of Christ. This is the only coming (*parousia*-G3952) mentioned in 2 Thessalonians chapter 2. Some church pastors/authors selling their fables suggest that the verse stating: [*even him*], *whose coming* (*parousia*) *is after the working of Satan* is speaking of a future man antichrist. However, that teaching is impossible because 2 Thessalonians 2:8 already mentioned *the brightness of His coming* (*parousia*). 2 Thessalonians 2:8 and 2:9 are using the identical word (*parousia*) speaking of the glorious return of Christ on the *last day*.

In other words, the coming (*parousia*) of Christ on the *last day* is after or against Satan and his *ministers* who practice *signs and lying wonders*. 2 Thessalonians 2 speaks of Jesus glorious return:

> **2 Thessalonians 2:8: And then shall that Wicked be revealed, whom the Lord shall consume with the spirit of his mouth, and shall destroy <u>with the brightness of his coming</u>: 2:9:** *Even him*, <u>**whose coming**</u> **is after the working of Satan with all power and signs and lying wonders, 10: And with all deceivableness of unrighteousness in them that perish; because they received not the love of the truth, that they might be saved. 11: And for this cause God shall send them strong delusion, that they should believe a lie…**

This causes us to wonder why Satan (the *Northern*) will not be fully destroyed until after a time of *consume and destroy* when the believers in Jesus take back the kingdom. Instead of being destroyed, he is removed by God into a land *barren and desolate* as Joel 2 mentions. This judgment process may span the final 3 ½ years past the year 2015. The halfway mark of the final seven years is significant since this is the time in which God will be magnified. Christ will finally annihilate the enemy on the *last day*.

Satan only has 3 ½ years to fully desolate, then the believers *consume and destroy* unto the end:

> **Daniel 7:25: And he shall speak** *great* **words against the most High, and shall wear out the saints of the most High, and think to change times and laws: and they shall be given into his hand <u>until a time and times and the dividing of time.</u> 26: But the judgment shall sit, and <u>they shall take</u>**

> **away his dominion, to consume and to destroy *it* unto the end. 27: And the kingdom and dominion, and the greatness of the kingdom under the whole heaven, shall be given to the people of the saints of the most High, whose kingdom is an everlasting kingdom, and all dominions shall serve and obey him.**

God removes the *Northern* (who magnified himself) into a land *barren and desolate:*

> **Joel 2:20: But I will remove far off from you the northern *army*, and <u>will drive him into a land barren and desolate</u>, with his face toward the east sea, and his hinder part toward the utmost sea, and his stink shall come up, and his ill savour shall come up, because he hath done great things. 21: Fear not, O land; be glad and rejoice: for the LORD will do great things.**

Obviously, the King James translators did not know what to do with *the Northern* so they inserted the word *army*. Yet, the language states that God will drive *him into a land barren and desolate, with his face toward the east sea*, etc... This has been a puzzle for some time as God mentions a land *barren and desolate*. When we look up the original Hebrew words for *barren and desolate* there can be only one answer.

Nineveh the Capital of Assyria

Zephaniah is an interesting part of God's Word. This book is only three chapters, but the main impact is God's judgment on false worship:

> **Zephaniah 1:12: And it shall come to pass at *that* time, that <u>I will search Jerusalem</u> with candles,**

and punish the men that are settled on their lees: that say in their heart, The LORD will not do good, neither will he do evil. 13: Therefore their goods shall become a booty, and their houses a desolation: they shall also build houses, but not inhabit *them*; and they shall plant vineyards, but not drink the wine thereof.

Whether the language is: *I sit a queen and am no widow, and shall see not sorrow* or *the LORD will not do good, neither will He do evil,* this is the same *peace and safety* message in which the houses of God feel so sure and secure in our time.

In Zephaniah 2 God speaks against Moab, Gaza, and Ashkelon. However, in verse 13 He also mentions that He *will make Nineveh a desolation, and dry like a wilderness*:

Zephaniah 2:13: And he will stretch out his hand against the north, and destroy Assyria; and will make Nineveh a desolation, and dry like a wilderness.

Why is God bringing up Nineveh, the capital of Assyria, and the place where Jonah was sent to warn against God's impending judgment? Zephaniah is speaking of the *day of the Lord,* and, yet, God is using past history and lands. This is a great example of how God has written His Word. He is using the examples of these lands in which years ago they went far from serving God and turned to worshipping other gods. Zephaniah 2:14 also mentions the *rejoicing city.* When we connect the dots, we see how the *rejoicing city* is, in fact, *fallen Babylon.* We know from the book of Revelation that *fallen Babylon* or *mystery Babylon* is, in fact, the fallen churches worldwide.

> **Zephaniah 2:15: <u>This is the rejoicing city</u> that dwelt carelessly, that said in her heart, I *am*, and *there is* none beside me: how is she become a desolation, a place for beasts to lie down in! every one that passeth by her shall hiss, *and* wag his hand.**

Babylon that *Rejoicing City*

> **Isaiah 21:9: And, behold, here cometh a chariot of men, *with* a couple of horsemen. And he answered and said, Babylon is fallen, is fallen; and all the graven images of her gods he hath broken unto the ground.**

> **Isaiah 22:2: Thou that art full of stirs, a tumultuous city, a joyous city: <u>thy slain *men are* not slain with the sword, nor dead in battle.</u>**

Does it seem odd to anyone else that the fallen houses of God use the term "slain in the spirit" as a good thing? That is unusual language considering Isaiah 22 mentions *thy slain men are not slain with the sword, nor dead in battle.*

Is there any other Biblical language that connects the names Jerusalem, Nineveh and Babylon? Does God relate these historical cities to the fallen houses of God worldwide? The answer is yes as He ties together these three cities with the term *great city.*

The Great City: Babylon

> **Revelation 18:10: Standing afar off for the fear of her torment, saying, Alas, alas, <u>that great city Babylon</u>, that mighty city! For in one hour is thy judgment come.**

> **Revelation 18:19: And they cast dust on their heads, and cried, weeping and wailing, saying, Alas, alas, <u>that great city</u>, wherein were made rich all that had ships in the sea by reason of her costliness! For <u>in one hour is she made desolate.</u>**

The Great City: Jerusalem

> **Revelation 11:8: And their dead bodies *shall lie* in the street <u>of the great city</u>, which spiritually is called Sodom and Egypt, <u>where also our Lord was crucified.</u>**

In the book of Revelation God is intertwining Babylon and Jerusalem (where the Lord was crucified), and calling both the *great city*. God also calls Nineveh a *great city*:

That Great City: Nineveh

> **Jonah 3:1: And the word of the LORD came unto Jonah the second time, saying, 2: Arise, go unto <u>Nineveh, that great city</u>, and preach unto it the preaching that I bid thee. 3: So Jonah arose, and went unto Nineveh, according to the word of the LORD. Now <u>Nineveh was an exceeding great city of three days' journey.</u> 4: And Jonah began to enter into the city a day's journey, and he cried, and said, Yet forty days, and Nineveh shall be overthrown.**

Nahum is three chapters long in the Bible. It starts off with the *burden of Nineveh*. God also mentions the *excellency of Jacob,* which transfers right into the *bloody city* in chapter three:

Nahum 2:2: For the LORD hath turned away the excellency of Jacob, as the excellency of Israel: for the emptiers have emptied them out, and marred their vine branches.

Nahum 3:1: Woe to the bloody city! It *is* all full of lies *and* robbery; the prey departeth not...

God then mentions His proclaimed judgment as the nations will look upon the *bloody city*:

Nahum 3:5: Behold, I *am* against thee, saith the LORD of hosts; and I will discover thy skirts upon thy face, and <u>I will shew the nations thy nakedness, and the kingdoms thy shame</u>. 6: And I will cast abominable filth upon thee, and <u>make thee vile, and will set thee as a gazingstock.</u> 7: And it shall come to pass, *that* <u>all they that look upon thee shall flee from thee</u>, and say, <u>Nineveh is laid waste</u>: who will bemoan her? Whence shall I seek comforters for thee?

We have now come full circle. Nineveh is laid waste. The nations will see the shame of the fallen houses of God. However, one thing the people of all nations must understand is that judgment on the houses of God is 3 ½ years prior to the judgment on the entire world. God will be magnified in this judgment, and many will fear God who has judged the houses which are called by His name. There comes a time in which God will no longer allow the polluting of His holy name:

Ezekiel 39:7: So will I make my holy name known in the midst of my people Israel; and I will not *let them* pollute my holy name any more: and the

heathen shall know that I *am* the LORD, the Holy One in Israel.

Thy Merchants were the Great Men of the Earth

God also uses the term *thy merchants* which means that as these great cities were consumed with money, so too are the fallen houses of God:

> **Nahum 3:16: <u>Thou hast multiplied thy merchants</u> above the stars of heaven: the cankerworm spoileth, and flieth away.**

> **Revelation 18:23: And the light of a candle shall shine no more at all in thee; and the voice of the bridegroom and of the bride shall be heard no more at all in thee: <u>for thy merchants were the great men of the earth</u>; for by thy sorceries were all nations deceived.**

God uses the same language of the *locust* and *cankerworm* destroying the vine and fig tree in Joel 2:

> **Joel 1:4: That which the palmerworm hath left hath the locust eaten; and that which the locust hath left hath the cankerworm eaten; and that which the cankerworm hath left hath the caterpillar eaten.**

This kind of natural destruction of a vineyard and a fig tree is one way of saying the enemy and evil spirits will come up against the houses of God.

Nineveh- The Land *Barren and Desolate*

The most difficult aspect of understanding God's Word as He used these cities of the past as "types" of the fallen houses of

God is figuring out what they represent. For instance, we have learned that God removes *the Northern* to a land *barren and desolate*. God identifies what that land represents by key phrases and words.

We also learned that God deemed Nineveh as one *great city* which becomes *barren and desolate*. Then we take it one step further and see how God interchanges the cities of Jerusalem, Nineveh and Babylon as representations of the fallen houses of God.

God calls these cities *great cities*. They were places on earth that were merchandising with the nations. Jesus overturned the moneychangers in the temple of Jerusalem. People were *buying and selling* as they turned God's house into a *house of merchandise*. Thus, the houses of God have become part of the world system, which, like the historical cities, will fall due to false worship and greed.

Nineveh was the capital of Assyria and was named the land of Asshur, the second son of Shem. There is one more time clue that God brings up in association with the King of Assyria who hired Moab and then turned on Moab. *The glory of Moab shall be contemned* is another warning to the houses of God. The time clue is *within three years*. It is hard to know when the three-year countdown of this prophecy began. Was the year 2011 the starting point or was the year 2012 the starting point of *within three years the glory of Moab will be contemned*? Either year means it will not be long until the glory of the houses of God will be despised (contemned).

I believe we are soon going to see the lowering of glory come upon the houses of God worldwide. The most likely timing of this judgment is at the anniversary of the cross in the year 2015. We will look carefully at this language as God is using past history as an example of a future judgment upon the houses of worship. The self-glory in their wealth and earthly status will be not be looked upon in high esteem by the nations.

Chapter 12—Within Three Years - The Glory of Moab will be Despised

Isaiah 16:14: But now the LORD hath spoken, saying, <u>Within three years, as the years of an hireling, and the glory of Moab shall be contemned</u>, with all that great multitude; and the remnant *shall be* very small *and* feeble.

It is astonishing to see how God has used so many historical examples that point us to this time just prior to judgment coming upon the houses of God. I became interested in past history the more I learned how the historical language in the Bible is pointing us to the final years of history. The Bible sometimes gives us a chapter or phrase that really seems like a time clue in which we can learn from. In order to understand the verses in question, past history must be looked at and understood.

We should always try to find the answer in the Bible by comparing verse upon verse and word upon word. There are times, however, where the historical record can really aid us in further understanding.

The Error of False Prophets Today: Greed

Before we look at historical Moab, we must look at the error of Balaam since Peter brings this up in speaking of the escalation of false prophets:

> **Jude 1:11: Woe unto them! For they have gone in the way of Cain, and ran greedily after the error of Balaam for reward, and perished in the gainsaying of Core.**

Jude 1:11 mentions three men whose actions of the past encapsulate the traits of false prophets of the final years.

Cain was a tiller of the ground who brought forth of the ground an offering to the Lord. His brother Abel brought forth the firstlings of the flock and the fat (riches and choicest). The Lord had respect unto Abel's offering. Cain became *wroth*, which is the same word associated with Sanballat's anger against the Jews as they built the wall. Satan is behind this anger that Cain had towards his brother. God warned Cain: *if you do not well* then *sin lies at the door*. Cain *rose up* and murdered his brother. Why would God mention Cain in the midst of the end time warning of false prophets?

> **Luke 11:50: That the blood of all the prophets, which was shed from the foundation of the world, may be required of this generation; 51: <u>From the blood of Abel</u> <u>unto the blood of Zacharias, which perished between the altar and the temple</u>: verily I say unto you, It shall be required of this generation.**

This same activity of *killing in great anger* the believers, who bring forth the truth of God's Word, is very present today. This is one of the most obvious traits of false prophets.

In Luke 11:46, after Christ called the Pharisees hypocrites, those of the law were offended. Jesus' words to the lawyers were words of condemnation as recorded in Luke 11:46:

> **Luke 11:46: And he said, Woe unto you also, *ye* lawyers! <u>For ye lade men with burdens grievous to be borne</u>, and ye yourselves touch not the burdens with one of your fingers.**

The lawyers of God's law placed heavy burdens on men which is the opposite of what Jesus offers. Today in some churches this is called legalism. Church members must dress a certain way, donate so much money, and behave a certain way or they are placed under real scrutiny and possibly even shunned. There is never true rest when legalism and burdens overwhelm a person. Jesus proclaimed that if people are heavy laden to turn to Him and He will give rest:

> **Matthew 11:28: Come unto me, all *ye* that labour and are heavy laden, and I will give you rest. 29: Take my yoke upon you, and learn of me; for I am meek and lowly in heart: and ye shall find rest unto your souls. 30: For my yoke *is* easy, and <u>my burden is light</u>.**

Gainsaying of Core

The word *gainsaying* means to speak against, to murmur, to complain. With Moses and Aaron, the complaining of Korah (Core in Greek) became so intense that Moses had to lay down a challenge. This uprising in the congregation included 250 men who were considered *the famous* and *men of renown*. The men who rose against Moses are spoken of in Numbers chapter 16:

> **Numbers 16:1: Now Korah, the son of Izhar, the son of Kohath, the son of Levi, and Dathan and Abiram, the sons of Eliab, and On, the son of Peleth, sons of Reuben, took *men*: 2: And they rose up before Moses, with certain of the children of Israel, two hundred and fifty princes of the assembly, famous in the congregation, men of renown.**

The historical setting was the Exodus out of Egypt, and the complaint (murmuring) was that Moses and Aaron had brought the people into the wilderness to perish. Moses, the one God had chosen, had to deal with many accusations/complaints from Korah, Dathan and Abiram:

> **Numbers 16:12: And Moses sent to call Dathan and Abiram, the sons of Eliab: which said, We will not come up: 13:** *Is it* **a small thing that thou hast brought us up out of a land that floweth with milk and honey, to kill us in the wilderness, except thou make thyself altogether a prince over us?**

Throughout this rebellion, Korah had complained about how Moses had taken too much upon himself when, in fact, it was God who placed the responsibly on Moses to lead the people through the wilderness. There is a sense of Korah being jealous of Moses as the forerunner to lead the congregation where God had directed him to do so. There was also a jealousy against Aaron. The names of Korah, Dathan, Abiram and On (son of Peleth) are mentioned in Numbers 16:1. God can use the number four as to show universality. I do not think this is an isolated incident of Moses' day since the fleeing out (Exodus) of the fallen houses of God is also happening today.

There will be *men of renown*, the famous of the houses of God who will oppose any fleeing out of the houses of God. The *men of name* or *men of renown* today would be the leaders in the congregations who will oppose the fleeing out of the fallen congregations. The pleading of Moses, by the command of God, was to get out from among these *wicked men:*

> **Numbers 16:23: And the LORD spake unto Moses, saying, 24: Speak unto the congregation,**

saying, Get you up from about the tabernacle of Korah, Dathan, and Abiram. 25: And Moses rose up and went unto Dathan and Abiram; and the elders of Israel followed him. 26: And he spake unto the congregation, saying, Depart, I pray you, from the tents of these wicked men, and touch nothing of theirs, lest ye be consumed in all their sins.

Moses pleaded with Korah and admonished him as a son of Levi. Moses was telling him that it is no small thing how God had set the Levites apart. Their duties were set apart from the congregation because they were responsible for serving the tabernacle of the LORD and also ministering unto the congregation. Yet, Korah was complaining against Moses and Aaron.

The challenge by Moses, as He pleaded with God, proved that God had chosen Moses to bring His people out of Egypt. It also proved that God had chosen Aaron for the role of high priest. Moses, after hearing what God would do, pleaded with God on behalf of the congregation. The first judgment came upon Korah and *all that appertained unto him* as the earth opened up from under them and they went down into the pit:

Numbers 16:32: And the earth opened her mouth, and swallowed them up, and their houses, and all the men that *appertained* unto Korah, and all *their* goods. 33: They, and all that *appertained* to them, went down alive into the pit, and the earth closed upon them: and they perished from among the congregation.

The second judgment was upon the 250 men who held the censors. They were destroyed by the fire of the Lord. The following day more murmuring began and a plague broke out in the congregation until Moses commanded Aaron to *stay the plague:*

> **Numbers 16:49: Now they that died in the plague were fourteen thousand and seven hundred, beside them that died about the matter of Korah. 50: And Aaron returned unto Moses unto the door of the tabernacle of the congregation: and the plague was stayed.**

Why is the gainsaying of Korah brought up in the warning against false prophets of our day? There is nothing new under the sun; the *wicked men* who Moses warned against are no different than the *wicked men* God warns about in the book of Jeremiah. Read Jeremiah 5:23-27 carefully as God mentioned the *early and latter rain* which is also mentioned in the book of James *unto the coming of the Lord.* The command of Jesus is not to condemn. The condition today is the *rich* in the houses of God do condemn believers for standing up for the truth of God's Word:

> **James 5:5: Ye have lived in pleasure on the earth, and been wanton; ye have nourished your hearts, as in a day of slaughter. 6: <u>Ye have condemned *and* killed the just</u>; *and* he doth not resist you.**

> **Luke 6:36: Be ye therefore merciful, as your Father also is merciful. 37: Judge not, and ye shall not be judged: <u>condemn not, and ye shall not be condemned</u>: forgive, and ye shall be forgiven...**

This is a very timely topic. There are leaders in the congregations who lay snares *to catch men* and have become *great and waxen rich*:

> **Jeremiah 5:23: But this people hath a revolting and a rebellious heart; they are revolted and gone. 24: Neither say they in their heart, Let us now fear the LORD our God, that giveth rain, both the former and the latter, in his season: he reserveth unto us the appointed weeks of the harvest. 25: Your iniquities have turned away these *things*, and your sins have withholden good *things* from you. 26: For among my people are found wicked *men*: they lay wait, as he that setteth snares; they set a trap, they catch men. 27: As a cage is full of birds, so *are* their houses full of deceit: therefore they are become great, and waxen rich.**

There is not much difference between Moses' warning by the command of God to come out from being with these wicked men, and the command of Christ to *come out of her my people*:

> **Revelation 18:4: And I heard another voice from heaven, saying, Come out of her, my people, that ye be not partakers of her sins, and that ye receive not of her plagues. 5: For her sins have reached unto heaven, and God hath remembered her iniquities.**

The Error of Balaam

Another name that is mentioned in association with false prophets of the last days is Balaam, a prophet for *hire*. I find this account most interesting since the Exodus out of Egypt relates to those who make the escape out of the fallen houses of God. Moab was concerned because the Israelites who came out of Egypt were many; this is recorded in Numbers 22:3:

281

Numbers 22:3: And Moab was sore afraid of the people, because they *were* many: and Moab was distressed because of the children of Israel.

Balaam was hired to curse the traveling Israelites. He was offered by Balak (the waster), the King of Moab, great riches and honor, but Balaam kept repeating that no amount of riches would influence him. That is very noble of Balaam, right?

Numbers 24:13: If Balak would give me his house full of silver and gold, I cannot go beyond the commandment of the LORD, to do *either* good or bad of mine own mind; *but* what the LORD saith, that will I speak?

Balaam was instructed originally by God not to go with the princes of Moab, and at first he obeyed, then came a greater offer by the King of Moab. Balaam then asked God the second time if he should go with them. The Lord's response the second time was qualified:

Numbers 22:20: And God came unto Balaam at night, *and* said unto him, <u>If the men come to call thee, rise up, and go with them</u>; but yet the word which I shall say unto thee, that shalt thou do. 21: And Balaam rose up in the morning, and saddled his ass, and went with the princes of Moab.

There is no record that the princes of Moab came to call upon Balaam but just that Balaam really wanted to go and so he saddled up and left. This is the first instance where he is seen *running greedily* as the New Testament proclaims of fellow false prophets that follow his ways:

282

Jude 1:11: Woe unto them! For they have gone in the way of Cain, and <u>ran greedily after the error of Balaam for reward</u>, and perished in the gainsaying of Core.

2 Peter 2:15: Which have forsaken the right way, and are gone astray, <u>following the way of Balaam *the son* of Bosor, who loved the wages of unrighteousness</u>; 16: But was rebuked for his iniquity: the dumb ass speaking with man's voice forbad the madness of the prophet. 17: These are wells without water, clouds that are carried with a tempest; to whom the mist of darkness is reserved for ever.

Balaam taught Balac to cast a stumbling block before Israel and Israel fell into false worship. This is such an important aspect of the final years that God placed this warning of the error of Balaam in three places in the New Testament. The warning to the church of Pergamos also included *the error of Balaam*. The verse below is Jesus speaking directly to the church at Pergamos and it does relate to the houses of God in our day:

Revelation 2:14: But I have a few things against thee, because <u>thou hast there them that hold the doctrine of Balaam</u>, who taught Balac to cast a stumblingblock before the children of Israel, to eat things sacrificed unto idols, and to commit fornication.

Balaam kept repeating to Balak how he could only do what the Lord tells him to do, right? There finally is a departure between Balak and Balaam, but later in the book of Numbers we read the final effect of what Balaam did. He would not curse Israel as Balak wanted him to do, but he knew the way

283

that would cause Israel would fall. We learn how Israel fell into false worship with the Moabites. From Revelation 2:14, we can know that Balaam taught Balak to cast a stumbling block before the children of Israel. This is exactly what happened as we read in Numbers chapter 25:

> **Numbers 25:1: And Israel abode in Shittim, and the people began to commit whoredom with the daughters of Moab. 2: And they called the people unto the sacrifices of their gods: and the people did eat, and bowed down to their gods. 3: And Israel joined himself unto Baalpeor: and the anger of the LORD was kindled against Israel.**

The error of Balaam eventually caught up with him as the Israelites slayed him:

> **Joshua 13:22: Balaam also the son of Beor, the soothsayer, did the children of Israel slay with the sword among them that were slain by them.**

In Joshua 13:22, Balaam was called a *soothsayer* or *diviner*. Soothsaying or divining is an ancient custom in which even the King of Babylon participated. However, in God's Word divining is forbidden. In fact, it is part of the end time deception which God judges:

> **Micah 3:11: The heads thereof judge for reward, and the priests thereof teach for hire, and the prophets thereof divine for money: yet will they lean upon the LORD, and say, *Is* not the LORD among us? none evil can come upon us.**

> **Ezekiel 22:27: Her princes in the midst thereof *are* like wolves ravening the prey, to shed blood, *and* to destroy souls, to get dishonest gain. 28: And her**

prophets have daubed them with untempered *morter*, seeing vanity, <u>and divining lies unto them</u>, saying, Thus saith the Lord GOD, when the LORD hath not spoke.

Cain rising up against his brother Abel, the deception of Balaam, and the complaining of Korah all relate to the false prophets of today. Jude 1:11 proclaims how people will act in the same way of Cain, Balaam and Core:

Jude 1:11: Woe unto them! for they have gone in the way of Cain, and ran greedily after the error of Balaam for reward, and perished in the gainsaying of Core.

Korah could have gone to Moses privately and humbly, but he instead chose to bring a large number of men who publicly stood against God's chosen. The book of Jude is actually proclaiming that this will transpire in the *last time* as mockers will come. Their judgment will not linger for long. At this present time, God is still being longsuffering with all mankind:

Jude 1:14: And Enoch also, the seventh from Adam, prophesied of these, saying, Behold, the Lord cometh with ten thousands of his saints, 15: To execute judgment upon all, and to convince all that are ungodly among them of all their ungodly deeds which they have ungodly committed, and of all their hard *speeches* which ungodly sinners have spoken against him. 16: These are murmurers, complainers, walking after their own lusts; and their mouth speaketh great swelling *words*, <u>having men's persons in admiration because of advantage</u>.

The account of Balaam, I believe, relates to the false prophets of today who divine for profit but also something else. Israel became part of Moab as they participated in the worship of the gods of the Moabites. This is very similar to the warnings in the book of Revelation as the houses of God have become part of the world system as God calls them *Mystery Babylon.* Whether God is using the historical names of Moab or Babylon, the reason is the same: this is where false worship takes place.

The Glory of Moab and Kedar

We now need to look at the following verses which seems very important to this time in history. God speaks of the glory of Moab being contemned, and the glory of Kedar failing. Obviously, God is yet again drawing from past Biblical history to show how He will bring down the pride and glory of the houses of God.

The verses concerning Moab are found in the context of a time clue, which is *within three years*. There is also the mention of another time clue (*within a year*) concerning Kedar:

> **Isaiah 16:14: But now the LORD hath spoken, saying, Within three years, as the years of an hireling, and the glory of Moab shall be contemned, with all that great multitude; and the remnant *shall be* very small *and* feeble.**

> **Isaiah 21:16: For thus hath the Lord said unto me, Within a year, according to the years of an hireling, and all the glory of Kedar shall fail:**

In the book of Jeremiah, as God speaks of the *year of visitation*, Moab is greatly highlighted. How is it possible that the historical illustration of Moab could relate to the houses of God in the final years of history? Let us look at the language from the book of Jeremiah:

> **Jeremiah 48:39: They shall howl,** *saying,* **How is it broken down! how hath Moab turned the back with shame! so shall Moab be a derision and a dismaying to all them about him. 40: For thus saith the LORD; Behold, <u>he shall fly as an eagle, and shall spread his wings over Moab.</u>**

Verse 40 above says that the enemy will *fly as an eagle and shall spread his wings over Moab.* This is familiar language since Hosea 8 also speaks of God sending the enemy *as an eagle* against the house of God. Thereby is the connection between Moab and the fallen house of God:

> **Hosea 8:1:** *Set* **the trumpet to thy mouth.** *<u>He shall come</u>* <u>**as an eagle against the house of the LORD**</u>**, because they have transgressed my covenant, and trespassed against my law. 2: Israel shall cry unto me, My God, we know thee. 3: Israel hath cast off** *the thing that is* **good: <u>the enemy shall pursue him.</u>**

> **Deuteronomy 28:49: The LORD shall bring a nation against thee from far, from the end of the earth,** *as swift* **<u>as the eagle flieth</u>; a nation whose tongue thou shalt not understand; 50: <u>A nation of fierce countenance</u>, which shall not regard the person of the old, nor shew favour to the young...**

Historically the Chaldeans and Assyrians came against Israel as a judgment. God uses language very carefully. The term *fierce countenance* is related to the enemy that God sends as a judgment who *flies like an eagle* over the land. The king of Babylon would historically fit this pattern. However, with the language of *fierce countenance* being used in the context of the *last days*, we can know God is speaking about Satan himself who understands dark sentences (God's parables):

> **Daniel 8:23: And in the latter time of their kingdom, when the transgressors are come to the full, <u>a king of fierce countenance</u>, and understanding dark sentences, shall stand up. 24: And his power shall be mighty, but not by his own power: and he shall destroy wonderfully, and shall prosper, and practise, and <u>shall destroy the mighty and the holy people.</u>**

We have learned in this chapter how Balaam caused Israel to fall in the land of Moab by participating in false worship. The connection with God sending the enemy against Moab is now understood. False worship will be judged. Israel became part of the false worship in Moab.

> **Numbers 25:1: And Israel abode in Shittim, and the people began to commit whoredom with the daughters of Moab. 2: And they called the people unto the sacrifices of their gods: <u>and the people did eat, and bowed down to their gods.</u> 3: And Israel joined himself unto Baalpeor: and the anger of the LORD was kindled against Israel.**

Therefore, historical Israel, as well as the houses of God, are in that sense related to Moab. We know that God has used past history concerning Moab, yet He also lets us know that this judgment on Moab will come in the *last days*. This is referenced in Jeremiah 48 where God speaks of the judgment upon Moab in the *latter days*. This language implies a reversal by God, so there seems to be some aspect of real hope after God judges. The hope comes when people begin to fear the power of the hand of God. His judgments/chastisements force people to seek the Lord for His help. Both Jeremiah 48 and Joel 3 speak of this reversal:

> **Jeremiah 48:47: Yet will I bring again the captivity of Moab in the latter days, saith the LORD. Thus far *is* the judgment of Moab.**

> **Joel 3:1: For, behold, in those days, and in that time, when I shall bring again the captivity of Judah and Jerusalem...**

The ISA renders Joel 3:1 as: ...*I shall return, I shall reverse captivity of Judah and Jerusalem.*

The Latter Days

The term *latter days* is used in various parts of Scripture. The following verses are four places where this term is used. Daniel's *people* are the believers in Christ and *David their king* is speaking of Christ Himself:

- **Daniel 10:14: Now I am come to make thee understand what shall befall thy people <u>in the latter days</u>: for yet the vision *is* for *many* days.**
- **Hosea 3:5: Afterward shall the children of Israel return, and seek the LORD their God, and David their king; and shall fear the LORD and his goodness <u>in the latter days</u>.**
- **Micah 4:1: But in <u>the last days</u> it shall come to pass, *that* the mountain of the house of the LORD shall be established in the top of the mountains, and it shall be exalted above the hills; <u>and people shall flow unto it.</u>**
- **Ezekiel 38:16: And thou shalt come up against my people of Israel, as a cloud to cover the land; it shall be <u>in the latter days</u>, and I will bring thee**

against my land, that the heathen may know me, when I shall be sanctified in thee, O Gog, before their eyes.

God is using Gog as a historical example of how Satan will come against *God's land* or, in other words, the houses of God. When this happens, God instructs His people to *come out of her* so that they do not participate in her sins and experience the plagues. Many will *flee to the mountains* as *the mountain of the house of the Lord* will be *established* in *the top of the mountains*. This language is indicating that people will be coming out of the houses of God and turning to God and His Word.

In Jeremiah 48:47, God promises to reverse the captivity of Moab. This may relate to God removing *the Northern* as found in the book of Joel. I believe the year 2015 will be a very significant year in these *latter days*.

Moab is Proud and Boastful - The History of Moab

Lot's two daughters made their father drunk with wine and lay with him to *preserve seed* of their father. The firstborn's son was named Moab:

Genesis 19:35: And they made their father drink wine that night also: and the younger arose, and lay with him; and he perceived not when she lay down, nor when she arose. 36: Thus were both the daughters of Lot with child by their father. 37: And the firstborn bare a son, and called his name Moab: the same *is* the father of the Moabites unto this day. 38: And the younger, she also bare a son, and called his name Benammi: the same *is* the father of the children of Ammon unto this day.

The Gods of Moab & Ammon- *Chemosh & Molech*

We have learned how Israel, during the Exodus, sojourned into the land of Moab. The Hebrew people fell prey to false worship of the land of Moab. King Solomon also did evil in the sight of the Lord and built a high place for both of the false gods named *Chemosh* and *Molech*. These were the gods of Moab and Ammon. This act by Solomon angered the Lord. God calls both the false gods of Moab and Ammon (*Chemosh* and *Molech*) an abomination:

> **1Kings 11:6: And Solomon did evil in the sight of the LORD, and went not fully after the LORD, as** *did* **David his father. 7: Then did Solomon build an high place for Chemosh, <u>the abomination of Moab</u>, in the hill that** *is* **before Jerusalem, and for Molech, <u>the abomination of the children of Ammon</u>. 8: And likewise did he for all his strange wives, which burnt incense and sacrificed unto their gods.**

The word *abomination* has been translated from the Hebrew word *shiqquets* (H8251). This is the same type of abomination which is associated with the 1,290 days. During the first fulfillment of the 1,290 days, Satan was active at the time of Christ. We can expect this same activity in the fallen houses of God during the second fulfillment from 2011 to 2015:

> **Daniel 12:11: And from the time** *that* **the daily** *sacrifice* **shall be taken away, and <u>the abomination</u> that maketh desolate set up,** *there shall be* **a thousand two hundred and ninety days. 12: Blessed is he that waiteth, and cometh to the thousand three hundred and five and thirty days.**

There Comes a Time- God Famishes All gods of the Earth

In Zephaniah 2, God links both Ammon and Moab with the overthrow of Sodom and Gomorrah. There comes a time when God will famish all false gods of the earth:

> **Zephaniah 2:9: Therefore *as* I live, saith the LORD of hosts, the God of Israel, Surely Moab shall be as Sodom, and the children of Ammon as Gomorrah, *even* the breeding of nettles, and saltpits, and a perpetual desolation: the residue of my people shall spoil them, and the remnant of my people shall possess them. 10: This shall they have for their pride, because they have reproached and magnified *themselves* against the people of the LORD of hosts. 11: The LORD *will be* terrible unto them: <u>for he will famish all the gods of the earth;</u> and *men* shall worship him, every one from his place, *even* all the isles of the heathen.**

I believe that with this language found in Zephaniah 2, God is using the former activity of false worship and comparing that with the false worship in the fallen houses of God. Since God is comparing the *children of Ammon* and the *children of Moab* with the overthrow of Sodom and Gomorrah, there must be another comparison that would relate to our day. In fact, there is such a comparison as God mentions that the punishment of the *daughter of my people* being greater than the punishment of the sin of Sodom. Perhaps the judgment on the houses of God is *greater* due the worldwide scope and duration the enemy has to desolate the *palaces* of God:

> **Isaiah 13:19: And Babylon, the glory of kingdoms, the beauty of the Chaldees' excellency, <u>shall be as when God overthrew Sodom and Gomorrah.</u>**

Lamentations 4:6: For the punishment of the <u>iniquity of the daughter of my people</u> is greater than the punishment of the sin of Sodom, that was overthrown as in a moment, and no hands stayed on her.

<u>Come Out From Among Them- Unequally Yoked</u>

Psalm 74 is an excellent section of God's Word that shows how the enemy has done wickedly in the sanctuary. The language includes *the enemies roar in the midst of the congregations* (Psalm 74:4). The questions are asked: *O God, how long shall the adversary reproach? Shall the enemy blaspheme thy name forever?* Then we read that even in the time of wickedness being done in the congregations, God is working salvation in the earth:

Psalm 74:12: For God is my King of old, working salvation in the midst of the earth.

God further qualifies the importance of not being *unequally yoked* with the people who worship false idols. This is important since God mentions this truth in the New Testament. Some people attempt to force the language of "unequally yoked" within the marriage of a husband and wife. This application to *unequally yoked* would be an obvious conclusion even without 2 Corinthians 6:14 as a reference scripture.

However, the context below is understood when we read all of the language. The believers in Christ should not be *unequally yoked* with people who are engaging in evil activity of Belial (Satan). This is why Jesus tells His people to *come out of her my people* (Revelation 18:4). That is the command when we see the abomination that makes desolate.

293

The command to *come out from among them* is found in the verses below:

> **2 Corinthians 6:14: <u>Be ye not unequally yoked together with unbelievers</u>: for what fellowship hath righteousness with unrighteousness? and what communion hath light with darkness? 15: And what concord hath Christ with Belial? or what part hath he that believeth with an infidel? 16: And what agreement hath the temple of God with idols? for ye are the temple of the living God; as God hath said, I will dwell in them, and walk in them; and I will be their God, and they shall be my people. 17: <u>Wherefore come out from among them, and be ye separate</u>, saith the Lord, and touch not the unclean thing; and I will receive you, 18: And will be a Father unto you, and ye shall be my sons and daughters, saith the Lord Almighty.**

According to the Years of an Hireling

There is a connection with Moab, Ammon, and Babylon all being places of false worship. Yet, God uses these names as types of what the fallen houses of God have become as they follow *signs and lying wonders*, and prosperity gospels etc… The topic of this chapter is how the *glory of Moab will be contemned* and the glory of Kedar will eventually fail. God uses a special time clue in Isaiah 16:13 concerning *Moab* and Isaiah 21:16 concerning *Kedar*. The phrase with this time clue is *according to the years of an hireling*. This clue helps set the course on discovering the length of time before the glory of the fallen houses of God is shamed or brought low.

I really believe this is speaking of the nations coming against the fallen houses of God as a judgment. Thus, their glory is shamed. However, the time frame of *the years of an hireling* must be defined. We have a great definition in Deuteronomy 15:18 which indicates that six years is a doubled time for a hired person. Therefore, this leaves three years as *the years of an hireling:*

> **Deuteronomy 15:18: It shall not seem hard unto thee, when thou sendest him away free from thee; for he hath been worth a <u>double hired servant *to thee*, in serving thee six years</u>: and the LORD thy God shall bless thee in all that thou doest.**

Deuteronomy 15:18 confirms that this time frame is a three year period. Isaiah 16:14 speaks of *within three years*, and, as we have discovered, the length of the years of a hireling is three years. The ISA renders "within three years" as *in three years.* So when we read Isaiah 16:13-14 a full three years is in view:

> **Isaiah 16:13: This *is* the word that the LORD hath spoken concerning Moab since that time. 14: But now the LORD hath spoken, saying, <u>Within three years</u>, as the years of an hireling, and the glory of Moab shall be contemned, with all that great multitude; and the remnant *shall be* very small *and* feeble.**

We have a time reference, but what other clues are in Isaiah 16 which will give us a reference point in time? Understanding these time clues is important since we are speaking of the glory of false worship being abased (brought low). Isaiah 16 speaks of a reversal in which, I believe, the timing of the 3 years is, in fact, from the years 2011-2012 to the years 2014-2015. The start point is very critical to understanding whether the three years end in 2014 or 2015. The *last end of the indignation*, I believe, ends in the year

2015. This is something we must be patient with but it does seem many paths lead to the year 2015. Here is the language of God's reversal as the *spoiler ceases*:

> **Isaiah 16:4: Let mine outcasts dwell with thee, Moab; be thou a covert to them from the face of the spoiler: for <u>the extortioner is at an end, the spoiler ceaseth, the oppressors are consumed out of the land</u>. 5: And in mercy shall the throne be established: and he shall sit upon it in truth in the tabernacle of David, judging, and seeking judgment, <u>and hasting righteousness.</u>**

Isaiah 16:5: is important because the book of Daniel speaks of God bringing in righteousness after a time of desolation:

> **Daniel 9:24: Seventy weeks are determined upon thy people and upon thy holy city, to finish the transgression, and to make an end of sins, and to make reconciliation for iniquity, <u>and to bring in everlasting righteousness</u>, and to seal up the vision and prophecy, and to anoint the most Holy.**

God bringing in *everlasting righteousness* fits the great reversal of Joel 2 where God is magnified after the *Northern* is removed. *The extortioner is at an end, the spoiler ceases and the oppressors are consumed out of the land*—this is important language which shows a precise time clue. I believe the conclusion of the three years in which *Moab's glory* (fallen houses of God) will be despised will occur somewhere within the year 2015. The anniversary of the cross in 2015 may turn out to be a very significant time of judgment upon the fallen houses of God. April 3, 2015 is the anniversary of the cross which occurred on April 3, 33 A.D. We are following the 3 ½ year pattern of Jesus' ministry days from 29 A.D. to 33 A.D. God was glorified at the time of the cross and He will be glorified again prior to and including the time of Pentecost in the year 2015. The final 3 ½ years ending in the year 2018 will be a time of great worldwide salvation.

We have learned that the double fulfillment of *blessed is he that waits and comes to the 1,335th day* lands in the year 2015. For me, that was a significant Biblical find because it fits the rest of the information concerning the final seven years ending in 2018.

Historical Moab and King Sennecherib

If historical Moab was *hired* by King Sennecherib only later to find that King Sennecherib would come against them (Moab the hireling), then this would be the historical application of *within three years according to the years of an hireling*. I normally try to stick solely with Scripture, but sometimes Bible commentaries can point out some scriptures that could apply to the verses in question. Below are quotes from two Bible commentaries concerning the three years and Moab's glory being despised by the attack of King Sennecherib:

"after those things, and the establishment thereof, Sennacherib king of Assyria came into Judah, 2 Chronicles 32:1 and at the same time sent Tartan to Ashdod, Isaiah 20:1 who overran the Ammonites and Moabites, who helped him when he besieged Samaria three years, that it might be fulfilled what is said, Isaiah 16:14 at the same time the king of Assyria sent Rabshakeh from Lachish to Jerusalem."

"Upon which Kimchi observes, as an interpretation of the phrase, "as the years of an hireling."

"it is as if it was said, because they helped the king of Assyria three years against Samaria, it was as if they had been hired; therefore they fell by his hand, and the glory of Moab was light in the hand of the king of Assyria."

~~Gill's Exposition of the Entire Bible[18]~~

~~~~~~~~~~~~~~~~

Wesley's Notes[19]:

"16:14 The Lord - Hath made this farther discovery of his mind to me. **Three years** *- This may well be understood of some great blow given to the Moabites, either by Sennacherib, or his son Esarhaddon, from which notwithstanding they recovered and flourished again 'till Nebuchadrezzar completed their destruction.* **Hireling** *- Within three years precisely counted; for hirelings are very punctual in observing the time for which they are hired. The glory - Their strength, and wealth, and other things in which they glory, shall be made contemptible to those who formerly admired them.* **With** *- With the great numbers of their people, of which they boasted."*

~~End of Bible Commentaries~~

If Wesley's and Gill's commentaries are accurate in mentioning Sennacherib who was the King of Assyria, there should be some Biblical reference of Sennacherib found in the book of Isaiah where the prophecy against Moab is found.

In Isaiah 37, Hezekiah prayed to the Lord due to the arrogant challenge of Sennacherib. The King of Assyria was on a rampage and had already destroyed many lands. Sennacherib mocked Hezekiah and reminded him that no other gods of the lands that he had conquered were able to save them. Why would Jerusalem be different? This account in Isaiah 37 does fit how the king of Assyria was destroying many lands, including the land of Moab. Thus, the historical shaming of the glory of Moab came at the hand of the King of Assyria. God could use any method to bring down the glory of the fallen houses of God. The nations opposing the houses of God is only one type of judgment that would shame the glory of the worldwide houses of worship.

The Times They are Changing

I want to bring up the topic of God's everlasting righteousness. We have all lived in such a dark time in history these past years. For those who are old enough to have lived through a different era, they know how rapidly things have changed. Even the best era though cannot compare to when God's righteousness will rule. Did you know that God is waiting for His people to turn to Him, to come to the mountain of His righteous? When we read in James that God waits for the *precious fruit of the earth,* we can begin to understand the longsuffering of God. Isaiah 30 also speaks of God waiting:

> **Isaiah 30:17: One thousand *shall flee* at the rebuke of one; at the rebuke of five shall ye flee: till ye be left as a beacon upon the top of a mountain, and as an ensign on an hill. 18: And <u>therefore will the LORD wait</u>, that he may be gracious unto you, and therefore will he be exalted, that he may have mercy upon you: for the LORD *is* a God of judgment: <u>blessed *are* all they that wait for him.</u>**

I am glad that we wait for God to take action. He will go before us in battle and His righteousness will triumph. God is the one who will *gather all nations* for His purpose. It is by

His hand that this unrighteous world will begin to experience His righteousness and power. We wait for Him for He will rise up to the prey:

> **Zephaniah 3:8: Therefore <u>wait ye upon me</u>, saith the LORD, <u>until the day that I rise up to the prey</u>: for my determination *is* to gather the nations, that I may assemble the kingdoms, to pour upon them mine indignation, *even* all my fierce anger: for all the earth shall be devoured with the fire of my jealousy.**

God also chastises His people so they can rest from the days of adversity; after judgment, there comes forth righteousness.

> **Psalm 94:12: Blessed *is* the man whom thou chastenest, O LORD, and teachest him out of thy law; 13: That thou mayest give him rest from the days of adversity, until the pit be digged for the wicked. 14: For the LORD will not cast off his people, neither will he forsake his inheritance. 15: But <u>judgment shall return unto righteousness: and all the upright in heart shall follow it.</u>**

Another aspect of the *glory of Moab* being *contemned* in three years is that God also mentions *Kedar*. At this time, I believe, that 2012 was approximately the start time of the three year countdown. This would be based on the Nisan to Nisan calendar similar to the years of Darius. Why it has been difficult to fully understand the timeline is because of how God also mentions Kedar as well as Moab.

Historically, God may be focusing on the King of Assyria who came against both Moab and Kedar. The King of Assyria hired Moab to come against Samaria. Then, when the *years of a hireling* were fulfilled, the King of Assyria wages war against Moab. We can know that the *glory of Moab* will be shamed and the all the *glory of Kedar* will fail. This illustration of the king of Assyria using Moab would be like Satan using the fallen houses of God as a *hireling* and then comes their own judgment for false worship. These historical illustrations signify the coming judgment upon the fallen houses of God during the time of *great tribulation.* All the glory of Kedar failing is mentioned in Isaiah 21:16:

> **Isaiah 21:16: For thus hath the Lord said unto me, Within a year, according to the years of an hireling, and all the glory of Kedar shall fail...**

In Isaiah 21:9, God is laying forth the fall of Babylon as the watchman continues to tell what he sees. This is the same chapter which mentions the glory of Kedar failing. Therefore, we know the connection between the *glory of Kedar* failing and *Babylon is fallen, is fallen*:

> **Isaiah 21:9: And, behold, here cometh a chariot of men, *with* a couple of horsemen. And he answered and said, <u>Babylon is fallen, is fallen</u>; and all the graven images of her gods he hath broken unto the ground.**

> **Isaiah 21:16: For thus hath the Lord said unto me, Within a year, <u>according to the years of an hireling</u>, and all the glory of Kedar shall fail:**

Notice the similar language of Revelation 14: *Babylon is fallen, is fallen.* It is the *hour* of God's judgment. This may be the forewarning of *all the glory* of the fallen houses of God failing in yet a further year (2016?). Revelation 14:6 mentions that the Gospel is still going forth into every nation:

> **Revelation 14:6: And I saw another angel fly in the midst of heaven, <u>having the everlasting gospel to preach unto them that dwell on the earth</u>, and to every nation, and kindred, and tongue, and people, 7: Saying with a loud voice, <u>Fear God, and give glory to him; for the hour of his judgment is come</u>: and worship him that made heaven, and earth, and the sea, and the fountains of waters. 8: And there followed another angel, saying, <u>Babylon is fallen, is fallen, that great city</u>, because she made all nations drink of the wine of the wrath of her fornication.**

The other place in the book of Revelation where God mentions *Babylon is fallen, is fallen* is Revelation 18:2. It is there where God mentions that the fallen houses of God have become a *habitation of devils*. Further on in Revelation 18 God commands His people to *come out of her*:

> **Revelation 18:2: And he cried mightily with a strong voice, saying, <u>Babylon the great is fallen, is fallen, and is become the habitation of devils</u>, and the hold of every foul spirit, and a cage of every unclean and hateful bird.**

> **Revelation 18:4: And I heard another voice from heaven, saying, <u>Come out of her, my people</u>, that ye be not partakers of her sins, and that ye receive not of her plagues.**

While looking at the glory of Moab being contemned and the glory of Kedar failing, God allows us to know something concerning Moab.

Pride Goes Before Destruction

> **Jeremiah 48:29: We have heard the pride of Moab, (he is exceeding proud) his loftiness, and his arrogancy, and his pride, and the haughtiness of his heart.**
>
> **Proverbs 16:18: Pride *goeth* before destruction, and an haughty spirit before a fall.**

Whether God uses the prince of Tyrus, or the King of Babylon as an illustration of the activity of Satan lifting himself up, the end result will be the same. God will abase the lofty and exalt the lowly. What is especially exciting is that from the beginning of creation, Satan has always been an antagonistic destroyer of man, but now we are a short time away from God removing his power.

Ezekiel 28 first mentions the *prince of Tyrus* and then switches right into the *anointed Cherub* who lifted himself up with pride. Isaiah 14 does the same identity change from the King of Babylon to Heylel (H1966) *son of the morning* who weakened the nations. God also uses phrases like *son of perdition* to apply to a man, namely Judas Iscariot, but also Satan himself. Ezekiel 28: 6-7 proclaims God's judgment upon this self-glorying:

> **Ezekiel 28:6: Therefore thus saith the Lord GOD; Because thou hast set thine heart as the heart of God; 7: Behold, <u>therefore I will bring strangers upon thee, the terrible of the nations</u>: and they shall draw their swords against the beauty of thy wisdom, and they shall defile thy brightness.**

Since Satan has dominion within the fallen houses of God, a real judgment of the *terrible of the nations* coming upon the houses of worship is very possible. According to the book of

2 Thessalonians, the falling away occurs in the houses of God when Satan lifts himself up to be as God:

> **2 Thessalonians 2:3: Let no man deceive you by any means: for *that day shall not come*, except there come a falling away first, and that man of sin be revealed, the son of perdition; 4: Who opposeth and exalteth himself above all that is called God, or that is worshipped; so that he as God sitteth in the temple of God, shewing himself that he is God.**

Satan accomplishes this exploit by working through his ministers who come with *signs and lying wonders.* Once the unveiling of the wicked occurs, Jesus shall consume with the *spirit of His mouth* to the advent of His coming (*parousia*). 2 Thessalonians 8-9 can be saying that the Word of God will be very powerful in bringing down the kingdom of Satan during the final year 3 ½ years of history (2015-2018). The words *shall destroy with the brightness of His coming* can be translated as *shall destroy to the presence of Him.* This does match well with the believers *consuming* and *destroying* the kingdom of Satan unto the end:

> **2 Thessalonians 2:8: And then shall that Wicked be revealed, whom the Lord shall consume with the spirit of his mouth, and shall destroy with the <u>brightness of his coming</u>: 9: *Even him*, <u>whose coming</u> is after the working of Satan with all power and signs and lying wonders, 10: And with all deceivableness of unrighteousness in them that perish; because they received not the love of the truth, that they might be saved.**

> **2 Corinthians 11:13: For such *are* false apostles, deceitful workers, transforming themselves into the apostles of Christ. 14: And no marvel; for**

Satan himself is transformed into an angel of light. 15: Therefore *it is* no great thing if his ministers also be transformed as the ministers of righteousness; <u>whose end shall be according to their works.</u>

When we therefore see how Moab was full of pride and how after three years Moab will howl for Moab, this is similar to Satan howling for His conquest. Satan will howl for his lost conquest of the fallen houses of God. Isaiah 16:7 proclaims this howling of Moab. Jeremiah 51:8 proclaims a similar howling for *fallen Babylon:*

> **Isaiah 16:7: Therefore shall <u>Moab howl for Moab</u>, every one shall howl: for the foundations of Kirhareseth shall ye mourn; surely *they are* stricken.**

> **Jeremiah 51:8: Babylon is suddenly fallen and destroyed: <u>howl for her</u>; take balm for her pain, if so be she may be healed.**

Have God's people within the fallen houses of God forsaken the *fountain of living waters?* Is this why their own glory will fail much like the *glory of Kedar* failed?

> **Jeremiah 2:10: For pass over the isles of Chittim, and see; and send unto Kedar, and consider diligently, and see if there be such a thing. 11: Hath a nation changed *their* gods, which *are* yet no gods? but <u>my people have changed their glory for *that which* doth not profit.</u> 12: Be astonished, O ye heavens, at this, and be horribly afraid, be ye very desolate, saith the LORD. 13: <u>For my people have committed two evils; they have forsaken me the</u>**

fountain of living waters, *and* hewed them out cisterns, broken cisterns, that can hold no water.

Judgment on the fallen houses of God is not an easy thing to proclaim. When pride is lifted up, there almost always is an accompaniment of wrath that will soon follow. God used the illustration of Ezekiel as a watchman. The watchman's duty was to warn and sound the trumpet when *the sword was coming upon the land.* The ones who hear the sound of the trumpet but do not take the warning seriously shall be taken away by *the sword.* Their blood shall be upon their own heads. If the watchmen sees the sword coming and does not blow the alarm, then the blood shall be upon the watchman's head because he failed to warn. God tells Ezekiel the following:

> **Ezekiel 33:7: So thou, O son of man, I have set thee a watchman unto the house of Israel; therefore thou shalt hear the word at my mouth, and warn them from me.**

> **Ezekiel 33:28: For I will lay the land most desolate, and the pomp of her strength shall cease; and the mountains of Israel shall be desolate, that none shall pass through. 29: Then shall they know that I *am* the LORD, when I have laid the land most desolate because of all their abominations which they have committed.**

The Mountains of Israel Shall be Desolate

We all need to deal with how God uses certain language in the Bible to represent something other than the obvious. The *mountains of Israel* are a reference to where false worship historically took place on the *high places.* God has some very

306

serious language concerning laying the land desolate. False worship will always be judged by a holy God:

> **Ezekiel 6:2: Son of man, set thy face toward the mountains of Israel, and prophesy against them, 3: And say, Ye mountains of Israel, hear the word of the Lord GOD; Thus saith the Lord GOD to the mountains, and to the hills, to the rivers, and to the valleys; Behold, I,** *even* **I, will bring a sword upon you, and I will destroy your high places. 4: And <u>your altars shall be desolate, and your images shall be broken: and I will cast down your slain</u> *men* <u>before your idols</u>.**

There is more than one historical example where God judges false worship. This seems to be a constant theme throughout Biblical history. How does God judge false worship? With the mountains of Israel God promised desolation. When Jesus warned in Matthew 24 about the deception happening prior to His coming, He was speaking of the abomination (within the houses of God) that makes desolate.

Satan, being full of pride and lifting himself up as God (similar to Moab, King of Babylon, Herod etc…), creates this desolation. This desolation is in a dimension most people in this world do not understand. However, they may see how things seem very wrong in the houses of God. The believers know this desolation is happening because God's Word proclaims that it must come to pass, and the evidence is ramping up worldwide. God promises judgment on the fallen houses of God (*Babylon is fallen, is fallen*), but by what means does this judgment come? This is the topic of the next chapter.

Chapter 13—Every Man's Sword Against His Brother

In the past couple of years, I became interested in the topic of the desolation which happens in the houses of God. After understanding certain passages of God's Word, it became apparent that the people inside the houses of God will feel secure and believe that no harm will come to them. The Bible speaks of this as *peace and safety*. This false sense of security is because those within the houses of God feel God is on their side, yet the Lord makes it clear that bringing the Gospel does not include covetousness and becoming wealthy off His good news that He offers freely. Whether it is a history lesson from the Old Testament or a warning from the New Testament, God will judge His houses that use His name:

> **Hosea 8:2: <u>Israel shall cry unto me, My God, we know thee. 3: Israel hath cast off</u> *the thing that is* <u>good: the enemy shall pursue him.</u> 4: They have set up kings, but not by me: they have made princes, and I knew *it* not: of their silver and their gold have they made them idols, that they may be cut off.**

<u>The Means by Which Previous Judgment has Come</u>

Historically, God has used the enemy to come against Israel for their sins. The King of Assyria, the King of Babylon, and Pharaoh King of Egypt were all used by God for chastisement. After the chastisement, then God *puts hooks* or

309

bridles into the enemy and turns them back around. However, is this language of the Old Testament only focusing on historical Kings and Pharaoh's or is it a grand illustration of how God uses Satan and then *puts hooks into his jaws* when his *little season* is over? Below are some verses that show how God turns back the enemy.

The hooks into the King of Assyria-Sennacherib:

- **Isaiah 37:29: Because thy rage against me, and thy tumult, is come up into mine ears, <u>therefore will I put my hook in thy nose</u>, and my bridle in thy lips, and I will turn thee back by the way by which thou camest.**

The hooks into the Pharaoh of Egypt-That *Great Dragon*:

- **Ezekiel 29:3: Speak, and say, Thus saith the Lord GOD; Behold, I *am* against thee, Pharaoh king of Egypt, the great dragon that lieth in the midst of his rivers, which hath said, My river *is* mine own, and I have made it for myself. 4: <u>But I will put hooks in thy jaws</u>, and I will cause the fish of thy rivers to stick unto thy scales, and I will bring thee up out of the midst of thy rivers, and all the fish of thy rivers shall stick unto thy scales.**

The hooks into Gog of Magog- The Chief Prince of Meshach and Tubal:

- **Ezekiel 38:3: And say, Thus saith the Lord GOD; Behold, I *am* against thee, O Gog, the chief prince of Meshech and Tubal: 4: <u>And I will turn thee back, and put hooks into thy jaws</u>, and I will bring thee forth, and all thine army, horses and horsemen, all of them clothed with all sorts of**

armour, even a great company with bucklers and shields, all of them handling swords...

The three examples above show how God turns back these historical leaders. However, we can know that God is using these historical leaders as an example of how God uses Satan and then turns him back by *putting hooks into his jaws*. We know this by the language of *the latter years*. Satan ascends and comes against the houses of God like a storm:

Ezekiel 38:8: After many days thou shalt be visited: <u>in the latter years thou shalt come into the land *that* is brought back from the sword</u>, and is gathered out of many people, against the mountains of Israel, which have been always waste: but it is brought forth out of the nations, and they shall dwell safely all of them. 9: Thou shalt ascend and come like a storm, thou shalt be like a cloud to cover the land, thou, and all thy bands, and many people with thee.

How will Gog come in the *latter days* or *latter years* when the historical land of Magog was named after a son of Japheth who was a son of Noah? Gog was an historical prince of Meshech and Tubal known for the trading of *persons of men* and *copper/brass* (Ez.27:13):

Genesis 10:2: The sons of Japheth; Gomer, and Magog, and Madai, and Javan, and Tubal, and Meshech, and Tiras.

Ezekiel 38:2: Son of man, set thy face against Gog, the land of Magog, the chief prince of Meshech and Tubal, and prophesy against him, 3: And say, Thus saith the Lord GOD; Behold, I *am* against

thee, O Gog, the chief prince of Meshech and Tubal...

Ezekiel 38:16: And thou shalt come up against my people of Israel, as a cloud to cover the land; it shall be <u>in the latter days</u>, and I will bring thee against my land, that the heathen may know me, when I shall be sanctified in thee, O Gog, before their eyes.

The answer can only be that God is using historical Gog as an illustration of what Satan does as he comes against the houses of God in these final years. The *house of Israel* or the *mountains of Israel* can be shown that this is where false worship took place historically. Ezekiel 36 is a great chapter and shows that even though the house of Israel did harm to God's name and they were shamed among the nations, God, for His holy name showed mercy once again as declared in Ezekiel 36:36:

Ezekiel 36:36: Then the heathen that are left round about you shall know that I the LORD build the ruined *places, and* plant that that was desolate: I the LORD have spoken *it*, and I will do *it*.

There are various ways God sends judgment when false worship is taking place. Already mentioned is how God can bring a nation (s) against His house as a chastisement. Even though the nations can come against the houses of God as a judgment, God also can reverse this as the following prayer of David reveals this truth:

Psalm 79:4: We are become a reproach to our neighbours, a scorn and derision to them that are round about us. 5: How long, LORD? wilt thou be

> **angry for ever? shall thy jealousy burn like fire?**
> **6: Pour out thy wrath upon the heathen that have**
> **not known thee, and upon the kingdoms that have**
> **not called upon thy name. 7: For they have**
> **devoured Jacob, and laid waste his dwelling place.**

If the nations of this world come up against the houses of God worldwide, they may come in various forms. In the United States, the churches have enjoyed a tax exempt status which can create animosity from tax payers who do not think the churches should be tax exempt. With the spirit of antichrist working in the hearts of mankind, anything is possible in the next couple of years. Currently, there are bills to terminate the tax exempt status of the churches in the United States. Has the coveting within the houses of God become apparent to the world? Is the challenge (from the people of the world) now being proclaimed to the churches to "pay your fair share" becoming more prevalent?

This is only one avenue in which the nations can come against the houses of God. There is also an error of political correctness in this world. If the unregenerate people of the nations do not like what the leaders in the houses of God are calling sin, there could be a backlash.

Every Man's Sword Against His Brother

A very common theme in the Bible during warfare is how the Lord himself creates an environment in which *every man's sword is against His brother*. God uses the above environment as judgment that comes upon Gog for coming against *Israel*.

> **Ezekiel 38:21: And I will call for a sword against**
> **him throughout all my mountains, saith the Lord**

GOD: every man's sword shall be against his brother.

This may be a possibility within the houses of God. In the past year there has been a movement nationwide that is speaking out against *strange fire* within the houses of God. Some pastors are speaking out against the strange activity that is going on in the fallen houses of God. This strange activity comes under the guise of *God Spirit* working but is, in fact, part of the falling away which features *signs and lying wonders*. The sword (Word of God) is coming against such activity in the houses of God.

God Sends a "Fire" to Swallow Up

In the book of Amos, God says that He *will send a fire*. This *fire* is yet another form of judgment in which, I believe, we have seen the evidence of in the past few years. On YouTube many videos including *Is this Fire from God?*[20] display the most bizarre activity coming from the so-called *men of God*. This, again, is part of the falling away spoken of in 2 Thessalonians. However, the answer to the YouTube video title may be that this *fire* is a judgment from God because of their rejection of true salvation and the truth of the Gospel of Jesus Christ (Note: Read about the *strong delusion* mentioned in 2 Thessalonians 2:11).

God *sends a fire* that consumes people in the sense that they are so caught up in this delusion that they no longer have real control. Satan has the control of their actions. In the book of Job, the interaction between God and Satan is an example of how Satan provoked God to allow him to *swallow up* or *destroy* Job:

Job 2:3: And the LORD said unto Satan, Hast thou considered my servant Job, that *there is* none

like him in the earth, a perfect and an upright man, one that feareth God, and escheweth evil? and still he holdeth fast his integrity, although <u>thou movedst me against him, to destroy him without cause.</u>

Six times God promises to send a *fire* which will swallow up/devour the *palaces* due to their iniquity of false worship:

- **Amos 1:4: But <u>I will send a fire</u> into the house of Hazael, which shall devour the palaces of Benhadad.**
- **Amos 1:7: But <u>I will send a fire</u> on the wall of Gaza, which shall devour the palaces thereof.**
- **Amos 1:10: But <u>I will send a fire</u> on the wall of Tyrus, which shall devour the palaces thereof.**
- **Amos 1:12: But <u>I will send a fire</u> upon Teman, which shall devour the palaces of Bozrah.**
- **Amos 2:2: But <u>I will send a fire</u> upon Moab, and it shall devour the palaces of Kerioth: and Moab shall die with tumult, with shouting, and with the sound of the trumpet...**
- **Amos 2:5: But <u>I will send a fire</u> upon Judah, and it shall devour the palaces of Jerusalem.**

God sending a *fire* that will *swallow up* or *devour the palaces* can be another way of saying that God will send the enemy (Satan) who will *swallow up* His houses due to false worship. This is a very real power by which people believe it is the power of God. However, believers is Christ know that this delusion comes as a judgment from God. We also have the example of Job coming under attack of Satan and the limitations God placed on his evil. There is a time limit that God has placed on the evil workings of Satan in our time also. The final *time, times and half a time* (3 ½ years) is all the time Satan has before God reverses the power and reign of wickedness.

Moab will Die with Tumult

The word tumult is a curious word in the Bible since it is associated with the *seas roaring*. Yet, it is the nations or people who are raging like mighty waves:

> **Psalms 65:7: Which stilleth the noise of the seas, the noise of their waves, and the tumult of the people.**

> **Isaiah 17:12: Woe to the multitude of many people, *which* make a noise like the noise of the seas; and to the rushing of nations, *that* make a rushing like the rushing of mighty waters! 13: The nations shall rush like the rushing of many waters: but *God* shall rebuke them, and they shall flee far off, and shall be chased as the chaff of the mountains before the wind, and like a rolling thing before the whirlwind. 14: And behold at eveningtide trouble; *and* before the morning he *is* not. This *is* the portion of them that spoil us, and the lot of them that rob us.**

Jesus, when speaking in parables, also mentioned the *seas and the waves roaring. Nation shall rise up against nation, kingdom against kingdom.* The nation/kingdom of Satan is coming against the nation/kingdom of God. This spiritual war will, in time, be settled by the Lord Himself:

> **Psalm 93:3: The floods have lifted up, O LORD, the floods have lifted up their voice; the floods lift up their waves. 4: The LORD on high is mightier**

than the noise of many waters, *yea, than* the mighty waves of the sea.

It is a good to know that God is in full control during the times of *tribulation* and *great tribulation*. God has released much information concerning these final seven years. The study of His Word is a good thing in anyone's life because it brings hope when there does not seem to be hope. To know that the Lord will go before His people in battle is a great comfort.

The year 2015 is going to be a great time in history. The title of this book could have been: *Three and a half years to a Better Tomorrow*, since God is going to create a great reversal at the midway point of the final seven years. On the date of Pentecost in 2015, we will also reach the 1,335th day spoken of in Daniel 12. However, within this book, the entire picture of the seven years needed to be covered. What happens after Pentecost 2015? The Gospel must go forth into the entire world as a *witness unto the nations*. The eternal house of God will be built according to the *years of Darius*. The nations will see God's power and He will be magnified. The people within the houses of God will know that God has judged His houses of worship.

The following chapter details what the churches have been teaching: *no man knows the day or hour*. Has this phrase been used wrongly? Why did Jesus give specifics of the end when the disciples asked Him concerning the *sign of His coming* and the *end of the age*? Why was Daniel granted certain understanding of the time of the end when He asked God? We need to look further at what Jesus wants all believers who are called unto salvation to know.

Chapter 14—"No man knows the Day or Hour" Repeat After Us...

At the risk of sounding too harsh with the leaders in the houses of God, I have never understood why such an attitude of "we cannot know" is coming from the pulpits worldwide. One would think that the houses of God would be first in line in asking God for understanding and wisdom as Daniel did concerning the things of the end. Granted, God only gave Daniel information up to the *time, times and half a time* (3 ½ years), yet he was still concerned about *what shall be the hereafter of these*. The disciples had this same interest in knowing information about the coming of the Lord Jesus Christ on the last day. The most spectacular event in human history is upon us all in a few short years.

What grateful soul, as a believer in the Lord Jesus Christ, would not want to know when He is going to judge this present world and usher in the *new heavens* and *new earth*? Have the leaders of houses of God become so complacent and content on this earth that warning of Christ's coming has become too "gloom and doom" for them? Are they afraid of losing membership in their congregations?

I think one of the problems in the houses of God has been a true discouraging of the study of God's Word on the topic of Christ's coming on the last day. We should never come to a conclusion by simply reading a single verse in the Bible. Every verse needs to be studied and compared with similar verses. Even the verse that is the title and theme of this chapter has been misquoted.

"No man knows the day or hour?"

I would like to break this verse down and compare other verses which relate. I will be the first to admit that man of himself can know nothing of the mysteries of God without God's guidance and leading by the Holy Spirit. It is God's Spirit that leads us into all truth. I believe this is why Christ sent us the *Comforter*:

> **John 14:26: But the Comforter, *which is* the Holy Ghost, whom the Father will send in my name, <u>he shall teach you all things</u>, and <u>bring all things to your remembrance</u>, whatsoever I have said unto you.**

> **John 15:26: But when the Comforter is come, whom I will send unto you from the Father, *even* the Spirit of truth, which proceedeth from the Father, he shall testify of me...**

The Bible is the Word of God and it is not an easy book to understand. God has written His Word with a full scope of history and has used the past to illustrate what will happen in the final years. As we study God's Word, we do not have the full scope of history, so we rely on the information God has given us in His Word. This is why we need God's Spirit leading us into all truth. This granting of understanding by God's Spirit is underscored in His Word. No man can know the things of God unless God reveals it through His Word by the Spirit granting understanding:

> **1 Corinthians 2:11: For what man knoweth the things of a man, save the spirit of man which is in**

him? even so the things of God knoweth no man, but the Spirit of God. 12: Now we have received, not the spirit of the world, <u>but the spirit which is of God; that we might know the things that are freely given to us of God.</u>

<u>Understanding Unveiled at the Time of the End</u>

At the time of the end, God freely gives understanding of the sealed knowledge in His Word. Daniel was instructed to seal the book *even to the time of the end*. Then, at the time of the end *knowledge will be increased*. The Hebrew word for knowledge is *da-ath* (H1847). We have seen in a previous chapter how this knowledge that increases at the time of the end is related to the understanding God's Word:

> **Daniel 12:4: But thou, O Daniel, shut up the words, and seal the book, *even* to the time of the end: many shall run to and fro, and <u>knowledge shall be increased.</u>**
>
> **Habakkuk 2:14: For the earth shall be filled with the <u>knowledge of the glory of the LORD,</u> as the waters cover the sea.**
>
> **Psalm 119:66: <u>Teach me good judgment and knowledge:</u> for I have believed thy commandments. 67: Before I was afflicted I went astray: but <u>now have I kept thy word.</u>**

However, there are those who do not fear God and who do not seek His knowledge. This is one of the things about the end that is a real informal fallacy-where the stated premise fails to support its proposed conclusion. There will be people who seek God's knowledge, and people who would rather misuse a Bible verse to avoid seeking the knowledge of God.

This lack of knowledge is the reason the houses of God go into captivity:

> **Isaiah 5:13: <u>Therefore my people are gone into captivity, because they have no knowledge</u>: and their honourable men are famished, and their multitude dried up with thirst.**

> **Revelation 13:10: He that leadeth into captivity <u>shall go into captivity</u>: he that killeth with the sword must be killed with the sword. Here is the patience and the faith of the saints.**

The verse that many pastors use, although incorrectly, is: *no man knows the day or hour.* 1 Corinthians 2:11 says that the spirit of man can know the things of man. However, verse 12 goes on to say that we who are believers have inherited the Spirit of God so *that we might know the things that are freely given us of God.*

Amos 3:7 is an incredible verse because it declares that before God does anything, He reveals it to His servants the prophets. If one accurately defines the word prophet, is it one who declares God's Word. Every believer in Christ should be prophesying (declaring) God's Word. It is true that God chose certain people to script His Word, which was sealed after the book of Revelation was complete, but the people who declare God's written Word are still prophesying His Word. We need to look at Amos 3:7 and focus on the word *revealeth:*

> **Amos 3:7: Surely the Lord GOD will do nothing, but he revealeth his secret unto his servants the prophets.**

Revealeth is from the Hebrew word *Sod* (H5475) and is a special word in that it means *close deliberation*. This is what God does with His people; He shares His plans with His people. God's Word was completed once the book of Revelation was finished, but we still gain understanding from the study of His Word.

What makes God's Word so incredible is that He can use a prophecy declared many years ago and doubles the fulfillment of it at the end of time. The 1,335 day prophecy is one example. Two years before the earthquake is another example. God revealed His secret to Amos, a herdsman of Tekoa, two years before God was going to do something important:

> **Amos 1:1: The words of Amos, who was among the herdmen of Tekoa, which he saw concerning Israel in the days of Uzziah king of Judah, and in the days of Jeroboam the son of Joash king of Israel, two years before the earthquake.**

Yet, Amos 5:2 speaks of *the day of the Lord*, so all of a sudden these words scripted many years ago for the time in which Amos lived are also the *secrets* which *God reveals* to his servants at the end of time. The days of Uzziah become an incredible learning lesson for us during the time just prior to the *day of the Lord*. An important lesson in the book of Amos is that God will send a fire of judgment upon the *palaces*, which today means the fallen houses of God. Yesteryear it was the palaces of Moab, Jerusalem, Benhadad, Gaza etc... All were examples of God's judgment upon the fallen houses of God in our day. The *palaces* upon the earth were for people seeking refuge with God:

> **Psalm 48:2: Beautiful for situation, the joy of the whole earth, *is* mount Zion, <u>*on* the sides of the</u>**

north, the city of the great King. 3: <u>God is known in her palaces for a refuge.</u>

Then the adversary, who is Satan, wants to establish his throne *on the sides of the North*, and the palaces of *refuge* become palaces of *tribulation*. However, God will have the last say as mentioned in Isaiah 14:

> **Isaiah 14:13: For thou hast said in thine heart, I will ascend into heaven, I will exalt my throne above the stars of God: I will sit also upon the mount of the congregation, <u>in the sides of the north</u>: 14: I will ascend above the heights of the clouds; I will be like the most High. 15: <u>Yet thou shalt be brought down to hell, to the sides of the pit.</u>**

<u>What Happened to the Command of Jesus to Watch?</u>

Why did Jesus underscore *watching* so many times in His Word? Why does Jesus single out *of that day* and *hour*? In other words: *about <u>yet</u> the day and the hour not yet one has perceived*.

> **Matthew 24:35: Heaven and earth shall pass away, but my words shall not pass away. 36: But of that day and hour knoweth no *man*, no, not the angels of heaven, but my Father only. 37: But as the days of Noe *were*, so shall also the coming of the Son of man be.**

The entire impact of the verses that most pastors use to instruct their congregations <u>not</u> to watch for Christ's coming is, in fact, telling us to be on the watch. We are commanded to *watch*!

Matthew 24:42: Watch therefore: for ye know not what hour your Lord doth come.

When the Lord tells us to watch, He even elaborates about the possible *hours* of His coming, which is something most pastors fail to bring up. Though admittedly, these periods of time listed below can have a greater meaning:

Mark 13:35: Watch ye therefore: for ye know not when the master of the house cometh, <u>at even, or at midnight, or at the cockcrowing, or in the morning</u>: 36: Lest coming suddenly he find you sleeping. 37: And what I say unto you I say unto all, Watch.

The ones who will be blessed (happy) are the ones who are watching. To be watching and ready is the command of Christ. The Lord challenges every believer to be ready and working. These are the ones who Jesus calls the *faithful and wise* servants. There is great reward for those who are watching:

Matthew 24:44: Therefore be ye also ready: for in such an hour as ye think not the Son of man cometh. 45: Who then is a faithful and wise servant, whom his lord hath made ruler over his household, to give them meat in due season? 46: Blessed *is* that servant, whom his lord when he cometh shall find so doing.

Meat in Due Season

What is the *meat* given in due season to the faithful and wise servant? Obviously, God is not talking about physical food for our strength and nourishment. After Saul (Paul) became blinded by Jesus on the road to Damascus, God commanded

Ananias came to the house where Saul was. He called Saul brother and told him that Jesus sent him to lay hands on Saul so that he would receive his sight, and also the Holy Spirit. Acts 9:19 then declares that Saul was nourished and strengthened after *he had received meat.*

> **Acts 9:18: And immediately there fell from his eyes as it had been scales: and he received sight forthwith, and arose, and was baptized. 19: And when he had received meat, he was strengthened. Then was Saul certain days with the disciples which were at Damascus. 20: And straightway he preached Christ in the synagogues, that he is the Son of God.**

The *meat* that God is focusing on involves the nourishment for our hearts. Like Saul, when we reach the season of *blessed is he that waits and comes to the 1,335ᵗʰ day,* we will all be nourished by God's actions.

The *Meat* is Nourishment for our Hearts

There is further Biblical evidence which suggests that God's *meat* or *food* is what gives us strength. Like Saul (Paul) when he was nourished and baptized by God's Spirit, he became a great witness. This is why Jesus is commanding us to be *watching* and *ready* for nourishment in *due season.* We are less than one year away from this *season,* which begins within the year 2015. The believers in Jesus Christ will become great witnesses after a *reviving* in the *midst of the years* (Habakkuk 3:2).

The following verse speaks of God doing good and sending *rain.* The spiritual rain periods of James 5:7 are coming in less than one year from the completion of this book (August of 2014). God, as the husbandman, is waiting for the *early and latter rain* that will produce the *precious fruit of the earth* (salvation). This will fill our hearts with *food and gladness*, thus producing a great witness for the Lord Jesus Christ:

> **Act 14:17: Nevertheless he left not himself without witness, in that he did good, and <u>gave us rain from heaven</u>, and fruitful seasons, <u>filling our hearts with food</u> and gladness.**

This understanding from God's Word is truly something to get excited about. Finally, after 23 years of *tribulation*, which ended in 2011, and the following 3 ½ year period of *great tribulation* (shortened from a full seven years), God is going to reverse the time of evil. Every believer with Jesus as their Lord and Savior should be anticipating this coming gladness and spiritual nourishment. This is why we as *faithful* and *wise servants* are watchful and ready for what God is going to do. God is going to use His people as witnesses after He sends the *good*. I really believe this is why the final 3 ½ years will be a time in which the believers will *consume and destroy* the kingdom of Satan unto the end.

<u>One of the Most Misunderstood Bible Verses</u>

> **Mark 13:32: But <u>of</u> that day and *that* hour knoweth no *man*, no, not the angels which are in heaven, neither the Son, but the Father.**

We know the impact of what Jesus is saying when He commands us to watch. We are to be watching and praying unto the coming of the Lord. The doorkeeper does not fall asleep, but rather, he keeps watch so that he will know when the time comes. When we use the ISA to look at the actual Greek words used in Mark 13:32, we find that this verse is teaching that in Jesus' time no one is *yet perceiving the day or hour*, not the angels, neither the Son, but the Father (if not the Father). Jesus said a few times that He declares what He has heard of the Father. This is a mystery, but no less a truth, which shows an order that God has established:

> **Hebrews 1:5: For unto which of the angels said he at any time, Thou art my Son, this day have I begotten thee? And again, I will be to him a Father, and he shall be to me a Son?**

> **John 15:14: Ye are my friends, if ye do whatsoever I command you. 15: Henceforth I call you not servants; for the servant knoweth not what his lord doeth: but I have called you friends; <u>for all things that I have heard of my Father I have made known unto you.</u>**

Jesus, as the Son of God, has made known unto His people all things that He has heard of His Father. At that precise time in history (just under 2,000 years ago) no one had perceived the *day or hour*. In other words, no one was made aware of the *day or hour*. This is not hard to grasp if we understand the order in which Christ obeyed as the Son who received things of the Father. When Jesus' *hour* had arrived, it was so intense that He prayed for the Father to remove the cup from Him, yet He endured it all:

> **John 13:1: Now before the feast of the passover, when <u>Jesus knew that his hour was come</u> that he should depart out of this world unto the Father, having loved his own which were in the world, he loved them unto the end.**

> **Luke 22:42: Saying, Father, if thou be willing, remove this cup from me: nevertheless not my will, but thine, be done.**

The disciples desired information about the *restoration of Israel*, but they were refused an answer because it was not for them to know *the times or seasons*. We can understand this because even with Daniel and his question: *what shall be the end of these?* he was told to *go thy way*. Why was Daniel denied the information he requested? This is because God had a plan to seal certain information until the time of the end. This is God's plan and the revealing of His plan is in His power to make known.

Who Can Know the Times and Seasons?

Jesus proclaimed to the disciples that the Father has put the *times and seasons* in His power. During the time of Jesus' ministry (3 ½ years) from 29 A.D. to 33 A.D., it was not the *time and season* for God to be revealing the details of the end. Instead the Lord made sure that the disciples understood their mission:

> **Acts 1:7: And he said unto them, It is not for you to know the times or the seasons, <u>which the Father hath put in his own power</u>. 8: But ye shall receive power, after that the Holy Ghost is come upon you: and ye shall be witnesses unto me both in Jerusalem, and in all Judaea, and in Samaria, and unto the uttermost part of the earth.**

What were the disciples asking that would cause the Lord to say *it is not for you to know the times or the seasons*? This is where it gets really interesting. The disciples were asking this question just prior to Jesus ascending into Heaven. This was the time prior to Pentecost when they were told to wait for the promise of the Father. The disciples had not yet experienced the *blessed is he that waits* prophecy, which occurred on Pentecost in 33 A.D. They were in a waiting mode until that great day arrived. So, what did the disciples ask?

When is the Restoration of *Israel*?

Below, we read what the disciples asked Jesus:

> **Acts 1:6: When they therefore were come together, they asked of him, saying, <u>Lord, wilt thou at this time restore again the kingdom to Israel?</u>**

I believe the first fulfillment of Pentecost in 33 A.D. (the 1,335th day) was not the time for God to restore the kingdom to the *Israel of God* i.e., the body of believers worldwide. That would come once *judgment sits* and the believers take back the kingdom after the *last end of the indignation* (after the 3 ½ years ending in 2015). Satan seeks to change *times and laws*. Why is that? Possibly to avoid his judgment:

> **Daniel 7:25: And he shall speak *great* words against the most High, and <u>shall wear out the saints of the most High, and think to change times and laws</u>: and they shall be given into his hand until a <u>time and times and the dividing of time</u>. 26: But the judgment shall sit, and they shall take away his dominion, to consume and to destroy *it* unto the end. 27: And the kingdom and dominion, and <u>the greatness of the kingdom under the whole heaven, shall be given to the people of the saints of the most High</u>, whose kingdom is an everlasting kingdom, and all dominions shall serve and obey him.**

Daniel 7 defines when the kingdom will be given to the believers or *Israel of God*. The kingdom will be given back to the believers after the *time, times and half a time* or 3 ½

330

years. As we read in Daniel 7:25-27 how the kingdom restoration comes after the 3 ½ years, then the year 2015 will be very significant in the kingdom of Christianity.

The disciples question was a good question, but it was simply not God's plan for the kingdom to be restored during the first fulfillment of the 1,335 day prophecy. Let us look once again at the 1,335 day chart and see why the year 2015 will be highly significant in satisfying the second fulfillment of the 1,335 day prophecy. The *Israel of God*- the believers will have the kingdom restored:

The Post Restoration- Reaching the 1,335th Day
9-28-29 A.D. Trumpets (Jesus is baptized) to 5-24-33 A.D. Pentecost = 1,335 days (This is not the season to restore the kingdom to *Israel*).
9-28-2011 A.D. Trumpets to 5-24-2015 A.D. Pentecost = 1,335 days (This is the season to restore the kingdom to *Israel-the believers*).

> **Galatians 6:15: For in Christ Jesus neither circumcision availeth anything, nor uncircumcision, but <u>a new creature</u>. 16: And as many as walk according to this rule, peace *be* on them, and mercy, and upon <u>the Israel of God</u>.**

Upon Jesus' ascension into heaven, we are promised that as He left so shall He return:

> **Acts 1:10: And while they looked stedfastly toward heaven as he went up, behold, two men stood by them in white apparel; 11: Which also said, Ye men of Galilee, why stand ye gazing up into**

heaven? this same Jesus, which is taken up from you into heaven, shall so come in like manner as ye have seen him go into heaven.

Jesus has commanded His people to be *watching and ready*. The command to *take ye heed* means to be looking. We must be looking and studying God's Word since God increases knowledge during the *time and season* of the end. If we read the following verses together and not isolate and paraphrase *no man knows the day or hour*, then we get a full understanding how important it is to be looking (taking heed), watching, and praying:

Mark 13:33: <u>Take ye heed</u>, watch and pray: for ye know not when the time is. 34*: For the Son of man is* **as a man taking a far journey, who left his house, and gave authority to his servants, and to every man his work, and commanded the porter to watch. 35: Watch ye therefore: for ye know not when the master of the house cometh, at even, or at midnight, or at the cockcrowing, or in the morning: 36: <u>Lest coming suddenly he find you sleeping.</u> 37: And <u>what I say unto you I say unto all, Watch.</u>**

Psalm 55:16: As for me, I will call upon God; and the LORD shall save me.

In the final chapter, we will be looking at various important topics concerning the years 2011-2018 and the coming of Christ on the last day. The *beautification of the temple* is something I did not understand at the start of this writing. The *beautification* of God's eternal house is something very important as it relates to salvation in the final days. We will also discover the importance of how some Biblical numbers show God's salvation plan during the final seven years from

2011 to 2018. Be prepared to share the gospel in the coming years as it will produce the *fruit of salvation*!

Chapter 15—2018 the Year of Possibility

This final chapter is important because we are talking about the next greatest event in the history of mankind. The coming of Christ on the last day is something the believers in Christ are very aware of. Unfortunately, many church leaders who should be lifting up this grand event are discouraging people from *watching* by misusing a Bible verse. Two other problems exist today within the houses of God; some people are trusting in a man-made fable of Christ reigning on this earth for 1,000 years and also the teaching of a *silent pre-rapture*. There is yet another teaching that has been lifted up in the houses of God, and that is: "Jesus can come at any time; therefore, we should always be ready." While this is a nice sentiment, it is far from what the Bible declares. Jesus' first coming was in the fullness of the time:

> **Galatians 4:4: <u>But when the fulness of the time was come</u>, God sent forth his Son, made of a woman, made under the law, 5: To redeem them that were under the law, that we might receive the adoption of sons.**

The ISA renders *the fullness of the time* as *the filling of the time*. Since creation, the focal point has been concerning the time in which God chose to send forth His Son, which was 7 B.C. I personally still use B.C. because God's salvation plan governs this world. In the book: *Time Has an End- A Biblical History of the World 11,013 B.C.-2011 A.D.,* Camping showed how the date of creation can be traced back to the year 11,013 B.C. This was done by using the Biblical

335

calendar contained in the Bible. I believe that most of the studies contained in *Time has An End* were accurate. God may have waited to reveal new information concerning what comes after the 8,400 days that ended on May 21, 2011. This is why we have explored these post-tribulation possibilities in this book. This book has become a presentation of the newer information that God has revealed through the study of His Word, the Bible. Let us look at how from the time of creation to Christ's birth in 7 B.C. there are 11,006 years.

11,006 Years and Counting

When we look at a number like 11,006 total years from creation in 11,013 B.C. to 7 B.C., it seems like an odd number of years. We know that the Bible speaks of the *fullness of the time* in regards to Jesus being born of a woman under the law. How does the *fullness of the time* relate to Biblical factors? Let's examine this idea further.

Jesus was born in the year 7 B.C., which was 11,006 years past the date of creation in 11,013 B.C.[21] 11,006 years = 2 x 5,503. Could God's Word be indicating the *fullness of the time* as representing a doubling of time? In this case 5,503 years would be doubled. Not only does the Word of God speak of the *fullness of the time*, but in Jesus all the fullness dwells:

> **Colossians 1:19: For it pleased *the Father* that in him should all fulness dwell; 20: And, having made peace through the blood of his cross, by him to reconcile all things unto himself; by him, *I say*, whether *they be* things in earth, or things in heaven.**

Since all completeness dwells in Christ, and He came in the fullness (completeness) of time, then the year 7 B.C. must relate somehow to His return on the last day. It is important to point out that the following numbers that show up as factors in the year 2018 are a compliment to the other information we have studied. I would never suggest the year of Christ's return based solely on Biblical factors. However, we have seen how the years of Darius line-up with the years ending in 2018 as well as the various rain periods of understanding (Elijah's rain). These numbers can become a great compliment to the new information from God's Word. Let's count the number of years from 7 B.C. to the year 2018 B.C. What do the factors of these years show?

From the birth of Christ in 7 B.C. to His possible return in 2018 A.D. there are 2,025 years. Then we must subtract one year since there is no year zero, which would be 2,024 total years. The factors of 2,024 are 2 x 2 x 2 x 11 x 23.

The number two in the Bible has been shown to represent the believers going out as witnesses with the good news. Jesus sent forth the disciples two by two. From the mouth of two or three witnesses every word may be established (Matthew 18:16):

> **Mark 6:7: And he called *unto him* the twelve, and began to send them forth by <u>two and two</u>; and gave them power over unclean spirits...**

The number 11 really seems related to Jesus. He was born in the year 7 B.C. (11,006 years after creation), which features the number 11,000. There are 77 names (7 x 11) mentioned in *the generation of Jesus Christ*, which are also important:

> **Matthew 1:1: The book of the generation of Jesus Christ, the son of David, the son of Abraham. 2: Abraham begat Isaac; and Isaac begat Jacob; and Jacob begat Judas and his brethren...**

337

From Abraham to Joseph (the husband of Mary), all the names listed in the generation of Jesus are significant. All people who would be saved by God's Spirit from all time would partake in the generation of Christ. Thus, 77 or 7 x 11 is very relevant to Christ's birth and His return on the *last day*.

The number 23, which is a factor of 2,024, is always a number of judgment in the Bible. I would suspect that this number would show up as a factor from 7 B.C. to whatever year Jesus will return in *power and great glory*. It will be *Judgment Day* for the entire world. The following points show us how the number 23 is related to judgment:

- There are 2,300 *evening mornings* spoken of in Daniel 8:4.
- 1 Corinthians 10:8 speaks of 23,000 that fell in the wilderness in one day.
- In the 23rd year of King Nebuchadrezzar, 4,600 (2 x 2,300) were recorded as having gone into captivity in Jeremiah 52:30.
- There were 23 years from 1988 to 2011, which was 8,400 days exactly. This is a shorter version of Judah's 70-year/840 month *tribulation* period.
- There were 23,000 numbered with the two sons of Aaron who offered *strange fire*. No inheritance of Israel was given to those 23,000 people who did this.

It is for the above reasons that the number 23 must be somehow connected with the coming of Christ. The study of Biblical numbers must never be confused with any other number system such as "numerology." God's use of numbers in the Bible is there for a good reason. The numbers show a real meaning from past Biblical history. God is the one who has orchestrated the use of certain numbers. This chapter is not a complete study of God's use of numbers in the Bible, but, if you are interested in further study of numbers as used in the Bible, E.W. Bullinger (1837-1913)[22] wrote a fairly extensive book on this topic.

Below are a few verses that show how the number 23 signifies judgment:

> **Numbers 26:61: And <u>Nadab and Abihu died, when they offered strange fire</u> before the LORD. 62: And those that were numbered of them were <u>twenty and three thousand</u>, all males from a month old and upward: for they were not numbered among the children of Israel, because there was no inheritance given them among the children of Israel.**

> **1 Corinthians 10:8: Neither let us commit fornication, as some of them committed, and fell in one day <u>three and twenty thousand.</u>**

> **Daniel 8:14: And he said unto me, Unto <u>two thousand and three hundred days</u>; then shall the sanctuary be cleansed.**

What About Other Years Within the Seven Years?

We have focused on the year 2018 as the most likely year for the return of Jesus on the *last day*. What about other years of possibility? Since the *last end of the indignation* is a period of 3 ½ years, which ends in 2015, we know that Christ's return will not be until at least that period of time has expired. Also, according to Joel 2, we know that God will be magnified for a period of time after the indignation is complete. This time of magnification comes after the *Northern* (Satan) is removed into *a land barren and desolate*.

God's magnification should sync-up with the anniversary of the cross in 2015- April 3, 2015.

We also know that the rain periods spoken of in both Joel 2 and James 5:7 must also come. Since Elijah's prayer for no rain was for a period of 3 ½ years, that again would place us in our upcoming year of 2015.

However, Elijah prayed again and God gave rain. The time of rain must occur so that the *precious fruit of the earth* will come forth. We must also consider the years of Darius. In the second year of Darius, God commands us to work. This command relates to building God's eternal house as people become saved worldwide. The historical temple was completed in the sixth year of Darius. The sixth year of Darius lines up with the year 2018. If we consider the year 2017 as a possibility for the end, we find instead that the factors relate more to salvation going forth in the world.

From the birth of Christ (7 B.C.) to 2017 there are 2,023 years (2,024 years less one year-no year zero = 2,023 years). While 2,000 years plus 23 years may seem important since 23 is a number of judgment, the factors show salvation in that year:

2,023 years = 7 x 17 x 17

I believe 2017 will be a great time of salvation worldwide as it appears that the *precious fruit of the earth* will be coming forth worldwide. The number 17 represents the times of salvation. Jeremiah 32:8 is one example of how God uses 17 in association with redemption and inheritance:

> **Jeremiah 32:6: And Jeremiah said, The word of the LORD came unto me, saying, 7: Behold, Hanameel the son of Shallum thine uncle shall**

> come unto thee, saying, Buy thee my field that *is* in
> Anathoth: for the right of redemption *is* thine to
> buy *it*. 8: So Hanameel mine uncle's son came to
> me in the court of the prison according to the word
> of the LORD, and said unto me, Buy my field, I
> pray thee, that *is* in Anathoth, which *is* in the
> country of Benjamin: <u>for the right of inheritance *is*
> thine, and the redemption *is* thine; buy *it* for
> thyself.</u> Then I knew that this *was* the word of the
> LORD.
>
> Jeremiah 32:9: And I bought the field of
> Hanameel my uncle's son, that *was* in Anathoth,
> and weighed him the money, *even* <u>seventeen
> shekels of silver.</u>

The above verses show one example of how 17 represents both redemption and inheritance. The 153 great fish caught by the disciples also shows 17 as a factor.

153 = 3 x 3 x 17

Since the disciples became *fishers of men*, the illustration of 153 great fish caught with Jesus' help shows how salvation is involved with this special number:

> John 21:10: Jesus saith unto them, Bring of the
> fish which ye have now caught. 11: Simon Peter
> went up, and drew the net to land full of great
> fishes, <u>an hundred and fifty and three</u>: and for all
> there were so many, yet was not the net broken.

From the time of the cross in 33 A.D. where Jesus became the first of the *firstfruits*, until the year 1988 A.D. there were 1,955 years. The year 1988 was also the beginning of the first *tribulation* of 8,400 days. This year was also the 13,000[th] year anniversary since creation. The factors of 1,955 show the number 5 and also salvation (17) & judgment (23):

1,955 years = 5 x 17 x 23

With the 1,955 years, it is not the 55 years past the 1,900 years that are significant, but rather, it is the factors of the 1,955 years. Likewise, it is more likely that factors of 2,023 years (7 x 17 x 17) are more significant than the number 23 linked to the number of 2,023 years.

The Temple Finished in the Month Adar

In chapter 10, we discussed the years of Darius that came after Judah's 70-year/840-month captivity in October of 539 B.C. It was then that Cyrus the Persian peacefully conquered Babylon. The kingdom was given by God to both Cyrus the Persian and Darius the Mede as spoken of in Daniel 5. Using the ascension year system employed in Darius' time, we find that the first year of Darius would have officially begun in Nisan of 538 B.C. Following this same pattern after our 8,400-day *tribulation* period, which ended in 2011, the official mirror of the first year of Darius would have begun in Nisan of 2012.

God had precise commands from the second year of Darius and upward, and it was during the sixth year of Darius that the temple was completed. With the pattern of Darius' first official year beginning in 2012 in our time, we find that the sixth year of Darius lines-up with the year 2018. I am pointing this out to show once again how the sixth year of Darius applies to the possible last year of 2018. Let's now look at the verses that show when the temple was complete:

Ezra 6:14: And the elders of the Jews builded, and they prospered through the prophesying of Haggai

the prophet and Zechariah the son of Iddo. And they builded, and finished *it*, according to the commandment of the God of Israel, and according to the commandment of Cyrus, and Darius, and Artaxerxes king of Persia. 15: <u>And this house was finished on the third day of the month Adar, which was in the sixth year of the reign of Darius the king.</u>

In the Hebrew Calendar, Adar is the 12th month of the year (sometimes the added extra 13th month also). The third day of Adar in the sixth year of Darius would be our February 18, 2018.[23] It has been fascinating reviewing this word *Adar* since there seems to be a real special meaning to it. There are two concordance numbers for the 12th Hebrew month: *Adar* (H143) and *Adar* (H144).

There is also *Adar* (H142) that God uses especially in association with Himself. The Hebrew letters for this word are *Adr* and it means: to be glorious, to be expanded (made wide), and to be magnificent. With this word there is a sense of greatness or excellency:

Here are some verses that show how this Hebrew word <u>*Adar*</u> <u>(*Adr*)</u> is used (besides being associated as a month). The word *glorious* has been used for the Hebrew word Adar:

Exodus 15:6: Thy right hand, O LORD, is become <u>glorious in power</u>: thy right hand, O LORD, hath dashed in pieces the enemy. 7: And in the greatness of thine excellency thou hast overthrown them that rose up against thee: thou sentest forth thy wrath, *which* consumed them as stubble.

Exodus 15:11: Who *is* like unto thee, O LORD, among the gods? who *is* like thee, <u>glorious in holiness</u>, fearful

in praises, doing wonders? 12: Thou stretchedst out thy right hand, the earth swallowed them.

Isaiah 42:21: The LORD is well pleased for his righteousness' sake; he will magnify the law, and make *it* <u>honourable.</u>

God has for a long time held His peace, yet there comes a time in which He will no longer allow His glory to be shared with *graven images*:

Isaiah 42:8: I *am* the LORD: that *is* my name: and my glory will I not give to another, neither my praise to graven images. 9: Behold, the former things are come to pass, and new things do I declare: before they spring forth I tell you of them.

Because Israel forsook the law, God sent judgment and then the law was magnified and made honorable. Will the houses of God proclaim the same thing that the people of Israel proclaimed? When the enemy pursued Israel these words of shock were proclaimed: *my God we know thee.* The years 2015 and 2018 are both significant when it comes to Adar, which is the name of the last Hebrew month, and it is also a word that has to do with God being magnified.

The Mordecai/ Esther Connection to Adar

The book of Esther holds some clues concerning the month of Adar. Haman's plot to destroy the Jews in the kingdom of Ahasuerus is curious simply because of how Haman's name possibly means *the destroyer or to disquiet.* The Hebrew word *Haman* (H2001) and *Hamam* (destroy-H2000) have a similar connection. Setting aside the meaning of Haman's name, we can know for sure that Haman was the enemy of the Jews and his plot was to destroy:

> **Esther 9:24: Because <u>Haman</u> the son of Hammedatha, the Agagite, the enemy of all the Jews, had devised against the Jews to destroy them, and had cast Pur, that *is*, the lot, to consume them, and <u>to destroy them</u>...**

This is an interesting Biblical account since the King of Babylon was also known for destroying (Jeremiah 51:34). Therefore, Haman can be a type or prefigure of Satan who desired to destroy God's people. The month Adar, which is the 12th month in the Hebrew calendar, is not only associated with the completion of the temple in the sixth year of Darius, but it is also associated with Purim. Haman's plot to destroy the Jews in the kingdom of Ahasuerus was foiled by Mordecai and Esther. *Pur* (the lot) was cast by Haman from the first of the year (Nisan) to the end of the year (Adar). Adar was also the month when the Jews had great joy due to the reversal of Haman's plot to destroy them:

> **Esther 9:20: And Mordecai wrote these things, and sent letters unto all the Jews that *were* in all the provinces of the king Ahasuerus, *both* nigh and far, 21: To stablish *this* among them, that <u>they should keep the fourteenth day of the month Adar, and the fifteenth day of the same, yearly</u>, 22: As <u>the days wherein the Jews rested from their enemies</u>, and the month which was turned unto them from sorrow to joy, and from mourning into a good day: that they should make them days of feasting and joy, and of sending portions one to another, and gifts to the poor.**

The number ten is present in the book of Esther as Haman had ten sons. Haman also encouraged the plot to destroy the Jews by suggesting to the king that 10,000 talents of silver be used to accomplish the work of destruction. The number ten is associated with *tribulation* and also completeness:

> **Revelation 2:10: Fear none of those things which thou shalt suffer: behold, the devil shall cast *some* of you into prison, that ye may be tried; and <u>ye shall have tribulation ten days</u>: be thou faithful unto death, and I will give thee a crown of life.**

The entire plot of Haman was to destroy God's people in the kingdom. Upon the king's enquiry, Esther told the king that it was Haman who sought to destroy her and her people. The Hebrew word used in Esther 7:4 for *destroyed* (H8045) is the same Hebrew word *shamad* used in Daniel 11:44 where Satan attempts to destroy near the end:

> **Esther 7:4: <u>For we are sold, I and my people, to be destroyed, to be slain, and to perish.</u> But if we had been sold for bondmen and bondwomen, I had held my tongue, although the enemy could not countervail the king's damage. 5: Then the king Ahasuerus answered and said unto Esther the queen, Who is he, and where is he, that durst presume in his heart to do so? 6: And Esther said, <u>The adversary and enemy *is* this wicked Haman.</u> Then Haman was afraid before the king and the queen.**

Not only is *shamad* (H8045) used in Daniel 11:44 but the outcome of Satan evil plot is very similar to Haman's outcome of demise. The aftermath for Satan, as he goes forth with *great fury to destroy* is that: *he will come to his end and none will help him*. This same outcome happened to Haman. Daniel 11:44-45 explains Satan's *great fury* and the end of his evil plot to destroy:

Daniel 11:44: But tidings out of the east and out of the north shall trouble him: therefore <u>he shall go forth with great fury to destroy</u>, and utterly to make away many. 45: And he shall plant the tabernacles of his palace between the seas in the glorious holy mountain; yet <u>he shall come to his end, and none shall help him</u>.

Esther 7:9: And Harbonah, one of the chamberlains, said before the king, Behold also, the gallows fifty cubits high, which Haman had made for Mordecai, who had spoken good for the king, standeth in the house of Haman. Then the king said, Hang him thereon. 10: <u>So they hanged Haman on the gallows that he had prepared for Mordecai</u>. Then was the king's wrath pacified.

<u>To be Destroyed, to be Slain, and to Perish</u>

The language Esther uses when warning the king of Haman's plot is also seen in other verses where Satan (*the adversary* and *wicked one*) attempts to destroy:

Esther 7:6: And Esther said, The <u>adversary and enemy</u> is this <u>wicked</u> Haman. Then Haman was afraid before the king and the queen.

When Satan magnifies himself against all in Daniel 11, he then hears an announcement (tidings) that cause him to *go forth with great fury to destroy, and utterly to make away many.*

What is curious is that the rumor or announcement comes from *the east* and from *the north*. At this time, I am not completely sure how God is using *the east* and *the north* as it is used in Daniel 11. In connection with the temple being judged by God as He sends a famine of hearing His Word, it is there that He uses the directional words *north and east* (Amos 8:12). This famine in the land can very well relate to the houses of God. Let us look again at the language of Satan going forth to *destroy* due to the rumor he hears *out of the east and out of the north*:

> **Daniel 11:44: But tidings out of the east and out of the north shall trouble him: therefore he shall go forth with great fury to destroy, and utterly to make away many.** **45: And he shall plant the tabernacles of his palace between the seas in the glorious holy mountain; yet he shall come to his end, and none shall help him.**

They Shall Wander from the North to the East

> **Amos 8:11: Behold, the days come, saith the Lord GOD, that I will send a famine in the land, not a famine of bread, nor a thirst for water, but of hearing the words of the LORD 12: And they shall wander from sea to sea, and from the north even to the east, they shall run to and fro to seek the word of the LORD, and shall not find *it*.**

Does the Bible disclose what the tidings are that Satan is made aware of? Are these the tidings concerning his own destruction that is soon to come? Perhaps he begins to understand that his time for the *last end of the indignation* is only 3 ½ years or a *time, times and half time*. Satan possibly thought that he had a full seven years. From the temptation of Christ in the wilderness, we know that Satan understands God's Word. However, does he know that God has shortened the time he has to destroy? Ezekiel 7 mentions the *day of trouble* coming upon the *four corners of the land*, which is a recompense for the abominations done.

In Isaiah chapter 45, God mentions Cyrus and speaks of Him as His *anointed*. Cyrus is also called *my shepherd*. God is using Cyrus as an historical illustration of what Jesus does as He establishes His kingdom worldwide. Christ goes before us all and makes the *crooked places straight*. He *breaks in pieces the gates of brass* and destroys *the bars of iron* (representing tribulation). This is important because in Isaiah chapter 46 there is mention of *the east*. There is also mention of Cyrus (who was an earthly picture of what Christ would perform). King Cyrus is mentioned in Isaiah 45 and also here in Isaiah 46 as the man that executes God's counsel. He is typed as a *ravenous bird*:

> **Isaiah 46:10: Declaring the end from the beginning, and from ancient times *the things* that are not *yet* done, saying, <u>My counsel shall stand, and I will do all my pleasure</u>: 11: Calling a ravenous bird from the east, the man that executeth my counsel from a far country: yea, I have spoken *it*, I will also bring it to pass; I have purposed *it*, I will also do it. 12: Hearken unto me, ye stouthearted, that are far from righteousness: 13: <u>I bring near my righteousness; it shall not be far off, and my salvation shall not tarry</u>: and I will place salvation in Zion for Israel my glory.**

Cyrus being typed as a *ravenous bird* has some historical backbone. The official symbol of the Persian flag during Cyrus' reign was the *Shahbaz* or royal falcon. The following statements refer to this symbolic emblem of Cyrus the Great:

In the excavations at Persepolis archaeologists found a standard depicting a golden eagle (Oghabe Talaii) or

Shahbaz with open wings. The current belief is that this was the official symbol of Iran under Cyrus the Great and his heirs.[24]

The idea of God assigning a symbolic term like *ravenous bird* to a man is not exclusive to Cyrus the Great. In Ezekiel 39, God performs a massive reversal with Gog and his multitude (Satan and his masses); He then calls for the *ravenous birds* and *the beasts of the fields* to devour. I believe this is spiritual language showing how God reverses evil:

> **Ezekiel 39:4: Thou shalt fall upon the mountains of Israel, thou, and all thy bands, and the people that is with thee: <u>I will give thee unto the ravenous birds of every sort, and to the beasts of the field to be devoured.</u>**

Isaiah 46 also mentioned God's *counsel*. God's *counsel* is an important aspect of performing His work to the *sons of men* according to their ways:

> **Jeremiah 32:19: <u>Great in counsel, and mighty in work</u>: for thine eyes are open upon all the ways of the sons of men: <u>to give every one according to his ways</u>, and according to the fruit of his doings...**

The Sun of Righteousness Arises from the East

There is another phrase used in Isaiah 46 that mentions the word *righteousness* (*tsdaqah* H6666). When does God *bring near His righteousness*? The word righteousness is used in association of the rain periods, which come in the year 2015. This is exciting information since we are now months away from these rain periods spoken of in Joel 2:23 and Hosea 10:12. In the verses below, the phrase *former rain moderately* should really read the *former rain righteously* (*tsdagah* H6666). God sending the *rain of righteousness* is truly something to look forward to in the coming year:

> **Joe 2:23: Be glad then, ye children of Zion, and rejoice in the LORD your God: for he hath given you the <u>former rain moderately</u>, and <u>he will cause to come down for you the rain, the former rain, and the latter rain</u> in the first *month*. 24: And the floors shall be full of wheat, and the fats shall overflow with wine and oil.**

> **Hosea 10:12: Sow to yourselves in righteousness, reap in mercy; break up your fallow ground: for *it is* <u>time to seek the LORD, till he come and rain righteousness upon you.</u>**

If Satan learns about God's plan of Christ (like King Cyrus performed) rising up to break the bonds of tribulation (brass and iron), then what is his defense? Satan will have no defense as the following verse demonstrates:

> **Daniel 8:25: And through his policy also he shall cause craft to prosper in his hand; and he shall magnify *himself* in his heart, and by peace shall destroy many: <u>he shall also stand up against the Prince of princes; but he shall be broken without hand.</u>**

There are yet two other verses concerning *the east* and *the north* that are worth mentioning. I believe the language of Isaiah 41 is speaking of a time when Christ goes forth in judgment and righteousness. The mention of *east* or *rising of the sun* is used in two places in Isaiah 41. The word *north* is also found in this chapter:

> **Isaiah 41:1: Keep silence before me, O islands; and let the people renew *their* strength: let them come near; then let them speak: let us come near together to judgment. 2: <u>Who raised up the righteous *man* from the east</u>, called him to his foot, gave the nations before him, and made *him* rule over kings? he gave *them* as the dust to his sword, *and* as driven stubble to his bow.**

> **Isaiah 41:25: I have raised up *one* from the north, and he shall come: from the rising of the sun shall he call *upon* my name: and he shall come upon princes as upon morter, and as the potter treadeth clay.**

Who is the *righteous one* who is *raised up* from the rising of the sun (east)? Of course it the Lord Jesus whose power is unmatched. We can know this because Isaiah chapter 40 ends with the following verse:

> **Isaiah 40:31: But they that wait upon the LORD shall renew their strength; they shall mount up with wings as eagles; they shall run, and not be weary; and they shall walk, and not faint.**

We can also know that the *sun of righteousness* is an illustration of Christ Himself bringing in righteousness starting in the year 2015:

> **Malachi 4:2: But unto you that fear my name shall the Sun of righteousness arise with healing in his wings; and ye shall go forth, and grow up as calves of the stall.**

352

Matthew 17:2: And was transfigured before them: and <u>his face did shine as the sun</u>, and his raiment was white as the light.

Satan doesn't have a chance once the judgment of Christ begins as He ushers forth His righteousness. Satan will somehow know that this final judgment has begun. He will go forth in fury and haste to destroy a great many. The Lord has shortened the days for the sake of the elect. We can all be thankful to God for His mercy as He ushers forth true righteousness because when Satan stands up against the Prince of Princes, he will be broken without any power left.

<u>The Rumor Heard in the Land</u>

Over the years I have become particularly interested in the *rumor* or *tidings* that *trouble* Satan. This troubling is not exclusive to Satan going forth in great fury to destroy, but it also involves the people in the *four corners* of the land of *Israel.* Ezekiel 7 seems to be speaking of the fallen houses of God. God performs a recompense for the abominations in the midst of the land:

> **Ezekiel 7:3: Now *is* the end *come* upon thee, and I will send mine anger upon thee, and will judge thee according to thy ways, and will recompense upon thee all thine abominations.**

In both instances the rumor comes and it is troubling due to the fact that it is the time of God's recompense:

> **Ezekiel 7:26: Mischief shall come upon mischief, and <u>rumour shall be upon rumour</u>; then shall they seek a vision of the prophet; but the law shall perish from the priest, and counsel from the ancients.**

> **Ezekiel 7:27: The king shall mourn, and the prince shall be clothed with desolation, and <u>the hands of the people of the land shall be troubled</u>: I will do unto them after their way, and <u>according to their deserts will I judge them; and they shall know that I *am* the LORD.</u>**

An Ambassador is Sent to the Nations

There is yet another interesting aspect of the rumor which causes both Satan and the people of the *four corners of the land* to be *troubled*. There is an ambassador sent.

Whatever the announcement is, Satan has great fury and goes forth to destroy many. This would be more disturbing if we did not have the illustration of Haman doing this same thing. Haman's wickedness was overturned as God worked through Mordecai and Esther to inform King Ahasuerus of Haman's evil plot to destroy.

Historical Evidence of Great Fury

In Haman's case, the king's men bowed and reverenced him, but Mordecai did not; this caused Haman to have great fury:

> **Esther 3:5: And when Haman saw that Mordecai bowed not, nor did him reverence, <u>then was Haman full of wrath.</u> 6: And he thought scorn to lay hands on Mordecai alone; for they had shewed him the people of Mordecai: <u>wherefore Haman sought to destroy all the Jews that *were* throughout the whole kingdom</u> of Ahasuerus, *even* the people of Mordecai.**

Since we have learned from 2 Thessalonians how Satan lifts himself up as God, it may be that more of God's people who refuse to worship under the pretense of *lying signs and wonders* will cause a great fury in Satan. This pattern is seen when Mordecai refuses to bow down to Haman. It is also seen in the book of Daniel when the three Hebrew men refuse to worship the false golden image that King Nebuchadrezzar had set up. This caused a great wrath to come from the king:

> **Daniel 3:18: But if not, be it known unto thee, O king, that we will not serve thy gods, nor worship the golden image which thou hast set up. 19: <u>Then was Nebuchadrezzar full of fury</u>, and the form of his visage was changed against Shadrach, Meshach, and Abednego: *therefore* he spake, and commanded that they should heat the furnace one seven times more than it was wont to be heated.**

The temple being complete in the sixth year of Darius is significant. The month Adar is also significant since it can mean *to be glorified*. The great reversal God performed working through Mordecai and Esther caused great joy and gladness in the month of Adar. If Haman was an historical type of adversary such as Satan, then Satan's destruction would also cause great joy in our day. Once the Jews in the Kingdom of Ahasuerus had experienced the great reversal, they had *light, gladness, joy and honor*:

> **Esther 8:16: The Jews had light, and gladness, and joy, and honour.**

Will the believers in Christ see a great reversal such as was seen in the book of Esther? Yes, when God reverses the times of *tribulation*, He will be magnified:

> **Jeremiah 33:7: And I will cause the captivity of Judah and the captivity of Israel to return, and**

will build them, as at the first. 8: And I will cleanse them from all their iniquity, whereby they have sinned against me; and I will pardon all their iniquities, whereby they have sinned, and whereby they have transgressed against me. 9: And <u>it shall be to me a name of joy, a praise and an honour before all the nations of the earth</u>, which shall hear all the good that I do unto them: and they shall fear and tremble for all the goodness and for all the prosperity that I procure unto it.

This is the righteousness of God. He has smitten but He heals. He has chastised His people, but with mercy He later causes them to rejoice with great joy and gladness. The adversary is only allowed to accomplish so much. God's time of a great reversal is coming in 2015 and will continue through the year 2018. It is also very possibly the time when things change as God *shakes the heavens and earth*. The nations will know the power of God as He judges the houses which use His name:

Jeremiah 31:10: Hear the word of the LORD, O ye nations, and declare *it* in the isles afar off, and say, He that scattered Israel will gather him, and keep him, as a shepherd *doth* his flock. 11: <u>For the LORD hath redeemed Jacob, and ransomed him from the hand of *him that was* stronger than he.</u> 12: Therefore they shall come and sing in the height of Zion, and shall flow together to the goodness of the LORD, for wheat, and for wine, and for oil, and for the young of the flock and of the herd: and their soul shall be as a watered garden; and they shall not sorrow any more at all. 13: Then shall the virgin rejoice in the dance, both young men and old together: for <u>I will turn their</u>

mourning into joy, and will comfort them, and make them rejoice from their sorrow.

God has orchestrated this great work so incredibly that it may seem hard to believe. Yet, the historical examples are before us in His Word the Bible. This incredible work God performs results is an incredible final period of history. God's salvation plan will govern the next few years. This is good news because we can see a better tomorrow is coming. Prior to this better tomorrow, God must perform His great work. He alone will overthrow the *strength of the kingdoms of the nations* (Haggai 2:22). This is all very exciting because God promises to accomplish this work that was proclaimed within the *years of Darius*. As of this writing (2014), we are now in the mirror of the third year of Darius. The sixth year is the year 2018 which completes the final seven years. We will soon see God reviving His Work *in the midst of the years* (2015):

> **Habakkuk 1:5: Behold ye among the heathen, and regard, and wonder marvellously: <u>for I will work a work in your days, *which* ye will not believe, though it be told *you*.</u>**

> **Habakkuk 3:2: O LORD, I have heard thy speech, *and* was afraid: O LORD, <u>revive thy work in the midst of the years, in the midst of the years make known; in wrath remember mercy.</u>**

We will soon arrive in the year 2018 which mirrors the sixth year of Darius in which the temple will be complete. Does this mean the month of Adar is the final month and salvation is complete? We have known how the Feast of Tabernacles has always been an important feast since Jesus stood up on the last day of that great feast and gave the cry of salvation:

> **John 7:37: <u>In the last day, that great *day* of the feast, Jesus stood and cried, saying, If any man thirst, let him come unto me, and drink</u>. 38: He that believeth on me, as the scripture hath said, out of his belly shall flow rivers of living water. 39: (But this spake he of the Spirit, which they that believe on him should receive: for the Holy Ghost was not yet *given*; because that Jesus was not yet glorified.)**

We also read in the book of Revelation this same invitation, which is given by Christ to *those who thirst* for eternal life. The following verses are prior to Jesus' warning concerning adding to or taking away from His Words (which many false religions with their ancillary books have done). These extra books add to what the Bible has already declared and they influence the teaching of these organizations. We still get the imploration from Jesus concerning salvation and drinking freely from the water of life:

> **Revelation 22:16: I Jesus have sent mine angel to testify unto you these things in the churches. I am the root and the offspring of David, *and* the bright and morning star. Revelation 22:17: And the Spirit and the bride say, Come. And let him that heareth say, Come. And let him that is athirst come. <u>And whosoever will, let him take the water of life freely.</u>**

The writing of this book began with understanding from God that the sixth year of Darius was crucial to the completion of the temple. This historical temple represents something much greater in our time i.e., the eternal house of God in which believers worldwide are the *living stones*. If you also study God's Word, you may be wondering at this point how we can justify the completion of God's eternal temple (saved believers in Christ) in the month of Adar in 2018 (February 18, 2018). After all, the last day of the Feast of Tabernacles in 2018 is October 2, which is a substantial Biblical feast in the Bible. I have been pondering this question since I began writing this book in January of 2014. God is continuing to reveal more truths from His Word as we study.

When one begins a writing such as this, one never really ceases from studying God's Word. In other words, during the writing of *Seven Years to a Better Tomorrow*, I have learned things which are extremely important concerning the timeline of the end. I have learned years ago that it is best to be patient and continue studying because God is the one who reveals more truth. As I was finalizing this last chapter before writing the summary, I began studying the book of Ezra again. After the temple was complete, the Israelites kept the dedication of the house of the Lord and the Feast of Passover:

> **Ezra 6:16: And the children of Israel, the priests, and the Levites, and the rest of the children of the captivity, kept the dedication of this house of God with joy…**
>
> **Ezra 6:19: And the children of the captivity kept the passover upon the fourteenth *day* of the first month.**

Now After These Things…

As we continue to read in the book of Ezra, we learn that God mentions a different Persian king:

> **Ezra 7:1 Now after these things, in the reign of Artaxerxes king of Persia, Ezra the son of Seraiah, the son of Azariah, the son of Hilkiah...**

In Ezra 6, when the temple was complete in the sixth year of Darius, three kings are mentioned. I think the secret to understanding the kings of Persia is the term *beyond the river* which would imply that Persia was sectioned off for different kings or they simply ruled at different times. Three kings are mentioned, but there is also something curious about these verses. The temple was built *according to the commandment of the God of Israel*:

> **Ezra 6:14: And the elders of the Jews builded, and they prospered through the prophesying of Haggai the prophet and Zechariah the son of Iddo. And they builded, and finished** *it*, **<u>according to the commandment of the God of Israel</u>, and <u>according to the commandment of Cyrus, and Darius, and Artaxerxes king of Persia.</u>**

The phrase, *according to the commandment of the God of Israel,* is as important now as it ever was back then. Artaxerxes even wanted things to be done speedily as we read in Ezra 7:21:

> **Ezra 7:21: And I,** *even* **I Artaxerxes the king, do make a decree to all the treasurers which** *are* **beyond the river, that whatsoever Ezra the priest, the scribe of the law of the God of heaven, shall require of you, <u>it be done speedily</u>...**

The Beautification of the Temple

There is also something in Ezra 7 that, I believe, relates to salvation going forth to the *last day*. Even though the temple was complete in the sixth year of Darius, there was still something to be done with the temple. The temple was to be beautified, and Artaxerxes was the king that made sure the beautification was done:

> **Ezra 7:27: Blessed *be* the LORD God of our fathers, which hath put *such a thing* as this in the king's heart, <u>to beautify the house of the LORD which *is* in Jerusalem</u>...**

<u>God Beautifies the Meek with Salvation</u>

While looking carefully at the words in Ezra 7, the word *beautify* really stood out as being important. This truly is an extraordinary word since it relates to the salvation of the meek. What is extremely important about the following Psalm is that there appears to be a reversal by God. There, God speaks of beautifying *the meek with salvation* and He also tells us that the two-edged sword is the Word of God:

> **Psalm 149:4: For the LORD taketh pleasure in his people: <u>he will beautify the meek with salvation</u>. 5: Let the saints be joyful in glory: let them sing aloud upon their beds. 6: *Let* the high *praises* of God *be* in their mouth, and a twoedged sword in their hand; 7: To execute vengeance upon the heathen, *and* punishments upon the people; 8: To bind their kings with chains, and their nobles with fetters of iron; 9: To execute upon them the judgment written: this honour have all his saints. Praise ye the LORD.**

> **Hebrews 4:12: <u>For the word of God *is* quick, and powerful, and sharper than any twoedged sword</u>, piercing even to the dividing asunder of soul and**

361

spirit, and of the joints and marrow, and *is* a discerner of the thoughts and intents of the heart.

It is not only Psalm 149 that speaks about God beautifying with salvation, but the language of salvation is also found in Isaiah 60. The word *glorified* in the passage below is the same word that was translated as *beautify*. Isaiah 60 is in the context of the gentiles coming to the light of Christ and kings to <u>the brightness of His rising</u>. I believe this is so important in the final years of history. This beautification of God's eternal house means more and more people will come into the Kingdom of Jesus Christ as eternal citizens:

Isaiah 60:9: Surely the isles shall wait for me, and the ships of Tarshish first, to bring thy sons from far, their silver and their gold with them, unto the name of the LORD thy God, and to the Holy One of Israel, <u>because he hath glorified thee</u>. 10: And the sons of strangers shall build up thy walls, and their kings shall minister unto thee: for in my wrath I smote thee, but in my favour have I had mercy on thee.

The Hebrew word for *beautify* is *paar* (H6286), and it is found four times in Isaiah 60 and once in Isaiah 61 where the *planting* of God (the believers in Christ) is highly spoken of. The reversal God speaks of in Isaiah 61 is very exciting because there is the language of everlasting life. This is another reason why the beautification of the eternal house of God may take place during the final seven months from February 18, 2018 (temple complete) to October 2, 2018 (last day of the Feast of Tabernacles).

When Jesus entered the temple to read the verses concerning *the acceptable year of the Lord,* he left out *the day of vengeance of our God.* I really believe this is due to the fact that these verses relate to both the time of Christ and also the final years of history:

> **Isaiah 61:1: The Spirit of the Lord GOD *is* upon me; because the LORD hath anointed me <u>to preach good tidings unto the meek</u>; he hath sent me to bind up the brokenhearted, to proclaim liberty to the captives, and the opening of the prison to *them that are* bound;**

> **Isaiah 61:2: <u>To proclaim the acceptable year of the LORD</u>, and the day of vengeance of our God; to comfort all that mourn; 3: To appoint unto them that mourn in Zion, <u>to give unto them beauty for ashes</u>, the oil of joy for mourning, the garment of praise for the spirit of heaviness; that they might be called trees of righteousness, <u>the planting of the LORD, that he might be glorified.</u>**

Jesus closed the book after He read: *to proclaim the acceptable year of the LORD*:

> **Luke 4:18: The Spirit of the Lord *is* upon me, because he hath anointed me to preach the gospel to the poor; he hath sent me to heal the brokenhearted, to preach deliverance to the captives, and recovering of sight to the blind, to set at liberty them that are bruised, 19: <u>To preach the acceptable year of the Lord</u>. 20: And he closed the book, and he gave *it* again to the minister, and sat down. And the eyes of all them that were in the synagogue were fastened on him. 21: And he began to say unto them, this day is this scripture fulfilled in your ears.**

Since the preaching of *good tidings* to the *meek* is mentioned by Christ Himself, we can know this is how salvation or *beautification of the meek* happens near the end. By the way, the day of vengeance, which is quickly coming, is spoken of in the following verses:

> **Isaiah 63:4: For <u>the day of vengeance</u> *is* <u>in mine heart</u>, and the year of my redeemed is come.**

> **Isaiah 34:8: For *it is* the <u>day of the LORD'S vengeance</u>, *and* <u>the year of recompences</u> for the controversy of Zion.**

> **Deuteronomy 32:35: <u>To me *belongeth* vengeance, and recompence</u>; their foot shall slide in *due* time: for the day of their calamity *is* at hand, and the things that shall come upon them make haste.**

One last thing, the word *meek* really can be translated as *humble ones*. Those who know the power of the Lord of Heaven know they cannot be proud or boastful because salvation is a gift from God. This knowledge creates a real humbleness within oneself. Moses was called *meek* (H6035), and God blesses the meek and allows the humble to inherit the new heavens and new earth:

> **Psalm 37:10: For yet a little while, and the wicked *shall* not *be*: yea, thou shalt diligently consider his place, and it *shall* not *be*. 11: But the meek shall inherit the earth; and shall delight themselves in the abundance of peace.**

Statutes and Judgments Come About by God's Spirit

After seeing that the year 2018 is a possible time for the return of Jesus in *power and great glory*, I cannot help but think that the year 2015 will be the time of God's reversal.

The beautifying of God's temple, the teaching of God's *statutes and judgments* in Ezra, and the building of the wall in Nehemiah all relate to the final years of history. The difference in our time, though, is that God is the one who beautifies His eternal house, builds the wall of salvation, and brings forth His *statutes and judgments* as He saves by His Spirit. Lastly, I want to present a few verses that show how the activity of Ezra and Nehemiah relate to our time and truly were forecasting God's incredible salvation plan:

> **Ezekiel 36:25: Then will I sprinkle clean water upon you, and ye shall be clean: from all your filthiness, and from all your idols, will I cleanse you. 26: A new heart also will I give you, and a new spirit will I put within you: and I will take away the stony heart out of your flesh, and I will give you an heart of flesh. 27: And I <u>will put my spirit within you, and cause you to walk in my statutes, and ye shall keep my judgments, and do them.</u>**

> **Isaiah 26:1: In that day shall this song be sung in the land of Judah; We have a strong city; <u>salvation will *God* appoint *for* walls and bulwarks.</u> 2: Open ye the gates, that the righteous nation which keepeth the truth may enter in. 3: Thou wilt keep *him* in perfect peace, *whose* mind *is* stayed *on thee*: because he trusteth in thee.**

We can all be anticipating something very incredible happening in the following months and years. We have all been living so long in a time of evil that when God *shakes the heavens and the earth* and executes a great reversal, His people will be rejoicing. Righteousness will come in *as a flood*. God's Word will be magnified and His glory will cover the earth. People will become saved by His Spirit and God will be magnified. I began this book being excited about the power and grace of God and now that has intensified.

This information is a blessing to know and to share with many people. I hope every reader will feel that same conviction to share this information freely. Pass out free copies to your friends and family. Use this book as a conversation piece with people you meet every day. This information must be shared. Who living in this present time does not want to know about a *better tomorrow* coming soon? Living in a turbulent world of uncertainty can be troubling. Just remember the times that Jesus told the disciples not to be *troubled* and *let not your heart be afraid.* He is in control of everything. His power and righteousness in the next few years will far surpass anything we have had to endure for His name.

Yes, God will judge His houses of worship and chastise His people, but this will cause many to know His power and turn to Him in a great way. For those people who have been saved by God's Spirit, the time to *work* and bring the good news is now. For those who do not know the Lord, and who desire His protection and salvation, the time to seek Him is now. God will save those of a contrite heart:

> **Psalm 34:17:** *The righteous <u>cry, and the LORD hereth,</u>* **and delivereth them out of all their troubles. 18: The LORD *is* nigh unto them that are of a broken heart; and saveth such as be of a contrite spirit.**

> **Isaiah 57:15: For thus saith the high and lofty One that inhabiteth eternity, whose name *is* Holy; I dwell in the high and holy *place*, with him also *that is* of a contrite and humble spirit, to revive the**

366

spirit of the humble, and to revive the heart of the contrite ones.

1Timothy 1:15: This *is* a faithful saying, and worthy of all acceptation, that Christ Jesus came into the world to save sinners; of whom I am chief.

1Timothy 1:16: Howbeit for this cause I obtained mercy, that in me first Jesus Christ might shew forth all longsuffering, <u>for a pattern to them which should hereafter believe on him to life everlasting.</u>

Since this chapter is concerning the year of possibility of Christ's coming, I wanted to note how 2 Thessalonians speaks of a revealing unto the coming of Jesus. In 2 Thessalonians there appears to be an unmasking of who Satan is and what he has done in creating desolation in the fallen houses of God:

2 Thessalonians 2:8: And then shall that Wicked be revealed, whom the Lord shall consume with the spirit of his mouth, and shall destroy with the brightness of his coming…

This is a difficult verse since the ISA renders the phrase *with the brightness of His coming* as *to the advent of presence of Him*. Since *consume and destroy* in Daniel 7:26 is the task given to the believers, it would make sense that the *wicked* is *consumed and destroyed* <u>unto</u> the advent of His coming, by the *spirit of His mouth*. The power of God's Word will be the method of this revealing and destruction of the *wicked*.

Whether it is *to* the advent of His coming or *with* the advent of His coming, the good news is the *wicked* will soon be destroyed by the Lord. This task is also given to His people as we have understood how the believers *consume and destroy* unto the end. Another word for *the wicked* is *the lawless,* which is a representation of Satan's works of blasphemy, accusing, and the self-glorying of himself to attempt to act as God. *Brightness* of His coming is implied since the Greek word *epiphaneia* (G2015) is related to *epiphaino* (G2014), which means *to shine upon* or *give light.* Jesus is coming in *power and great glory*!

Summary of Chapters

I hope you have found this book worth your time. I believe the information in this book contains some of the most important topics of our time. The coming of Christ on the *last day* will be an event unsurpassed in human history. It will be the culmination of everything that has gone on before us. The Creation in 11,013 B.C., the Noachian Flood in 4990 B.C., and the Cross of Christ in 33 A.D. were similar in significance except for the fact that none of the three events were witnessed by over 7 billion people; although, the time of the cross surely was a turning point for the Kingdom of God.

God has been very merciful in revealing these truths before they happen. His power and mercy will be known, and this world is going to experience some great changes. Below is a quick summation of this book's chapters.

In Chapter 1, we looked at the grand worldwide announcement of Judgment Day in the year 2011. Besides a major world disaster, I have never seen any topic travel throughout the world so fast. If it were not for 2011 being the 7,000[th] anniversary of the flood, we may not have focused so much on that year being the possible year of our Lord's powerful return.

We know now (according to 2 Peter 3) that God is not willing that any would perish (as they did with the flood), but rather, He wants people to come to repentance and become saved. This is done by God's Spirit creating an eternal change in a person's life. Peter pointed us to what Paul understood about God's longsuffering. We are currently living in the time of God's longsuffering.

We also looked at the Bible term *the day of the Lord*. We explored how this was a period of time in which God's judgment process begins with the houses of worship. Obadiah 1:15 uses the term *the day of the Lord* in which the nations also experience God's judgment. The *day of the Lord* is a period of time of God recompensing for evil. The Bible uses the language of *as thou hast done, it shall be done unto thee: thy reward shall return upon thine own head.*

We touched on the parable of Job 29:23 as God proclaims: *and they waited for me as for the rain; and they opened their mouth wide as for the latter rain.* This is all about God giving understanding to His Word at a precise time during the *latter rain*. This time of *latter rain* is around Pentecost 2015 when God performs a great reversal.

In Chapter 2, we studied how it was possible that some Bible students grouped the two *tribulation* periods together as one and the same time. We know now that God separated the time of *tribulation* from the time of *great tribulation*. In other words, the completion of the 8,400-day *tribulation* period, which ended on May 21, 2011, was the end of the mirror of Judah's 840 months/70-year *tribulation* period.

Likewise, our current *great tribulation* period (2011-2018) is a mirror of the 7-year famine of Jacob's day that God also called *great tribulation*. This current *great tribulation* period is a time of famine of hearing God's Word and a time of judgment on the fallen houses of God. Mercifully, the Lord has shortened the time of *great tribulation* to the first 3 ½ years.

God shortened the days for the sake of salvation. After a period of a *time, times and half time* (3 ½ years) God sends a spiritual rain of understanding His Word to produce the *precious fruit of the earth* (salvation). Satan is only allowed the 3 ½ years, and then according to Joel 2, God removes the *Northern* (Satan) into a land *barren and desolate*. The gospel goes forth into the *all the world* for the final 3 ½ years. This is a very similar task Jesus gave to the disciples prior to His ascension into heaven. Jesus proclaimed to the disciples: *go ye into all the world, and preach the gospel to every creature*.

Gospel Goes into All the World- 33 A.D. & 2015 A.D.		
Date	**Event**	**Verse**
33 A.D.	Command to the disciples by Christ, after the Cross and before Pentecost, just prior to His ascension into Heaven: *And he said unto them, Go ye into all the world, and preach the gospel to every creature*.	Mark 16:15
2015 A.D.	Declaration by Christ: *And this gospel of the kingdom shall be preached in all the world for a witness unto all nations; and then shall the end come*. Pentecost 2015 onward.	Matthew 24:14

We looked at the reason why Daniel had to wait 21 days before he was given understanding concerning the things of the end. This is important in our time, since God revealed more information past the 8,400 days (4 x 2,100). God reveals even more information from the jubilee of 1994 to Pentecost of 2015 (21 years).

The nature of the *tribulation* and *great tribulation* is how many people will be proclaiming "I am anointed." This deception comes under the delusion of *lying signs and wonders*. This is a grand deception that attempts to mimic the only true anointed of God who is Jesus the Christ (anointed).

In Chapter 3, we studied how God will be magnified when judgment comes upon the fallen houses of God. This will be a similar time of magnification to that of the time of the cross. The after effect will be that many people become saved by God's Spirit worldwide. How this judgment on the fallen houses of God occurs is more difficult to understand. However, because we have the historical Biblical examples of Israel's judgment, we are proclaiming a worldwide judgment on the fallen houses of God.

How will God bring this to pass? Will the unsaved gentile nations come against the fallen houses of worship just as God previously sent Assyria and Babylon against sinful Israel? False worship is always judged. The *falling away* includes seeking after *signs and lying wonders,* and prosperity gospels instead of the true gospel of Jesus Christ. In the book of Revelation, there is language that fallen Babylon (the fallen houses of God) has become *a habitation of devils*. That in itself is a judgment, and the importance of fleeing out by the command of Christ should be taken seriously.

We also studied the mystery of Matthew 24 concerning the days being shortened for the elect's sake. This equates the time of *Jacob's trouble* or *great tribulation* being shortened from 7 full years to 3 ½ years ending in 2015. God's salvation governs the time line of the final years.

The *gospel of the kingdom* was reviewed in this chapter. When Jesus declared the *gospel of the kingdom* He told people to *repent and believe*. This will be the focus from 2015 onward as the gospel of the kingdom goes forth; the kingdom of God will truly be *at hand*. We also learned, according to the timeline of the years of Darius, how the proclamation of Satan being rebuked will come within the years of Darius, most likely lining up with the year 2015. This grand event may coincide with the *latter rain* of understanding which God promises to send in Joel chapter 2 and James chapter 5. This understanding that is sent by God leads to the salvation of people worldwide.

In Chapter 4, we introduced the idea of the 1,335 day prophecy having a double fulfillment in history. The first fulfillment of *blessed is he that waits and comes to the 1,335th day* was Pentecost in 33 A.D. The second fulfillment lands on Pentecost in the year 2015. The 1,335 chart on page 103 illustrates this double fulfillment.

The all-important feast celebrations were reviewed. From the Feast of Trumpets in 29 A.D. to the Feast of Weeks (Pentecost) in 33 A.D., there were 1,335 days. These feasts that were established by God many years ago were all pointing to fulfillment in Christ. The Feast of Weeks (Pentecost) should prove to be an important feast in God's salvation plan worldwide: *Not by might, nor by power, but by my spirit, saith the LORD of hosts* (Zechariah 4:6).

We also looked at the 1,260, 1,290 and 1,335 day prophecies as being important during the 3 ½ years of *great tribulation.* The timing of the cross in 33 A.D. was an important time marker in history as the *prince of this world* (Satan) was cast out. Therefore, the anniversary of the cross in 2015 should be the timing of God rebuking Satan. According to Joel 2, God removes the *Northern* after a time in which Satan had magnified himself.

In Chapter 5, we focused on *perilous times* as defined by the Bible. *Perilous times* can be defined as *fierce times* by the example of the two men possessed by devils who came out of the tombs in the country of the Gergesenes. They were exceedingly fierce. We also focused on the term *last days* and understood that scoffers would follow their own desires proclaiming: *where is the promise of His coming?*

We began to explore the Biblical language of judgment coming on the fallen houses of God; the example being the overthrowing of Sodom. We also explored the language of Micah chapter 4 as God rebukes the nations. Whether God rebukes the nations, the Red Sea or Satan himself, God's rebuke produces results.

The truth of God's judgment beginning with the fallen house of God was only one aspect of His Judgment. Micah 4 declares that God will *rebuke the strong nations from afar off*. In Micah 5:15, God promises to execute vengeance in *anger and fury upon the heathen*, such as they have not heard. The ISA makes a bit more sense in that Micah 5:15 reads: *and I do in anger and in fury vengeance with the nations which not they listen*. Most of the time, the language of *they listened not* is related to the house of God being in rebellion. However, this language is reserved for the nations. This underscores how the *day of the Lord* will affect the nations as well as the fallen houses of God.

We also explored the term the *latter days* in which we are all living. We looked at how the title of this book could have been *One Year to a Better Tomorrow*, since the year 2015 is a grand time of God's turn around. The anniversary of the cross, the 1,335[th] day of God's blessing by His Spirit, and also the promise from God to rebuke Satan, all of these truths would make a better tomorrow. However, the completion of the building of God's eternal temple (salvation) lines-up with the mirror of the 6th year of Darius, which is the year 2018. The year 2015 will still be very significant.

In this chapter there was also mention of the price for rejecting the knowledge of God. Are the houses of God rejecting the information concerning Christ's return on the last day? I believe some of the pastors are rejecting God's knowledge. Doctrines of a "silent rapture" and a thousand year reign of Christ on this sin-cursed earth have overrun the truth of the Bible. These man-made doctrines were introduced in the late 1800's. They are not the original teachings of Christ or the gospels of the disciples.

In Chapter 6, we explored how the final seven years are a time of God being longsuffering. We looked at modern day attacks on the Apostle Paul by men who claim Paul was *a ravening wolf.* Paul understood God's longsuffering and knew of His longsuffering/patience first hand. Paul was the first example of God's longsuffering. Being such, it is no surprise that the spirit of Antichrist, working through men, would begin to attack God's first example of His enduring patience with mankind. Satan wants people to think there is no hope left. Christ proclaims: *If any man thirst, let him come unto me, and drink.* Jesus proclaimed this on the *last day*, that great day of the Feast of Tabernacles.

We explored how false accusers would come in the last days. This is a trait of Satan who is the accuser of the brethren. He worked through other people who do not have God's Spirit to accomplish this evil.

The Apostle Paul understood the book of Isaiah as he expounded on God being the potter, making His power and mercy known to the vessels that He has created. This all ties-in to the judgment coming in the year 2015 once the *last end of the indignation* is over.

We looked at what was missed in the year 2011 as the grand announcement of judgment day was proclaimed. The years of

Darius, the *last end of the indignation,* the 3 ½ years of Elijah praying for no rain, God removing the *Northern,* what Daniel was allowed to know, and the separation of the *tribulation* period (23 years) from the *great tribulation* (7 years) all needed to be revealed by God.

In Chapter 7, we discovered how much information Daniel was allowed to know concerning the things of the end. Daniel had prayed for understanding, and it took 21 days before he received an answer. The *tribulation* period that ended on May 21, 2011, was 8,400 days (4 x 2,100). This 23-year period (8,400 days) followed the pattern of Judah's captivity of 70 years (840 months) of tribulation. Once the 8,400 days ended on May 21, 2011, God began to reveal more.

From the year 2011 onward God gave much more information concerning the final seven years of God's longsuffering. This information came from studying God's Word and the patterns contained in His Word. Daniel was given information that was disconcerting to him. This information was concerning God's people during the *time, times and half a time* (3 ½ years). Daniel wanted to know what would be the hereafter of *these.* That is when the information was cut off. Daniel was told to *seal up the words* until the time of the end when knowledge would be increased by God.

It was shown in chapter six how this *knowledge* was information concerning the things of the end. Daniel was also informed how the *wise* (those who are given wisdom by God) would understand, but none of the wicked would understand. The book of Daniel also explained how the *wise* would turn many to righteousness and *shine* (*zawhar*) like the stars in the firmament of heaven. We learned that the Hebrew word *zawhar* actually means to warn or to enlighten.

It is the task of the believers in Jesus Christ to warn the world of the coming judgment that will first come upon the fallen houses of God and then upon the entire world. The way of escape is through the good news (Gospel) of Jesus Christ. Many people will be fleeing to God and the Gospel will continue to go into *all the world* during the last half of the final seven years. Daniel was told to *go thy way* until the end (extremity) of the time when he would stand in his lot (inheritance). While Daniel was not given the *hereafter of these*, he was given the comfort that like other believers in Christ, he would arise to inherit eternal life.

Chapter 8 is an important chapter because in the book of James God gave two men to whom we are to look toward as examples. Elijah was one of the men and Job was the other. If I may suggest, read James chapter 5 and focus on the details of being patient unto the coming of the Lord. Why is God urging patience? God, as the husbandman, is being patient waiting for the *early and latter rain* to produce the *precious fruit of the earth*. This, once again, is focusing on the longsuffering which both Peter and Paul understood. It is also focusing on the latter rain of understanding/salvation once God removes Satan *into a land barren and desolate*.

Job was an important illustration because he came under the attack of Satan. Satan is active in the first half of the final seven years. The last half of the seven years is reserved for God's *short work* (logos) which He performs on the earth:

Romans 9:28: For he will finish the work, and cut *it* short in righteousness: because a short work will the Lord make upon the earth.

The number seven is listed seven times in the book of Job with the eighth time being a repeat of Job's "seven sons." Why is God focusing on the number seven in the book of Job? God restored Job double at the end of his trial. Does this relate to the final seven years? I believe it does relate to either the midway point in the year 2015 or the end of the seven years in 2018.

Elijah was the other man in whom God wants us to learn from. In Chapter seven we looked at Elijah's prayer of no rain where false worship was taking place. He prayed again and there was great rain. What was the length of the no rain period? There were 3 ½ years of no rain in Samaria where Ahab and Jezebel caused the people of the land to fall into false worship. I believe this is a grand picture of the final seven years with the first half being the *time, times and half a time,* which is *the last end of the indignation.* We then get to the halfway mark where God promises to remove the *Northern* (Satan) to a land *barren and desolate.* At that time things will begin to change, and God will be magnified in a great way.

We are months away from this incredible change. James 5:8 instructs all believers to be patient, establish (stand fast) your hearts, for the coming (*parousia*) of the Lord is near. Since Joel 2 mentions the removing of Satan into a land *barren and desolate*, it will not be until the coming (*parousia*) of Christ (on the last day) until Satan is fully destroyed (2 Thessalonians 2).

The believers get the privilege to *consume and destroy* Satan's kingdom unto the end (Daniel 7:27). This fits the pattern of the final seven years which are divided into two 3 ½ year sections. It fits the example of Job and Elijah. It also fits how Elisha got a double portion of Elijah's spirit. The

<u>Power of Elisha</u> is the title of a study I am reserving for the *2011studies* (YouTube) channel. Feel free to join the YouTube channel entitled: *2011studies* (one word).

We learned how the sin of Samaria is similar to the falling away in the houses of God. Jesus uses the language of casting those who participate in false worship into a bed of *great tribulation* with *Jezebel* (Revelation 2:22). Historically, Jezebel did not repent of her evil. It was Jezebel who *stirred up* King Ahab to perform wickedness in the land:

> **1Kings 21:25: But there was none like unto Ahab, which did sell himself to work wickedness in the sight of the LORD, <u>whom Jezebel his wife stirred up</u>.**

Jezebel's death as recorded in 2 Kings Chapter 9 may very well relate to the year 2015 since the time of *great tribulation* will come to a close.

We read how God defines *"Mystery Babylon"* by the adorning of the women in Revelation 17. The colors, precious stones, and gold were all decorations of God's temple in the Old Testament. This translates to the fallen houses of God today which commit *adultery* against God by the practice of false worship, lying signs and wonders, prosperity gospels etc... We also learned how the fallen houses of God eventually become a *habitation of devils*.

God has chosen very distinct language of the believers being *fruitful and multiplying*. This relates to salvation of many people worldwide. We also know that after three days we shall be *revived* and *live in His sight* as we go on to *know the Lord*. This relates to God reviving us after the *last end of the indignation*. This means that God will be giving His people strength to accomplish the task of bringing the saving Gospel into all the world in the year 2015.

In Chapter 9, we covered the patterns of *tribulation* mentioned in the Bible. Harold Camping did some incredible ground work on the *patterns of tribulation* in his books: *Time has an End* and also *1994?* Much of that information concerning Judah's 70-year *tribulation* period (840 months) being the pattern for the 8,400 day *tribulation* period still holds true.

I believe what was missed prior to 2011 was the post *tribulation* time period. What happened to the Judean captives who returned from Babylon back to their homeland during the *years of Darius*? This is where we explored the language of *good and comfortable words.* After all, it was during the *years of Darius* that the rebuilding took place.

The temple was complete in the month Adar in the sixth year of Darius. This completion of the temple relates to our year 2018, according to the mirror of the *years of Darius.* The completed temple represents the believers worldwide who become saved by God's Spirit and are as living stones in the house of God. This rebuilding process today involves the *Gospel of the kingdom* going forth during the mirror of the years of King Darius. The *letters of peace and truth* in the book of Esther also represent the Gospel of Christ being published into all lands once the enemy is removed. Haman, who was a picture of Satan, was the historical *destroyer* in the book of Esther.

God has established these patterns so we can know how He will orchestrate His salvation plan right to the *last day.* We produced some charts in this book to illustrate the important timelines such as the years of Darius and how those years of rebuilding relate to our current years post 2011.

In this chapter we also covered the Biblical command to *wait for it.* Though it seems like it may be a time of lingering, the vision concerning the things of the end will come and will not tarry any longer. Habakkuk stood upon his watch to answer when he was being reproved or questioned. This is an important aspect of the time after the 7,000[th] year anniversary of the flood (2011). This waiting period is for the sake of salvation of people worldwide. The vision is *for an appointed time, but at the end it shall speak.* We also learned that the *soul which is lifted up is not upright in him.* The opposite of this *lifting up* is how the believers in Jesus will live by *His faith (Habakkuk 2:4).*

We began to explore the years of Darius and what happened historically in each year. God wants us to know how the command to work came in the 2nd year of Darius. Since the proclamation of *no more salvation* was made by some people after 2011, it was reviewed how God has a covenant with day and night. The covenant cannot be broken by any man or any such declaration of *salvation is over.* In fact, the waiting and coming to the 1,335[th] day in Pentecost 2015 is enough to disqualify such a teaching. So we pray that anyone who declared such a teaching of *no more salvation* would think different and join in the task of bringing the gospel during the final years of history.

The two witnesses of Revelation chapter 11 coming back to life and once again standing *before the God of the earth,* suggests how God's Word will regain power once we reach the year 2015. The *last end of the indignation* will have ended. The time of *no rain* where false worship was occurring will have ended. God will then be magnified and His rain of understanding will go forth. Revelation chapter 11 must be studied in the light of Zechariah chapter 4.

<u>In Chapter 10</u>, we broke down the years of Darius and learned what was commanded in those years after the captivity of Judah. I believe these *years of Darius* relate to the final seven years after the year 2011. In the first year of Darius, information concerning the things of the end was given to Daniel. After the year 2011 the learning process began for us; it became a time of God revealing more truth through the study of His Word.

The second year of Darius was very important because God commanded the rebuilding of the temple. The command to work that was given by God was also followed up with *from this day and upward will I bless you*. This was encouraging to learn because the believers must know that the command to send forth the Gospel has not stopped. God is commanding us to work.

The third year of Darius is not mentioned in the Bible, so the command to work continues into the third year and onward.

In the fourth year of Darius, God demands true judgment and for every man to show mercy and compassion to his brother. Zechariah 7 mentions the fourth year of Darius and the recollection of when Jerusalem prospered, but then they became corrupt and imagined evil against their brothers. The *poor and needy* were not taken care of either. The *widow* and the *fatherless* were also ignored. Zechariah may be forecasting judgment in the houses of God because this recollection happened in the fourth year of Darius, which would be 2015-2016 (Nisan to Nisan) in our time.

The fifth year of Darius is not mentioned in the Bible. The sixth year, however, is mentioned, and this was the year in which the temple was completed. The elders of the Jews built the temple, and they prospered through the prophesying of Haggai and Zechariah. The Word of God is an active part of

382

finishing the eternal house of God in our time. The believers need to know that God is commanding us to work during these final seven years. Also, we all need to know that God will bless the work for He is with us.

Another phrase we covered was how God is forecasting that He will *shake the heavens and the earth*. This imperative *shaking* is mentioned twice in Haggai 2 where God says, *Yet once, it is a little while, and I will shake the heavens, and the earth, and the sea, and the dry land . . .* This warning from God comes in the second year of Darius, so anytime during the years of Darius (after the second year) this great change from God will take place. The timing is most likely in the year 2015 since the mirror of the 2nd year of Darius is our 2013-2014 (Nisan to Nisan). God is going to change this world and Satan's kingdom is coming down by God's powerful hand.

Shaking the heavens and earth is mentioned in Isaiah 13:13, Joel 3:16, Haggai 2:6, and Haggai 2:21. In Joel 3:16, God is the hope and shelter for His people. I suspect that the *shaking of heavens and earth* is spiritual language for the coming judgment, yet the believers will be protected. God is our shelter and hope. Though I avoided mentioning physical earthquakes in this chapter, the emphasis in Luke 21:11 is on *great earthquakes*. So I would expect great earthquakes to continue in this world.

One of the greatest promises from God's Word is that He will remove the reproach of His people. Christian's worldwide face this reproach but not for long. For those believers who were persecuted unto death, they will be coming back with Christ on the last day to be part of the judging process. We are living in a time of evil and Christian persecution is on the rise worldwide. Kingdom is now rising against kingdom. I believe this is one reason that there will be great joy when God removes this reproach. This was my favorite chapter because the "mirror years" of the years of Darius really do hold some great promises.

Chapter 11 followed the chapter concerning the *years of Darius* because it involves the blood moon tetrad, which happens in the years 2014 and 2015. The reason I decided to talk about this tetrad (four blood moon eclipses) is because these eclipses land on very precise Biblical feast days. God mentions in the book of Genesis how the moon is for *seasons* or *appointed times*. The *appointed times* relate to the precise feast days which God has established in His Word. In this chapter we explored why it is possible that these certain feast days joined to blood moons are significant markers for judgment coming on the fallen houses of God. The two feasts related to the eclipses are *Unleavened Bread* and *Tabernacles*—both relate to the exodus out of Egypt and also the fleeing out of the fallen houses of God (spiritually called *Sodom and Egypt*).

Some pastors are suggesting that these blood moons could signal something significant for the nation of Israel. I would not eliminate the parallel between Israel and the churches (the worldwide *house of Israel*). However, since so many things are lining up with judgment coming upon the fallen houses of God (*Babylon is fallen, is fallen*), I believe the main focus of these blood moons is concerning God's warning to the fallen houses of God. The timing of this judgment seems to line-up with the year 2015. Therefore, the blood moons in the year 2015 and especially the one near Passover (unleavened bread) should be a significant time of judgment.

The other important topics in this chapter included the importance of the blowing of *shophar* or trumpets, and the *parousia* or coming of Christ. We also looked at how God uses the term *great city* and applies it to Babylon, Jerusalem and Nineveh. All these historical *great cities* are an end-time illustration of the judgment which comes upon the fallen houses of God.

In Chapter 12, we looked at the prophecy concerning the glory of Moab being contemned *according to the years of the hireling*. The Biblical *years of the hireling* were a three-year contract and if the contract was doubled it was six years. The Bible mentions the *glory of Moab being contemned* in three years. Since Moab was involved in false worship, and proud and exalted, this could be a prophecy of how the fallen churches are brought low and despised (contemned).

We also looked how, historically, the king of Assyria had *hired* Moab, and then after three years he invaded the land of Moab where false worship was. The language of the timing of this does seem to fit the year 2015 since the following language is found in Isaiah 16:7: *...the extortioner is at an end, the spoiler ceaseth, the oppressors are consumed out of the land.* God uses the *spoiler* as a picture of one who desolates (Jeremiah 48:8), and Babylon is a good example of desolation when God decrees a judgment on Babylon:

> **Jeremiah 51:48: Then the heaven and the earth, and all that *is* therein, shall sing for Babylon: for the spoilers shall come unto her from the north, saith the LORD. 49: As Babylon *hath caused* the slain of Israel to fall, <u>so at Babylon shall fall the slain of all the earth.</u>**

With the above language, God is using history to illustrate the judgment which comes upon the fallen houses of God.

We also looked at what happens near the end as we saw what happened to the three men mentioned in Jude:

> **Jude 1:11: Woe unto them! for they have gone in the way of Cain, and <u>ran greedily after the error of Balaam for reward</u>, and perished in the gainsaying of Core.**

Judgment is then ushered forth first in the year 2015 and then finally as Christ comes with ten thousands of His saints (Jude 1:14-15); 10,000 is a number of completeness. This grand event on the last day comes after a time of false prophets.

There comes a time in which God will famish all the gods of the earth. False worship will have a day of recompense. God commands His people in various ways to: *depart out, come out from among them,* and also *come out of her my people.* All these commands are for His people to flee from the abomination which makes desolate. God asks in 2 Corinthians chapter 6: *what concord hath Christ with Belial?* What harmonious agreement does Christ have with Satan? Jesus' kingdom is the antithesis of Satan's kingdom:

> **2 Corinthians 6:17: Wherefore come out from among them, and be ye separate, saith the Lord, and touch not the unclean *thing*; and I will receive you...**

<u>In Chapter 13</u>, we explored the possible judgments coming upon the fallen houses of God. *Every man's sword against his brother* is something that God has previously brought about which creates great confusion. God's judgment on Gog (Satan) shows this confusion and judgment:

> **Ezekiel 38:21: And I will call for a sword against him throughout all my mountains, saith the Lord**

GOD: every man's sword shall be against his brother.

God has also previously used a nation such as Babylon or Assyria to come against Israel for false worship. Will the nations come against the houses of God as a judgment? There is one thing the Bible makes clear and that is God will be magnified in the eyes of the nations:

> **Ezekiel 38:23: Thus will I magnify myself, and sanctify myself; and I will be known in the eyes of many nations, and they shall know that I *am* the LORD.**

God also uses a spiritual *fire* as a judgment. The language of God sending a fire upon the palaces, I believe is a historical picture of the spiritual fire which comes on the fallen houses of God:

> **Amos 1:12: But I will send a fire upon Teman, which shall devour the palaces of Bozrah.**

One reason for this judgment is the pursuing and mistreatment of their brothers:

> **Amos 1:11: Thus saith the LORD; For three transgressions of Edom, and for four, I will not turn away *the punishment* thereof; <u>because he did pursue his brother with the sword</u>, and did cast off all pity, and his anger did tear perpetually, and he kept his wrath for ever...**

Much of the language in Amos 1 is spiritual, such as *sword,* which can represent the Word of God. The misuse of God's Word as a *sword* is a common problem coming from some "evangelists" today. We know the *fire* God sends is spiritual since the Bible says that the *people work and weary*

387

themselves for vanity in the *fire*. The online YouTube video, *Is this Fire from God?* shows this kind of strange activity:

> **Habakkuk 2:12: Woe to him that buildeth a town with blood, and stablisheth a city by iniquity! 13: Behold, _is it_ not of the LORD of hosts that the people shall labour in the very fire, and the people shall weary themselves for very vanity? 14: For the earth shall be filled with the knowledge of the glory of the LORD, as the waters cover the sea.**

The book of Revelation also speaks of *fallen Babylon* which has become a *habitation of devils*. This in itself is a judgment and the reason Jesus commands His people to: *come out of her my people*. This command by Christ should be taken seriously.

> **Revelation 18:4: And I heard another voice from heaven, saying, Come out of her, my people, that ye be not partakers of her sins, and that ye receive not of her plagues. 5: For her sins have reached unto heaven, and God hath remembered her iniquities.**

Chapter 14 is a review of what the believers in Christ can know about His glorious return on the *last day*. We explored the reason why the houses of God in their current state hide from the topic of the coming of Christ. The isolation and use of *but of that day and hour knoweth no man,* which for the most part is misquoted, has become a wall of defense against seriously looking at the topic of the coming of Christ on the *last day*.

There are some things I did not mention in chapter 14 which I do feel needs to be presented in this book. God always seems to warn a couple years before His judgment comes to pass. I believe the houses of God today are sleeping the sleep of drunkenness, which God mentions in Jeremiah 51. We know that once *peace and safety* are proclaimed, then comes sudden destruction:

> **1Thessalonians 5:1: But of the times and the seasons, brethren, ye have no need that I write unto you. 2: For yourselves know perfectly that the day of the Lord so cometh as a thief in the night. 3: For when they shall say, Peace and safety; then sudden destruction cometh upon them, as travail upon a woman with child; and they shall not escape.**

In Jeremiah 51, there is language of a *perpetual sleep* which comes as a judgment:

> **Jeremiah 51:39: In their heat I will make their feasts, and I will make them drunken, that they may rejoice, and sleep a perpetual sleep, and not wake, saith the LORD.**

This *perpetual sleep* may be the reason why the declaration of *no man knows the day or hour* is an unceasing repetition by some pastors. Unfortunately, they have mostly adopted John Darby's late 1800's fable, so they are not looking for the coming of Christ on the *last day* in *power and great glory*. Jesus cannot return at any time; judgment must first come upon the fallen houses of God. This judgment arrives prior to Jesus coming on the *last day*. This is all part of the judgment process that God has spoken of in His Word.

Daniel and the apostles are our examples in showing interest and looking for the coming of the Lord. Daniel asked questions and God gave him understanding. The disciples asked Christ upon the Mount of Olives concerning the *sign of*

His coming and *the end of the world* (age). Jesus gave much information to the disciples, and this information is for us to learn from. Furthermore, the real focus in the Gospels is that we are to be watching, since of ourselves we do not know of the *day* or *hour*. If we are watching then God will give us *meat* in *due season*.

We watch because Christ commanded us to watch. We watch for the following reasons:

- To know when the thief comes and when to flee out of the fallen houses of God
- To warn fellow believers of God's coming judgment
- So the Lord can give us *meat* (understanding of God's Word) in *due season*
- To *shine* (warn, admonish, enlighten) as the firmament in the heavens
- To obey the Lord from Heaven who commands us to watch

Mark 13:34: *For the Son of man is* as a man taking a far journey, who left his house, and gave authority to his servants, and to every man his work, and commanded the porter to watch. 35: Watch ye therefore: for ye know not when the master of the house cometh, at even, or at midnight, or at the cockcrowing, or in the morning: 36: Lest coming suddenly he find you sleeping. 37: <u>And what I say unto you I say unto all, Watch.</u>

Luke 12:37: Blessed *are* those servants, whom the lord when he cometh shall find watching: verily I say unto you, that he shall gird himself, and make

them to sit down to meat, and will come forth and serve them.

Jesus comes *like a thief* for those who are not watching:

> **Revelation 3:3: Remember therefore how thou hast received and heard, and hold fast, and repent. <u>If therefore thou shalt not watch</u>, I will come on thee as a thief, and <u>thou shalt not know</u> what hour I will come upon thee.**

> **Luke 12:38: And <u>if he shall come in the second watch, or come in the third watch</u>, and find *them* so, blessed are those servants.**

> **Psalm 90:4: For a thousand years in thy sight *are but* as yesterday when it is past, <u>and *as* a watch in the night</u>.**

Two notable topics Jesus mentioned was who will know the *times and seasons*, and also when the restoration of *Israel* will be. It was not for the disciples to know the *times and seasons* which the Father has placed in His power. It was also not after the time of the cross in which God would restore the kingdom to *Israel* (the body of believers). We know that the restoration was not for the time of 33 A.D. in which the disciples asked this question of Jesus. Christ commanded them to go forth and be witnesses of Him unto the uttermost part of the earth:

> **Acts 1:7: And he said unto them, <u>It is not for you to know the times or the seasons, which the Father hath put in his own power</u>. 8: But ye shall receive power, after that the Holy Ghost is come upon you: and ye shall be witnesses unto me both in**

Jerusalem, and in all Judaea, and in Samaria, and unto the uttermost part of the earth.

The restoration of the kingdom to God's people can only come once Satan is removed. Jesus knew what Satan would do near the time of the end. Therefore, the timing of this important restoration was way out of the reach of the disciples in the year 33 A.D. This restoration will come in the year 2015 as the believers will *consume and destroy* once the *judgment shall sit* and the believers take back the kingdom (Daniel 7:26-27). In other words, the restoration of the kingdom to *Israel* (believers in Christ) would only come at a precise time in history. We are soon approaching that time in history.

In Chapter 15, we looked at the important numbers in the Bible. God established numbers in the Bible for a reason. Jesus was the one who proclaimed that we forgive 70 x 7, which produces the number 490. Both 490 and 49 are special numbers. Seventy years and seven years are also the times of *tribulation* and *great tribulation* in the Old Testament. These *tribulation* examples are repeated as shorter *tribulation* periods near the end with seven representing the final seven years.

The numbers of 153 and the factors of 3 x 3 x 17 show the importance of salvation and the feeding of Christ's sheep. This command given to Peter by Jesus is carried out by believers after the 153 days from May 21, 2011 to October 21, 2011. This book is part of the feeding of God's sheep as we all join together in sharing this information. A very important aspect of the final seven years is feeding Christ's sheep by presenting information God has revealed.

We also looked at any possible years within the years 2011-2018 which would present a possibility of Christ's return in *power and great glory*. The conclusion was that 2018 is the most likely year for Christ's return.

In this final chapter we explored some very important topics such as when the temple was finished in the 6th year of Darius, the Mordecai and Esther connection, and the importance of the month Adar (to enlarge). The temple was finished in the month of Adar in the 6th year of Darius. The final seven months in the year 2018 that lead to the Feast of Tabernacles (October 2, 2018) seem to be extremely related to the *beautification of the temple*. God uses the language of how He *beautifies the meek* with salvation. Therefore, we can know salvation will go right up to the last day of the Feast of Tabernacles in the upcoming and anticipated year of 2018 (October 2, 2018). The work of Nehemiah and Ezra were important in the rebuilding of Jerusalem and the temple. In our day, it is God who will build the wall of salvation and cause people to understand His *statutes and judgments*:

> **Isaiah 26:1: In that day shall this song be sung in the land of Judah; We have a strong city; salvation will *God* appoint *for* walls and bulwarks.**

> **Ezekiel 36:26: A new heart also will I give you, and a new spirit will I put within you: and I will take away the stony heart out of your flesh, and I will give you an heart of flesh. 27: And I will put my spirit within you, and cause you to walk in my statutes, and ye shall keep my judgments, and do *them*.**

The very works that Nehemiah and Ezra performed are now the works of God Himself in these final years. He will build the wall of salvation and He will cause His people to walk in His statutes and keep His judgments.

This book has been an ongoing study these past seven months. Studying and learning more about the *rumor* that Satan hears was another important piece of this endless seam of truth woven throughout God's Word. How God relates Cyrus the Great to "my shepherd" is a dramatic illustration of how Christ's power (as the good shepherd) will rule the world. We can know that Satan in all his delusion will attempt to stand up against the *Prince of Princes* and he will be broken without hand (power). Praise God for His power.

The Significance of Biblical Numbers and Numbers in Parables

One- There is one body, one Spirit, one hope, one faith, one Lord, one baptism, one God and Father of all (Ephesians 4: 4-6).

Two- Two represents the witness of Christ and establishing of God's truth. Jesus sent forth the disciples two by two. Out of the mouth of two or three witnesses, God's Word is established (Mark 18:16). Two can also represent a doubling or the fullness of time. Jesus came in the fullness of time— 11,006 years past creation or 2 x 5,503 years. God divided the waters from the waters on the second day of creation. The *two anointed ones* which stand by the God of the whole earth represent God's Word. When *they* are resurrected, God's Word becomes powerful (Revelation 11:11).

Three- This is the number of the Trinity—the Father, the Word (Jesus is the Word who became flesh), and the Holy Spirit; these three are one (1 John 5:7). Three is also seen many times at the event of the Cross in 33 A.D. At the trial of Jesus, three times the crowd shouted *crucify him*. Two men plus Jesus were crucified to total three. There were three inscriptions above the cross. Jesus was betrayed for 30 pieces of silver (3 x 10). Three women came to anoint the body on resurrection morning. The number three seems to mean the purpose of God. Daniel lamented three full weeks in which the number 21 is shown to be a time of waiting (21 days or three full weeks) before God gives understanding. Jesus' ministry was 3 ½ years. The *time, times and half a time* (3 ½ years) is also the time Satan is allowed before God judges evil. This precise time period, which is half of seven years, is highly related to the years 2011 to 2015. God repeats many times: *for three transgressions and for four, I will not turn away* (see Amos chapter 1).

Four- The number four and the meaning of universal or worldwide go hand in hand in the Bible. God gathers His elect from the four winds (Mark 13:27). Before Lazarus' resurrection, he was in the tomb four days. Satan goes forth into the *four quarters of the earth* to deceive during the final years (Revelation 20:8). God sends a *breath* from the *four winds* to revive the slain of the dry bones so that they may live (Ezekiel 37:9).

In Genesis 2, the river of Eden, which watered the garden, was separated and became four heads: Piyshon, Gihon, Hiddekel and Perath (Euphrates). There were four horns of the gentiles who scattered Jerusalem, Judah, and Israel, and four carpenters who came to fray or make afraid the four horns (Zechariah 1:18-21). The four horns that scatter and the four carpenters that rebuild represent a universal illustration of the mighty rebuilding of God's eternal house in the last days. This comes after a time of desolation.

Five- Certain Biblical numbers have a dual meaning. The number 5 can mean judgment or salvation, wise and unwise, etc... This is seen with the five wise virgins who had oil for their lamps and the five foolish who did not have enough oil for their lamps. Since there were ten virgins, this is a grand picture of the times of *tribulation* (8,400 days) and also the final seven years.

When the cry was made to go out and meet the bridegroom the five wise virgins had enough oil and the five foolish virgins were told to go and buy from those who *buy and sell*. Jesus used this parable to illustrate how we must be *watching*. His Words at the end of this parable were: *watch therefore...* (Matthew 25:13). The people who were in the temple of Jesus' day were *buying and selling.* Are the majority of people in the churches watching for Christ's return, or are they being told *no man knows the day or hour?* Are the church leaders too busy "marketing" within the houses of God? We can know who the wise and foolish are by reading Matthew 7. In that parable, those who cry Lord, Lord are those that work iniquity (see also Hosea 6:8). We must be watching and bringing the Gospel. If it requires that we depart out of the fallen houses of God, then we depart out in order to be watching (by Jesus' command).

In Acts chapters three and four, as Peter was preaching to the people to repent (think differently) and convert, many of the 5,000 believed. The five barley loaves that fed the multitude also represents Christ's compassion and salvation (John 6:13). Revelation 9:5 speaks of the five months of torment or vexing by the evil that comes forth from the *bottomless pit.* So there are illustrations of the number five representing both salvation and judgment.

Six- Since man was created on the sixth day, the number six seems related to mankind. God began the flood at the 600th year of Noah's life. Since violence filled the earth and it grieved God that He had created man, the 600th year of Noah's life seems significant.

Parable Involving the Number 6- When Jesus turned the water into wine; it involved six water pots that were for the purifying/cleansing of the Jews. Purifying from sins is spoken of in Hebrews 1:3. This is what happened when Jesus' *hour* of His arrest, trial, and cleansing of our sins by His blood had come. Christ's focus was on the purification of His people.

Jesus' mother was at this wedding in Cana of Galilee; she had informed Jesus that there was no more wine. Jesus' response was focused on *His hour* of payment for the sins of His people: *woman, what have I to do with thee? my hour has not yet come.* At first blush that may seem like an odd response Jesus gave to His mother; however, Jesus was really focusing on the purification from sins by changing the six water pots into wine (which represented the cleansing by His blood for His people). Jesus was also focusing on *His hour*. We can know this because Jesus prayed to the Father to save Him from *the hour* which had come (John 12:27).

Jesus gave the command to <u>draw out</u> the water that had been turned into wine. The word *draw* is *antleo* (G501) and is used four times in the New Testament. *Antleo* was used in this wedding feast miracle of Christ. The servants knew where this wine came from.

However, the governor of the feast did not know but was duly impressed that the *good wine* from Jesus was saved for last. The credit went to the bridegroom of the wedding, but the servants of Jesus know that He is truly the bridegroom and His bride is the body of believers worldwide. This was an incredible foreshadowing of what the blood of Christ being shed would do for His people.

The second time this Greek word *antleo* (draw forth) is used is in association with the Samaritan women at the well whom Jesus asked for water from. After Jesus taught her about the true water of life, she ended up requesting the *water of life* in which Jesus alone can provide. Her witness to the Samaritans, after Jesus stayed with the Samaritans for two days, caused many to believe on Jesus' Words.

John 4:15: The woman saith unto him, Sir, give me this water, that I thirst not, neither come hither to draw.

Seven- God rested on the seventh day. The year 2011 was the 7,000[th] anniversary of the flood in 4990 B.C. When we add 7 more years and arrive at the year 2018, there will have been 7,007 years since the flood. The prime factors for 7,007 are 7 x 7 x 11 x 13. All of these numbers are significant Biblical numbers relating to the coming of Christ.

There were originally seven churches that Christ addressed in the book of Revelation. This was a representation of all churches as the number seven can represent completeness or fullness.

The times of *tribulation* involve the 70-year period of Judah's captivity and the 7-year period of *great tribulation*, which is from 2011 to 2018 and is the mirror of Jacob's *great tribulation*.

God gave Noah a final 7-day warning before the flood began (Genesis 7:4). God uses the same *seven standard* since we are now living within the final seven years of history.

Ezekiel stood stunned with the people of the captivity for seven days by the river Chebar. After seven days God instructed him to be a watchman for the house of Israel. This can represent those who are warning the houses of God of impending judgment coming after the 7,000[th] year anniversary of the flood in the year 2011.

In the wilderness Jesus fed the multitude with seven loaves and a few fish. Seven angels have the seven last plaques according to Revelation 15:1. The stone (*eben*) laid before Joshua had *seven eyes* and represented God removing the iniquity of the land in one day. In Revelation 5:6 the lamb slain (Jesus) had the spiritual *seven eyes,* which are the seven spirits that go forth into the entire world. This represents God's complete salvation being accomplished as also mentioned in Zechariah 4:10:

> **Zechariah 4:10: For <u>who hath despised the day of small things</u>? for they shall rejoice, and shall see the plummet in the hand of Zerubbabel *with* those seven; they *are* the eyes of the LORD, which run to and fro through the whole earth.**

Since Zechariah 4 also relates to the two candle sticks/olives branches which stand by the God of the whole earth, I suspect the year 2015 will usher in the final great time of worldwide salvation. The two witnesses of Revelation, which are the two olives branches, stand upon their feet after *3 ½ days*. God's Word will be very powerful in the final 3 ½ years from the year 2015 and leading up to the year 2018. Will seven years complete the time of God's longsuffering from 2011 to 2018?

Jesus told His disciples that they were to forgive 70 x 7 times. This may represent the times of *tribulation,* with the seven being the final seven years of *great tribulation.* It can also represent the number 490. The seventy weeks of Daniel 9 show the number 490 (70 sevens = 490):

> **Daniel 9:24: Seventy weeks are determined upon thy people and upon thy holy city, to finish the transgression, and to make an end of sins, and to make reconciliation for iniquity, and to bring in everlasting righteousness, and to seal up the vision and prophecy, and to anoint the most Holy.**

God will bring in *everlasting righteousness* during the final week (seven years). However, this comes after the *overspreading of abominations* in the fallen houses of God.

Eight- The eight souls saved by water (Noah and his family) represent the baptism by God's Spirit that saves people:

> **1 Peter 3:20: Which sometime were disobedient, when once the longsuffering of God waited in the days of Noah, while the ark was a preparing, wherein few, that is, <u>eight souls were saved by water. 21: The like figure whereunto *even* baptism doth also now save us </u>(not the putting away of the filth of the flesh, but the answer of a good conscience toward God,) by the resurrection of Jesus Christ.**

Ten, One Hundred, One Thousand- Many verses with the numbers of 10, 100, 1,000, etc... show completeness of what God has in view. In Revelation 2:10, God uses 10 days to show a completeness of *tribulation*. In Revelation 20:7 the 1,000 years also shows God's completeness. There are 1,000 generations, 1,000 hills, and 10,000 *saints* mentioned in the Bible:

> **1 Chronicles 16:15: Be ye mindful always of his covenant; the word *which* he commanded <u>to a thousand generations</u>...**

> **Psalm 50:10: For every beast of the forest *is* mine, *and* <u>the cattle upon a thousand hills.</u>**

> **Jude 1:14: And Enoch also, <u>the seventh</u> from Adam, prophesied of these, saying, Behold, <u>the Lord cometh with ten thousands of his saints</u>...**

Eleven- The number eleven shows up many times as Biblical factors. For instance the 77 generations of Jesus would be 7 x 11. This number seems to be related to Christ's coming. In the 99th (9 x 11) year of Abram's life, God appeared to him and promised him that He would multiply him exceedingly (Genesis 17:1). The Abrahamic covenant represents the completed work of Jesus and the salvation of His people. The promise includes all who would believe on Jesus and His resurrection from the dead. This is why Paul introduced David also as one whose sins were forgiven.

God forgives the iniquity of His people and brings back the *captivity of Jacob*:

> **Psalm 85:2: Thou hast forgiven the iniquity of thy people, thou hast covered all their sin. Selah.**

Concerning David:

> **Romans 4:6: Even as David also describeth the blessedness of the man, unto whom God imputeth righteousness without works, 7: *Saying,* Blessed *are* they whose iniquities are forgiven, and whose sins are covered.**

Concerning the promise given to Abraham:

> **Romans 4:23: Now it was not written for his sake alone, that it was imputed to him; 24: <u>But for us also, to whom it shall be imputed</u>, if we believe on him that raised up Jesus our Lord from the dead...**

Let's review the factors from the date of creation (11,013 B.C.) to the year 2011 A.D. (the grand announcement of Judgment Day). If we add 2,011 years to the creation date of 11,013 B.C. there are 13,023 years (3 x 3 x 1,447). If we do the same with the year 2018 (11,013 plus 2018 and less one year since there is no year zero) it is 13,030 years or 10 x 1303. I became interested in the year 7 B.C. since it is 11,006 years from creation. The number 11,006 (2 x 5,503) may be significant since the Bible speaks of the coming of Jesus as *the fullness of time*. From Jesus' birth in 7 B.C. to 2018 A.D. there are 2,024 years or (2 x 1,012).

The Bible uses both phrases of the *fullness of time* and the *fullness of times* (plural). It does seem that the *fullness of time* relates to the first coming of Christ and the *fullness of times* (plural) relates to the gathering of the believers in heaven with the believers who are on earth. This is why it is possible that the *fullness of times* could be from 7 B.C. to 2018 A.D. or 2,024 years (2 x 1012). The *fullness of times* may very well relate to God's set seasons/feasts and the fullness of these feasts:

> **Ephesians 1:9: Having made known unto us the mystery of his will, according to his good pleasure which he hath purposed in himself: 10: That <u>in the dispensation of the fulness of times he might gather together in one all things in Christ, both which are in heaven, and which are on earth</u>;** *even* **in him: 11: In whom also we have obtained an inheritance, being predestinated according to the purpose of him who worketh all things after the counsel of his own will: 12: That we should be to the praise of his glory, who first trusted in Christ. 13: In whom ye also** *trusted*, **after that ye heard the word of truth, the gospel of your salvation: in whom also after that ye believed, <u>ye were sealed with that holy Spirit of promise</u>...**

The *fullness of times* (plural) is related to the times and seasons that the believers in the final years will understand. The fullness of seasons (times) is related to these following verses from 1 Thessalonians 5:

> **1 Thessalonians 5:1: But of the times and <u>the seasons</u>, brethren, ye have no need that I write unto you. 2: <u>For yourselves know perfectly that the day of the Lord so cometh as a thief in the night.</u> 3: For when they shall say, Peace and safety; then sudden destruction cometh upon them, as travail upon a woman with child; and they shall not escape. 4: But ye, brethren, are not in darkness, that that day should overtake you as a thief. 5: Ye are all the children of light, and the children of the day: we are not of the night, nor of darkness. 6: <u>Therefore let us not sleep, as *do* others; but let us watch and be sober</u>.**

<u>11,000 as a Number</u>

From the start of the first *tribulation* period (May 21, 1988) to last day of the Feast of Tabernacles in 2018 (October 2, 2018), which includes the 3 ½ years of *great tribulation*, there are 11,092 days. The number 11,000 is again featured in the second coming of Christ, much like it was featured at His birth in 7 B.C., which was 11, 006 years past creation. When we go to the last day of the Feast of Tabernacles, there are an extra 91 days (7 x 13) past the 11,000th day. There are 92 days (4 x 23) if we include the last day of the Feast of Tabernacles—October 2, 2018.

Twelve- Like the number seven, the number 12 is seen repeatedly in God's Word. God uses the number 12 to show fullness, for example, the 12 disciples, the 12 tribes of Israel, and the 12 gates with 12 pearls. There were 12 disciples and one was lost (Judas, the son of perdition). Judas was replaced soon after his death by the casting of lots by the disciples. The lot fell upon Matthias and he was numbered with the eleven. I believe God's hand was in this choosing of Matthias since Paul had to become the 13th apostle sent unto the gentiles. The number 144,000 is a spiritual number (not literal) that shows the fullness of God's elect (12 x 12 x 1,000). We see this fullness with the 12 foundations of the wall of the city spoken of in Revelation 21:14. The jubilee year of 1994 was 2,000 years after the birth of Jesus, and from 1994 to 2018 there are 24 years (2 x 12).

Thirteen- Thirteen in the Bible can represent the overflowing of fullness or the fullness of the gentiles. There were twelve apostles (delegates sent by God), but even after Judas was replaced after his death, Paul considered himself an apostle. He said that he was the least of the apostles because he previously persecuted the church of God; nevertheless, he was a delegate sent to the Gentiles by Jesus:

> **1 Corinthians 15:8: And last of all he was seen of me also, as of one born out of due time. 9: For I am the least of the apostles, that am not meet to be called an apostle, because I persecuted the church of God. 10: But by the grace of God I am what I am: and his grace which *was bestowed* upon me was not in vain; <u>but I laboured more abundantly than they all: yet not I, but the grace of God which was with me.</u>**

I have often wondered, since Paul would have been the 13th apostle sent by Jesus, if a repetition of his ministry to the gentiles would also be seen in a great way after the 13,000 year anniversary (1988) since creation. There are verses which indicate that the *nations* will say *let us go up to the mountain of the Lord* (Isaiah 2:3). This will result in great salvation of the people of the gentile nations, completing the work which Paul began as a delegate to the gentiles. We can know the timing of this great time of salvation due to the language of *in the last days*. This represents the time in which we are all living:

> **Micah 4:1: But <u>in the last days</u> it shall come to pass, *that* the mountain of the house of the LORD shall be established in the top of the mountains, and it shall be exalted above the hills; and people shall flow unto it.**

<u>Fourteen & Forty Two</u>- The number 14 is the number seven doubled and is seen in association with God blessing Job double. This doubling of Job's possessions came after the attack from Satan. Seven thousand sheep became fourteen thousand sheep. I believe the doubling Job received is somehow related to the salvation of people worldwide in the last years of history. Job and Elijah are our examples of *unto the coming of the Lord.* Job's endurance can be an illustration of Satan's final attack during the *time, times and half a time* (3 ½ years—2011 to 2015). The number 14 is also seen in association with the Feast of Tabernacles because at this feast 14 lambs were sacrificed (Numbers 29:13).

There were 14 generations from Abraham to David, 14 generations from David to the carrying away into Babylon, and 14 generations from the carrying away into Babylon unto Christ. Therefore, we have 42 generations: 14 + 14 + 14 = 42.

The number 42 is known as the *time, times and half a time* or 3 ½ years as 12 + 12 + 12 + 6 months = 42 months. Both Revelation 11:2 and 13:5 speak of this time where Satan engages in great blasphemies. The court of the temple and the holy city are given unto the gentiles. This can be a picture of how the houses of God are overrun by *gentiles*. The churches will be trampled underfoot. Satan was very active at the time of Christ as Herod and later Satan himself attempted to thwart God's salvation plan. In this sense, all of the *14 generations* can be an encapsulation of the times of *captivity* and the *great tribulation* of 3 ½ years (another focus on 42 will be explored in a dedicated section for the number 42).

Fifteen- The number 15 is seen in connection with the flood. The waters increased and prevailed for 150 (15 x 10) days. The waters also rose 15 (3 x 5) cubits above the highest mountain. Since the number 15 has 5 as a factor, we can see how both judgment and salvation are related to the flood:

> **1 Peter 3:18: For Christ also hath once suffered for sins, the just for the unjust, that he might bring us to God, being put to death in the flesh, but quickened by the Spirit: 19: By which also he went and preached unto the spirits in prison; 20: Which sometime were disobedient, when once the longsuffering of God waited in the days of Noah, while the ark was a preparing, wherein few, that is, eight souls were saved by water. 21: <u>The like figure whereunto *even* baptism doth also now save us (not the putting away of the filth of the flesh, but the answer of a good conscience toward God,) by the resurrection of Jesus Christ...</u>**

So the number 15 was associated with the flood. There was also a 15-year extension period of Hezekiah's life. Again, there is both mercy and judgment seen with Hezekiah and Jerusalem. God's hand forced Sennacherib, the King of Assyria, back to his land with shame. Hezekiah's heart was lifted up and he became sick. He then humbled himself and wept great tears as he pleaded with God. God then added 15 years to his life. In this instance, 15 (3 x 5) was a number of God's mercy.

Seventeen- The number 17 is a very significant Biblical number. It is a prime number and, therefore, shows no factors. It is, however, a factor of 153 (3 x 3 x 17). The number 153 is very important in relation to the catching of great fish by the disciples. I really believe the Bible illustrates the number 17 as a number of salvation or times of salvation. The disciples were called to be *fishers of men*. When the disciples decided to go fishing in John 21, they did not catch any fish as they fished the Sea of Galilee (Tiberius).

Peter was the one who said: *I go a fishing*, and the other disciples followed. On the boat were Peter, Thomas, Nathanael of Cana, the sons of Zebedee (James and John), and two other disciples. There were seven in total, including Peter who began this fishing expedition. They fished all night until the morning at which time Jesus stood by the shore and asked the disciples if they had caught anything. When they answered no, Jesus commanded them to cast forth their net on the right side of the boat. It was John who recognized that it was Jesus, and then he told Peter who it was. Jesus commanded them to bring the fish which they had caught. Peter then drags to shore the net full of *153 great fishes*.

Jesus asked them all to *come and dine*. It was there that Jesus asked Peter if he loved Him. The command to *feed my sheep* and *feed my lambkins* is very significant. In the year 2011, from May 21 (anniversary of the flood) to October 21 (the last day of Tabernacles), there were 153 days. I believe this was a time of great salvation since it was Jesus who initiated the call to *cast forth the net on the right side*. The 153 days was the beginning of a time to feed Christ's sheep and newly born-again *lambs*. The entire final seven years is a time of feeding God's sheep.

God's Spirit saves people, but God also gives teachers to feed His flock. I have been learning so much about this present time of God's longsuffering from 2 Peter chapter 3. Peter pointed us to what Paul understood. In this sense, Peter is still *feeding God's sheep*. His instruction to us has been a great blessing in knowing why we passed the year 2011 at the 7,000[th] year anniversary of the flood.

From the time of the cross in 33 A.D. to 1988 (the 13,000 year anniversary of creation), there were 1,955 years (5 x 17 x 23). God saved many during those years represented by the number 17. Then we get to the start of the first *tribulation* period in 1988 represented by the number 23, which is a number of judgment. The number 17 really seems to underscore the times of salvation. We gather this from the book of Jeremiah when he purchased the field of Anathoth for 17 shekels of silver. The *right of inheritance* and the *right of redemption* was Jeremiah's to purchase the land (Jeremiah 32:8-9).

King David understood this heritage/inheritance as we observe from Psalm 61:5-6:

> **Psalm 61:5: For thou, O God, hast heard my vows: <u>thou hast given *me* the heritage</u> of those that fear thy name. 6: Thou wilt prolong the king's life: *and his years as many generations.***

The believer's inheritance through Christ is eternal life. What could be more exciting or of greater value than eternal life? David understood this truth and sung praises to God. Peter understood this and blessed God; Paul understood this great inheritance and rejoiced even in tribulation. This inheritance of life everlasting will never fade away:

> **1 Peter 1:3: Blessed *be* the God and Father of our Lord Jesus Christ, which according to his abundant mercy hath begotten us again unto a lively hope by the resurrection of Jesus Christ from the dead, 4: <u>To an inheritance incorruptible, and undefiled, and that fadeth not away, reserved in heaven for you...</u>**

Below are a couple of examples of how 17 shows up as a factor in important time spans. Keep in mind that 2015 is the year in which the $1,335^{th}$ day will be reached—a time of great salvation similar to Pentecost in 33 A.D.

- May 21, 2011 (end of the 8,400 day *tribulation* and also the $7,000^{th}$ year anniversary of the flood) to October 21, 2011 (last day of the Feast of Tabernacles) = 153 days or 3 x 3 x 17.
- 587 B.C. (destruction of Jerusalem by the King of Babylon) to 2015 A.D. (judgment on the houses of God and also the duplication of Pentecost worldwide) = 2,601 years or 17 x 153 (also 3 x 17 x 3 x 17).
- 7 B.C. (birth of Christ in Bethlehem) to 2017 A.D. (one year before the final seventh year) = 2,023 years or 7 x 17 x 17.

Eighteen- The number 18 can be associated with being vexed and bound. The ruler of the synagogue accused Jesus of healing on the Sabbath. Jesus, responding to the ruler of the synagogue whom He called a hypocrite, stated the following:

> **Luke 13:16: And ought not this woman, being a daughter of Abraham, <u>whom Satan hath bound,</u>**

410

lo, these eighteen years, be loosed from this bond on the sabbath day?

The children of Israel did evil in the sight of the Lord and served Eglon the King of Moab for 18 years. When the children of Israel served other gods and not the Lord, God sent enemies to vex and oppress the Israelites who lived in the land of the Amorites for 18 years:

> **Judges 10:7: And the anger of the LORD was hot against Israel, and he sold them into the hands of the Philistines, and into the hands of the children of Ammon. 8: And that year they vexed and oppressed the children of Israel: eighteen years, all the children of Israel that *were* on the other side Jordan in the land of the Amorites, which *is* in Gilead.**

There is one other aspect of the number 18. The number 666 is well known for representing the time in which Satan rules. The 23-year *tribulation* period (8,400 days) and the *time, times and half a time* (3 ½ years) are both periods in which Satan causes desolation. The latter is considered to be the *last end of the indignation*. The number 666 shows 18 x 37 as factors. Both 18 (bound and vexed by the enemy) and 37 (a number which can represent judgment) are not good numbers, especially in the case of the number 666.

> **Revelation 13:18: Here is wisdom. Let him that hath understanding count the number of the beast: for it *is* the number of a man; and his number is Six hundred threescore *and* six.**

Twenty One- Daniel waited three full weeks for understanding. I believe the number 21 can be important in the two tribulations periods of the end. God gives

411

understanding during these important times of tribulation as well as the time of Judah's captivity:

> **Daniel 10:13: But the prince of the kingdom of Persia withstood me one and <u>twenty days</u>: but, lo, Michael, one of the chief princes, came to help me; and I remained there with the kings of Persia. 14: Now I am come to make thee understand what shall befall thy people in the latter days: for yet the vision *is* for *many* days.**

It has been my experience that God reveals more and more during precise times in history. After the 8,400 days, which ended May 21, 2011, much more information concerning the final seven years came forth.

8,400 days = 4 x 2,100

1994 (a Jubilee year) to 2015 = 21 years

I really believe that the 21 years from the jubilee year of 1994 to the year 2015 is a time of God revealing more truth from His Word. The latter rain of understanding in the year 2015 will help many people worldwide to understand God's Word.

<u>**Twenty Three**</u>- A number of judgment or desolation:

- In Daniel 8:14 God speaks of the time of 2,300 *evening mornings* until the sanctuary is cleansed (made righteous).
- In 1 Corinthians 10:8, 23,000 fell in the wilderness in one day.
- There were 4,600 (2 x 2,300) Israelites that went into captivity in the 23rd year of Nebuchadrezzar.
- The first *tribulation* period (1988-2011) = 23 years or 8,400 days.

- From 7 B.C (Jesus' birth) to 2018 (the most probable year for Jesus' return in *power and great glory*) there are 2,024 years or 2 x 2 x 2 x 11 x 23.

The Numbers 37 and 43- In the book, *Time has an End*[25], there is a noteworthy chart called: *Important Time Interval Relationships*. This chart shows important time intervals from one key Biblical date to another key Biblical date. There, Camping lists the following time intervals with their factors:

- From the time Sodom was destroyed and Isaac was born in 2067 B.C. to the destruction of Judah in 587 B.C. there are 1,480 years or 2 x 2 x 10 x 37.
- From the time Israel leaves Egypt in 1447 B.C. to the cross of Christ and the beginning of the church age in 33 A.D. there are 1,480 years or 2 x 2 x 10 x 37.

The factor 37 can show both judgment and salvation since both the judgment at the time of Jesus' crucifixion and Pentecost occurred in 33 A.D. Likewise, the factor 43 can also show judgment and salvation:

- From the time Israel enters Egypt in 1877 B.C. to the time Israel leaves Egypt in 1447 B.C. there are 430 years or 10 x 43.
- From the time Judah is destroyed in 587 B.C. to 1994 A.D. (Jubilee year) there are 2,580 years or 3 x 2 x 10 x 43.

God's salvation and judgment unfolds throughout history.

Forty- When found in the Bible, the number 40 underscores a time of testing. There were 40 days and 40 nights of rain during the flood; Moses spent 40 days and 40 nights with the Lord as he received the commandments on Mt. Sinai. With the murmuring Israelites there were 40 years of wilderness sojourn. Numbers 14:34 uses the *day-for-a-year principle*:

> **Numbers 14:34: After the number of the days in which ye searched the land, *even* forty days, each day for a year, shall ye bear your iniquities, _even forty years_, and ye shall know my breach of promise.**

Forty stripes were allowed by the law as spoken of in Deuteronomy 25. The number 40 is highlighted when Paul was judged by the Jews:

> **2 Corinthians 11:24: Of the Jews five times received I forty *stripes* save one.**

Having abstained from food, Jesus was tempted in the wilderness for 40 days and 40 nights. Israel was delivered into the hand of the Philistines forty years:

> **Judges 13:1: And the children of Israel did evil again in the sight of the LORD; and the LORD delivered them into the hand of the Philistines forty years.**

Forty two- Much like the number 23, the number 42 can represent a time of tribulation in the Bible. The 42 months (3 ½ years) spoken of in Revelation is related to *the time, times and half a time* or 3 ½ years of the *last end of the indignation*. It is during this time that Satan has great wrath and goes to take away a great many:

Revelation 13:5: And there was given unto him a mouth speaking great things and blasphemies; and _power was given unto him to continue forty _and_ two months_.

During this time Satan works through other people who have been transformed into *ministers of righteousness* who speak blasphemies while lifting themselves up to be as God. This *last end of the indignation* is also the time in which Satan wages war on the believers to overcome them. The good news is that after the 3 ½ years (the year 2015) the believers are given back the kingdom of God, and then we *consume and destroy* the kingdom of Satan unto the end.

Revelation 13: 5 and the following verses are speaking of the same period of time as we approach the reversal in the year 2015:

> **Daniel 7:25: And he shall speak *great* words against the most High, and shall wear out the saints of the most High, and think to change times and laws: and they shall be given into his hand until a time and times and the dividing of time. 26: But the judgment shall sit, and <u>they shall take away his dominion</u>, to consume and to destroy *it* unto the end. 27: <u>And the kingdom and dominion, and the greatness of the kingdom under the whole heaven, shall be given to the people of the saints of the most High</u>, whose kingdom *is* an everlasting kingdom, and all dominions shall serve and obey him.**

In one sense the number 42, which is half of 84, can represent times of *tribulation*. The 8,400 days, which ended on May 21, 2011, was patterned after the 840 months or Judah's 70-year captivity. While the final seven years from 2011 to 2018 are patterned after the *great affliction* of Joseph's time in Egypt (7 years of famine), God, in His mercy, has shortened the *great tribulation* to 3 ½ years ending in the year 2015. The year 2015 is significant since this seems to be the timing of the believers regaining the kingdom to *consume and destroy* Satan's dominion. Doesn't that sound incredible? Truly, this is one of the most important truths concerning the final years prior to Christ's coming on the *last day.*

It is also significant how God uses the number 42 with the prophet Elisha who received a double portion of Elijah's spirit by the hand of God. 2 Kings 2 describes how Elisha was mocked by children, and then two bears came out of the woods and tare 42 of the children. Why would this mocking and the number 42 be featured with the prophet Elisha? This historical account truly may be pointing us to the judgment which takes place after the 42 months, the *time, times and half a time* or 3 ½ years, which ends in the year 2015. There was mocking that came after the 8,400 days (after May 21, 2011), and the number 8,400 is 42 x 200.

In Amos 5 God refers to the *house of Israel* and declares not to enter into Bethel (Beth-el house of God). God will *pass through thee* and it will be a time of lamentation. God then uses the analogy of two animals and a serpent regarding the *day of the Lord.* This features the language of judgment: a lion, a bear and a serpent:

> **Amos 5:18: Woe unto you that desire the day of the LORD! to what end *is* it for you? the day of the LORD *is* darkness, and not light. 19: As if a man did flee from a lion, and a bear met him; or went into the house, and leaned his hand on the wall, and a serpent bit him.**

The *day of the Lord* does seem to be a longer period of time in which judgment comes upon the fallen houses of God but also the nations. Since the number 42 was featured in the mocking of Elisha, the end of the 42 months (*time, times and half time*) should start the *day of the Lord.* The command to *come out of her my people* should be taken very seriously by every believer. Judgment is coming upon the fallen houses of God.

I believe that the mocking that occurred after the *tribulation* will be judged after the 3 ½ years of *great tribulation.* Elisha's *double spirit* may relate to the believers in the final 3 1/2 years when they *consume and destroy* Satan's kingdom. It was very significant when Elijah prayed for no rain, and then 3 ½ years later he prayed again for rain shortly before he was taken up into Heaven by the chariot of fire. This prayer for rain could be the signal for when God's Word (in power) will be standing before the God of the earth. Elijah was a mystery since Jesus said that John the Baptist in some mysterious way was Elijah. This is perhaps why Elijah was taken up into Heaven:

> **Matthew 11:12: And from the days of John the Baptist until now the kingdom of heaven suffereth violence, and the violent take it by force. 13: For all the prophets and the law prophesied until John. 14: And if ye will receive *it*, this is Elias, which was for to come. 15: He that hath ears to hear, let him hear.**

Below is the comparison of Elijah and John:

Elijah- **2 Kings 1:8: And they answered him, *He was* an hairy man, and girt with a <u>girdle of leather</u> about his loins. And he said, It *is* Elijah the Tishbite.**

John- **Matthew 3:1: In those days came John the Baptist, preaching in the wilderness of Judaea, 2: And saying, Repent ye: for the kingdom of heaven is at hand. 3: For this is he that was spoken of by the prophet Esaias,**

saying, The voice of one crying in the wilderness, Prepare ye the way of the Lord, make his paths straight. 4: And the same John had his raiment of camel's hair, and <u>a</u> <u>leathern girdle</u> about his loins; and his meat was locusts and wild honey.

Since the announcement of the coming of Christ comes from the believers in Jesus, and this world has been turned into a wilderness by Satan (Isaiah 14:17), this *voice crying in the wilderness* are those broadcasting God's Word. John was the messenger in Jesus' time crying, *Prepare ye the way of the Lord.* Since the believers are now the ones crying, *Prepare ye the way of the Lord,* the following verses also apply to these final years of history. It is at this time that the warfare will be accomplished and God will be bringing down the exalted and raising the low:

> **Isaiah 40:1: Comfort ye, comfort ye my people, saith your God. 2: Speak ye comfortably to Jerusalem, and cry unto her, that her warfare is accomplished, that her iniquity is pardoned: for she hath received of the LORD'S hand double for all her sins. 3: The voice of him that crieth in the wilderness, Prepare ye the way of the LORD, make straight in the desert a highway for our God. 4: Every valley shall be exalted, and every mountain and hill shall be made low: and <u>the</u> <u>crooked shall be made straight</u>, and the rough places plain: 5: And <u>the glory of the LORD shall</u> <u>be revealed</u>, and all flesh shall see *it* together: for the mouth of the LORD hath spoken *it*.**

I believe the 42 months (3 ½ years) coming to a close in the year 2015 is extremely important. This will usher in the time of the magnification of God. The *voice* calling out to *repent and believe* will ring louder and louder. The kingdom of God will truly be *at hand.*

Seventy- See the number Seven.

Eighty Four- The number 84 can represent the times of *tribulation* and 42 (being half of 84) can represent the shortening of the days of *great tribulation.* A full seven years of *great tribulation* would have been 84 months. Judah's captivity at the hand of the King of Babylon was 70 years or 840 months. The 8,400-day *tribulation* period and the falling away in the houses of God began on May 21, 1988, which was also the 13,000 year anniversary since creation. The 8,400 day period went to the 7,000[th] anniversary of the flood which was May 21, 2011. Then, just before the 153 days ended on October 21, 2011, we arrived at the start of the *time, times and half a time* (Trumpets—September 28, 2011) which will end at a precise time in 2015 when God will be rebuking Satan. The Gospel will then go forth into all the world (Matthew 24). Please refer to the charts at the back of the book for time references.

One Hundred Fifty Three- The number 153 is a special number in the Bible that shows the salvation of God's people. The number 153 shows the factors of 3 x 3 x 17. The catching of the 153 great fish by the disciples at the command of Christ displays how Christ is the vine and the believers are the branches. We cannot produce fruit without Him. We also cannot be "fishers of men" without Him. The number 153 can also show the importance of *feeding the sheep* of the *Great Shepherd.* This was illustrated by Jesus telling Peter that, if you love me then *feed my sheep.* Peter's concern for believers at the end of time was seen as he referred us to Paul's understanding of God longsuffering. We continue this work of feeding God's sheep by sharing the unfolding truths from God's Word.

Two Hundred Seventy Six- The number 276 is also a very special Biblical number. The number 276 stands out in the Bible because the men who were with Paul during the storm (including Paul) were 276. Why would God's Word make sure we knew the number of the men onboard the ship during this massive storm? The storm or tempest in Acts 27 was no small tempest. The Greek word for tempest used in Acts 27 is *cheimon* (G5494). This identical word is used by Christ in association with praying that our fleeing out of the fallen houses of God would not be during the *winter* or *tempest*. This would indicate a time of great spiritual warfare and tempest. The first *tribulation* period of 8,400 days breaks down to 276 months. The Great Tribulation of 7 years is shortened to 3 ½ years. Thus, the 3 ½ years are the years of *tempest* or *winter*.

Was this great tempest tossing the 276 men a figure of the 8,400 days? Or is this a picture of the 3 ½ years of *great tribulation,* which has been shortened from the original 7-year *great tribulation* of Joseph's time? I believe the answer could be that the *last end of the indignation* (3 ½ years) is the time of *winter* since Paul and the men switched ships. Consequently, the time of tribulation and the time of *great tribulation* are thereby defined. The information from Mark 13 indicates that this time of *winter* shall never be again. Therefore, the magnification of God after the 3 ½ years ending in 2015 would mean the time of *winter* is over. Mark 13:18 speaks of the time of *winter* (tempest):

> **Mark 13:18: And pray ye that your flight be not in the winter. 19: For *in* those days shall be affliction, such as was not from the beginning of the creation**

which God created unto this time, neither shall be. 20: And except that the Lord had shortened those days, no flesh should be saved: but for the elect's sake, whom he hath chosen, he hath shortened the days.

On one hand the 276 months (8,400 days) seems important, but on the other hand the *great tribulation* seems to be a final wrap of Satan's time of desolation. This parabolic historical event of Paul and the other men is most fascinating due to the language. Could it be that both *tribulation* periods are featured in this historical account? That is a very real possibility. Paul and the prisoners were in one ship in which the winds were contrary or opposing:

Act 27:4: And when we had launched from thence, we sailed under Cyprus, because <u>the winds were contrary</u>.

We know from God's Word that people themselves can be opposing or contrary toward the believers in Christ as presented in Titus 2:8:

Titus 2:8: Sound speech, that cannot be condemned; that he that is <u>of the contrary part</u> may be ashamed, having no evil thing to say of you.

Paul admitted that he, as Saul, was contrary to the name of Jesus of Nazareth and imprisoned believers in Christ:

Acts 26:9: I verily thought with myself, that I ought to do many things <u>contrary to the name of Jesus of Nazareth</u>. 10: Which thing I also did in Jerusalem: and many of the saints did I shut up in prison, having received authority from the chief

priests; and when they were put to death, I gave my voice against *them*.

We can now understand how this event concerning the first ship with 276 men onboard can represent a time of people being contrary towards the believers in Christ. The first ship, perhaps, represented the first *tribulation* period of 8,400 days or 276 months. The number 276 is 12 x 23 and 23 always represents a time of judgment. The same time period of 8,400 days is also 23 years. However, they did eventually switch ships, and this is where Paul had great concern. Paul perceived this trip would cause *harm and loss*, but the centurion trusted the ship's owner more than Paul. God's Word then inserts that the south winds were calmer, and they set sail and eventually encountered a great tempest called *Euroclydon*.

The storm can be translated as the *east raging* or *east wind*. This storm was so fierce that casting forth cargo from the ship (the wheat) was deemed a protective measure. The Bible does use the *east wind* as a type of tribulation or judgment. God uses the *east wind* as an example of calamity:

> **Jeremiah 18:15: Because <u>my people hath forgotten me</u>, they have burned incense to vanity, and they have caused them to stumble in their ways *from* the ancient paths, to walk in paths, *in* a way not cast up; 16: To make their land desolate, *and* a perpetual hissing; every one that passeth thereby shall be astonished, and wag his head. 17: <u>I will scatter them as with an east wind before the enemy</u>; I will shew them the back, and not the face, in the day of their calamity.**

There is also a possibility that the prisoners in the ship (276) represent those saved (12) during the time of tempest or *great tribulation* (23). I say this due to Paul's instruction to them to *be of good cheer and eat* (they had been fasting). Paul was instructed by the Lord that these men were given to him. Why is this word *given* so important? It is the Greek word *charizomai* (G5483). The following verse is one instance where God uses this word as *forgiven*:

> **Colossians 2:13: And you, being dead in your sins and the uncircumcision of your flesh, hath he quickened together with him, <u>having forgiven you</u> all trespasses; 14: Blotting out the handwriting of ordinances that was against us, which was contrary to us, and took it out of the way, nailing it to his cross...**

It is no wonder these men, after eating and hearing Paul's words, were of *good cheer*. Let us review a few points:

1) The 276 (12 x 23) men were all involved in a great tempest (winter) and this can represent the time of *great tribulation.*

2) God instructed Paul that He had graced (given) the men to him on the ship.

3) Paul tells them to be of *good cheer*. This *good cheer* is a very exclusive phrase in the New Testament reserved for believers in Jesus. Besides this account in Acts, the only other place this word is used is when James instructs fellow believers who are of *good cheer* to sing Psalms (James 5:13).

4) If that is not enough, Paul also told the saved prisoners *for there shall not an hair fall from the head of any of you..* Jesus, in His discourse on the *tribulation*, makes a very similar statement in Luke 21:17-19. Believers will be hated for Jesus' name sake: *But there shall not an hair of your head*

perish. In your patience possess ye your souls. We have further commentary of this phrase concerning *no hair perishing* in 2 Samuel chapter 14. From 2 Samuel chapter 14 we can know that it is impossible for a believer to lose the *inheritance of God* (2 Samuel 14:16). *No hair perishing* is spiritual language indicating the security of eternal life that the believer in Jesus possesses. Please read 2 Samuel chapter 14 to get the full understanding of this truth. Is not this account of Paul and the prisoners making more sense now that the language is studied? God has written His Word in an incredible way.

5) Acts 27: 35 indicates that Paul took the bread, gave thanks to God in the presence of them all and then they began to eat. This is very similar to remembering the Lord's last supper.

There are two more things I want to present concerning how the 276 men finally got out of the storm and onto the Isle of Melita. I believe the truth of remaining in the ship is a picture of enduring the times of *tribulation*. The four anchors show a universal *great tribulation*. When they finally got to the point of rescue, the first part of the ship was thrust into shore and remained unmovable. However, the hinder part was broken in pieces by the violence of the waves.

I believe this storm and the ship, which the 276 must abide in, seem to represent the Kingdom of Heaven and the assault upon it near the end. The ships hinder part was broken in pieces by the violence of the waves. This Greek word for *violence* (G970) is related to Jesus' Words concerning the kingdom of heaven being taken by *violence* (G971):

> **Matthew 11:12: And from the days of John the Baptist until now the kingdom of heaven suffereth violence, and the violent take it by force.**

Remember also that since there is a repeating of the 1,290 days of Christ's time (29 A.D. to 33 A.D.) within the 1,335 days from 2011 to 2015, the kingdom of heaven also suffers *violence* as the violent take it by force. When John the Baptist baptized Jesus at Trumpets in 29 A.D., this ushered in the start of the 1,290 days. This period of 1,290 is why the last part of the *great tribulation* will be more difficult for the fallen houses of God worldwide.

The attack on the fallen houses of God in the 3 ½ years will be an all-out assault by Satan and possibly the nations coming against them. In Christ's parable of the sower, the wicked one *snatches away* (*harpazo*) the Word (seed) of the kingdom out of the heart of a person. This happens when one hears the message of the kingdom but does not understand it; other people may also discourage the person hearing the Word of God. The attitude of a religious hypocrite of Jesus' day who shut up the *Kingdom of Heaven* so men could not enter in is also symptomatic of our time.

It is interesting that the Greek word *harpazo* in a good way is associated with Jesus catching up His people on the last day.

> **1Thessalonians 4:17: Then we which are alive *and* remain shall be <u>caught up</u> together with them in the clouds, to meet the Lord in the air: and so shall we ever be with the Lord. 18: Wherefore comfort one another with these words.**

The final outcome of the 276 men, and especially Paul, was that the Gospel was brought to those on the isle of Melita. Paul shakes the serpent into the fire as no harm comes to him. All of this is an illustration of how that after the 3 ½ years of the *last end of the indignation,* the Gospel of Jesus Christ goes into all the world. Satan's power is removed until He is eventually destroyed on the *last day* at the coming of the Lord. This is all very good news since we are months away from God's great reversal.

The men who could swim cast themselves first into the water to get to shore. The other men rode in on planks from the ship. They all, however, made it to shore. They were all saved (*diasozo* G1295) as were also Noah and his family:

> **Act 27:44: And the rest, some on boards, and some on *broken pieces* of the ship. And so it came to pass, that they escaped <u>all safe</u> to land.**

There is so much great information contained in Acts 27 concerning this *smoky storm* called *Euroclydon*. Many times in a study of God's Word, I attempt to study the root word of a certain word in hopes it will help better define the verse. Acts 27:14 uses tempestuous wind which arose as the 276 men were on the ship:

> **Acts 27:14: But not long after there arose against it a tempestuous wind, called Euroclydon.**

This can be translated as smoky stormy or dusky wind. The Greek word for tempestuous is *tupho-nikos* (G5189). The root word is *tupho* (G5188). The root word is used once in the New Testament. The verse in which *tupho* is used has always been a puzzle due to the language of "smoking flax." Within this verse is somewhat of a time reference. Let's look at this verse keeping in mind that Jesus said this during His 3 ½ year ministry which equates our 3 ½ years also:

> **Matthew 12:20: A bruised reed shall he not break, and smoking flax shall he not quench, till he send forth judgment unto victory. 21: And in his name shall the Gentiles trust.**

Jesus uses a reference of not putting out *smoking flax* until He sends forth *judgment unto victory*. I believe this is a very veiled reference to the end of the *great tribulation* period when *judgment* (2015 onward) will go forth unto *victory* (the coming of Jesus on the last day). The Greek word for victory is *nikos* (G3534). Besides the *smoking flax* verse of Matthew 12:20, this victory is a result from the defeat over death. However, the proper order is *judgment unto victory*:

> **1 Corinthians 15:54: So when this corruptible shall have put on incorruption, and this mortal shall have put on immortality, then shall be brought to pass the saying that is written, <u>Death is swallowed up in victory</u>. 55: O death, where *is* thy sting? O grave, where *is* thy victory? 56: The sting of death *is* sin; and the strength of sin *is* the law. 57: <u>But thanks *be* to God, which giveth us the victory through our Lord Jesus Christ</u>. 58: Therefore, my beloved brethren, be ye stedfast, unmoveable, always abounding in the work of the Lord, forasmuch as ye know that your labour is not in vain in the Lord.**

When is this victory coming for all believers in Christ? If one becomes saved by God's Spirit then this victory will come at the last trump:

> **1 Corinthians 15:52: <u>In a moment, in the twinkling of an eye, at the last trump</u>: for the trumpet shall sound, and the dead shall be raised incorruptible, and we shall be changed. 53: For this corruptible must put on incorruption, and this mortal must put on immortality.**

We have first the judgment from God, and then comes the time in which *death is swallowed up in victory*. This *tempestuous storm* of *great tribulation* will come to an end and the kingdom of Christ will be victorious. Note: Isaiah chapter 42 contains the *smoking flax* verse from which Jesus was further illustrating *judgment unto victory*. He is the light unto the gentiles during His first coming and also just prior to His coming on the last day:

> **Isaiah 42:6: I the LORD have called thee in righteousness, and will hold thine hand, and will keep thee, and give thee for a covenant of the people, for a light of the Gentiles; 7: To open the blind eyes, to bring out the prisoners from the prison, *and* them that sit in darkness out of the prison house.**

God is letting us know by using two similar verses that *judgment unto victory*, and also *judgment unto truth* are coming very shortly. This is not a contradiction between the two verses, but God is showing His people how both verses will come to pass. *Truth* and *victory* will be attained once judgment is enacted by God:

> **Isaiah 42:3: A bruised reed shall he not break, and the smoking flax shall he not quench: <u>he shall bring forth judgment unto truth</u>. 4: He shall not fail nor be discouraged, till he have set judgment in the earth: and the isles shall wait for his law.**

For further study on this subject, the two words to perform a Bible study would be truth (*emeth* H571), and victory (*nikos* G3534).

<u>**Six Hundred Sixty and Six**</u>- If there was ever a number in the Bible more spoken about in our time, it is the number 666. If we count each digit in the number 666, as some people may suggest, we get: 6 + 6 + 6 = 18. Though adding

428

numbers in our number system compared to the Greek letters for the number 666 does not seem accurate. We have seen already how the number 18 can mean *being bound by Satan* as the woman in Luke 13:16 was bound by Satan for 18 years. Likewise, the number 666 shows the factors of 18 x 37.

The only way we can understand the number 666 in Revelation 13:18 is by looking at how God uses this number in other places within His Word. The first place we find God using the number 666 is when God tells us that there were 666 children of Adonikam that came out of the captivity of Babylon (Ezra 2:13). Therefore, the time of tribulation/captivity is at the forefront of understanding. The second place where 666 is highlighted in the Bible relates to King Solomon who had built Jerusalem and the temple magnificently, yet he fell into false worship:

> **2 Chronicles 9:13: Now <u>the weight of gold that came to Solomon in one year was six hundred and threescore and six talents of gold</u>.**
>
> **1Kings 10:23: So king Solomon exceeded all the kings of the earth for riches and for wisdom.**
>
> **1Kings 11:5: For Solomon went after Ashtoreth the goddess of the Zidonians, and after Milcom the abomination of the Ammonites. 6: And <u>Solomon did evil in the sight of the LORD</u>, and went not fully after the LORD, as *did* David his father.**

The last and probably the most significant place that 666 is found in the Bible is when the King of Babylon built a golden image for everyone in the kingdom to fall down and worship once music was played. This golden image was 60 cubits in height, 6 cubits in width, and 6 instruments were to be played to signal when it was time to bow down to the image. One important aspect of the King of Babylon is found in Isaiah where God uses him as a type of the *son of the dawn (Heylel)* who has fallen from heaven (Isaiah 14:12).

Therefore, the evil actions of King Nebuchadrezzar, who desired worship by setting up the golden image, were an illustration of what Satan does in the final years. There is also language in Daniel that is forecasting the *time, times, and half a time* (our 3 ½ years of *great tribulation*) where this false image (false worship) is *set up*.

The Hebrew word *arise* is the same Hebrew word translated as *set up* as the image of King Nebuchadrezzar was *set up*. Both verses presented below show how the golden image *arose* (set up) in Babylon and also how Satan shall arise for *a time, times and half time:*

> **Daniel 7:24: And the ten horns out of this kingdom *are* ten kings *that* shall <u>arise</u>: and <u>another shall rise after them</u>; and he shall be diverse from the first, and he shall subdue three kings. 25: And he shall speak *great* words against the most High, and shall wear out the saints of the most High, and think to change times and laws: and <u>they shall be given into his hand until a time and times and the dividing of time.</u> 26: But the judgment shall sit, and they shall take away his dominion, to consume and to destroy *it* unto the end.**

> **Daniel 3:1: Nebuchadrezzar the king made an image of gold, whose height *was* threescore cubits, *and* the breadth thereof six cubits: he <u>set it up</u> in the plain of Dura, in the province of Babylon.**

This historical demand for worship by King Nebuchadrezzar was heralded to the following: *all people, nations, and languages.*

These three Hebrew words as a group are seen seven times in the Old Testament. Eventually, though, there is a great turn around with King Nebuchadrezzar's heart. After being used by God for His purpose, Nebuchadrezzar praised the God of Heaven. While this may seem strange since he was a type or illustration of what Satan does near the end, nevertheless, he was only an earthly King.

To All People, Nations and Languages- Praise the God of Heaven

>**Daniel 4:1: Nebuchadrezzar the king, unto all people, nations, and languages, that dwell in all the earth; Peace be multiplied unto you. 2: I thought it good to shew the signs and wonders that the high God hath wrought toward me. 3: How great *are* his signs! and how mighty *are* his wonders! his kingdom *is* an everlasting kingdom, and his dominion is from generation to generation.**

King Darius also addresses *all people, nations, and languages.* This is very significant since we are mirroring the *years of Darius* from 2011 to 2018. Read below what King Darius proclaimed as recorded in Daniel chapter 6:

>**Daniel 6:25: Then king Darius wrote unto all people, nations, and languages, that dwell in all the earth; Peace be multiplied unto you. 26: I make a decree, That in every dominion of my kingdom men tremble and fear before the God of Daniel: for he *is* the living God, and stedfast for ever, and his kingdom *that* which shall not be destroyed, and**

> **his dominion *shall be even* unto the end. 27: He delivereth and rescueth, and he worketh signs and wonders in heaven and in earth, who hath delivered Daniel from the power of the lions. 28: So this Daniel prospered in the reign of Darius, and in the reign of Cyrus the Persian.**

God's dominion will go unto the end, not Satan's dominion. King Nebuchadrezzar eventually proclaimed this very truth when his understanding returned to him. The book of Revelation also speaks of similar language in which all nations will hear the prophecy of salvation through Christ for one final declaration. At a time when time itself should be no longer, and in the days when the mystery of God will be finished, something incredible happens:

> **Revelation 10:11: And he said unto me, Thou must prophesy again before many <u>peoples, and nations, and tongues, and kings.</u>**

> **Matthew 24:12: And because iniquity shall abound, the love of many shall wax cold. 13: But he that shall endure unto the end, the same shall be saved. 14: And <u>this gospel of the kingdom shall be preached in all the world for a witness unto all nations; and then shall the end come.</u>**

Yes, it is true that two divided into three produces .666... It is also true that the number 666 is 18 x 37 and can represent being bound by Satan (18) in a time of judgment (37). However, when we are focusing on a man, the illustration of the King of Babylon showing what Satan does during the final years is something that cannot be denied. Incredibly, God has shown from past Biblical history that He has power and control over the affairs of mankind.

Eventually, peace and truth will be multiplied in the entire world once Satan is removed into a land *barren and desolate*. False worship will be judged, and the believers in Christ will *consume and destroy* the kingdom of Satan unto the end. Adonakim's descendants of 666 who came out of captivity, Solomon's 666 drams of gold received in one year, and the golden image which was *set up* by King Nebuchadrezzar all represent some form of false worship and also tribulation/captivity. Remember though how God reverses things, and this requires the patience of His people:

> **Revelation 13:10: He that leadeth into captivity shall go into captivity: he that killeth with the sword must be killed with the sword. Here is the patience and the faith of the saints.**

This list of Bible numbers is in no way complete. It is an example of how God uses numbers in the Bible to show their spiritual significance. Many numbers have been presented on the *2011studies* YouTube channel. Everyone is welcome to subscribe to the channel for ongoing studies. God willing, we will continue to study these important topics in these few remaining years of history. This book should be officially published very near the 3-year anniversary of October 21, 2011. If it is God's will, this book will help feed His sheep as God's mercy endures.

I recorded the song below shortly after 2011 based on Habakkuk standing on the watch and asking God: *what shall I tell them when I am reproved* (questioned)? After my last book: *Countdown to the Last Day*, there were many questions and some mocking. Being patient and learning to trust God's Word is the key to gaining further understanding. God does not reveal things all at once. When God gave me this song, I, at that time, did not know some of the information contained in this book. The lyrics: *I'll tell them be ready, be ready for that day* was the answer I thought important to give at that time. Today, with this further understand from God's Word and with more urgency, I would change those lyrics to: *I'll tell them get ready, get ready for that day.*

What Shall I Tell Them (Be Ready) ♪♪

©Marty Cattuzzo -2012

I Stand upon Your watch

Waiting for that great day

Lord, what shall I tell them…What words do I say?

What do I tell them…What words do I say?

I'm simply amazed at Your mercy and grace

I'm simply amazed at Your mercy and grace

I'll tell them be ready

Be ready for that day

And though it may tarry

There are souls for You to save

Your mercy endures

As long as there is day

Your mercy endures

As Long as there is day

And what shall I tell them…Oh what words will I say

Your mercy endures

There are souls yet to save

Your mercy endures

There are souls yet to save

For this I am thankful and praise your Holy Name

For this I am thankful and praise your Holy Name

So Great a Salvation

In this present world in which people show enmity towards the name of Jesus, one could argue that this very enmity proves how the Words of Jesus given to the disciples are reliable truth. His Words from Mark 13:13 apply to every believer in Christ worldwide. The hatred towards Jesus and His believers is especially true during the time of *tribulation* and *great tribulation*. We are all witnessing this murderous hatred on a worldwide scale as *kingdom rises against kingdom*. The context of Mark 13 is the timeframe of *great tribulation*. We read about this hatred in the following verse:

> **Mark 13:13: And ye shall be hated of all *men* for my name's sake: but he that shall endure unto the end, the same shall be saved.**

Jesus, in speaking to the sons of Zebedee (James and John), mentioned that they would surely *drink of His cup*. Every believer in Christ must pick-up the cross and follow after or behind Him. We have this dramatic illustration as Christ walked forth to Golgotha and Simon of Cyrene was called to bear His cross:

> **Matthew 10:38: And he that taketh not his cross, and followeth after me, is not worthy of me.**

> **Mark 15:21: And they compel one Simon a Cyrenian, who passed by, coming out of the country, the father of Alexander and Rufus, <u>to bear his cross.</u>**

In some parts of the world, drinking of *His cup* can mean persecution and death for some believers. Every believer in

Christ understands, though, that Jesus has the power over death and the power to raise people from the grave. There is even a direct connection to a better place for those in Christ who depart from their body as Paul stated in 2 Corinthians 5:8:

> **2 Corinthians 5:8: We are confident, *I say*, and willing rather to be absent from the body, and to be present with the Lord.**

This salvation from the true God and creator of this universe is so great and so incredible that if any Christian's writing is void of mentioning this free gift by Christ, then the author has failed in bringing the good news. Throughout this book I used many Bible verses because I know how faith comes by hearing the Word of God. God is no respecter of persons as the Lord saves both Jew and Gentile:

> **Romans 10:12: For there is no difference between the Jew and the Greek: for the same Lord over all is rich unto all that call upon him. 13: <u>For whosoever shall call upon the name of the Lord shall be saved.</u>**

Attempting to explain the incredible act of salvation is a difficult task for the believer. It is difficult because when Christ explained it, He compares the Spirit of God (which saves us) to the wind which blows:

> **John 3:6: That which is born of the flesh is flesh; and that which is born of the Spirit is spirit. 7: Marvel not that I said unto thee, Ye must be born again. 8: The wind bloweth where it listeth, and thou hearest the sound thereof, but canst not tell whence it cometh, and whither it goeth: so is every one that is born of the Spirit.**

We do not control the wind any more than we control the Spirit of God that He has sent forth into the entire world to seek and save those people who are lost. This removes all control from the hands of mankind and places it in the power of God to accomplish His salvation. God's Word, however, lets us know that in seeking salvation and eternal life, we must approach God in prayer with a certain attitude. God's Word speaks against pride because it is a trait of Satan. How then do we approach the throne of God to ask for this great salvation? The Bible defines how we approach God in order to ask Him for this free gift of eternal life and forgiveness.

> **Psalm 34:18: The LORD *is* nigh unto them that are of a broken heart; and saveth such as be of a contrite spirit.**

> **Psalm 51:17: The sacrifices of God *are* a broken spirit: a broken and a contrite heart, O God, thou wilt not despise.**

A *broken and contrite heart* God will not despise. One of the best Biblical illustrations of a *broken and contrite heart* is the parable of the Pharisee and the Publican:

> **Luke 18:9: And he spake this parable unto certain which trusted in themselves that they were righteous, and despised others: 10: Two men went up into the temple to pray; the one a Pharisee, and the other a publican. 11: The Pharisee stood and prayed thus with himself, God, I thank thee, that I am not as other men *are*, extortioners, unjust, adulterers, or even as this publican. 12: I fast twice in the week, I give tithes of all that I possess. 13: And the publican, standing afar off, would not lift up so much as *his* eyes unto heaven, but smote upon his breast, saying, God be merciful to me a**

439

sinner. 14: I tell you, this man went down to his house justified *rather* than the other: for every one that exalteth himself shall be abased; and he that humbleth himself shall be exalted.

The greatest thing we can take away from this parable is that there are two kinds of people. There are those who judge other people and think they themselves are not sinners. They actually have the lofty pride to thank God that they are not like the sinner, yet, they are not at all free from sin.

There is also the admitted sinner who, like Peter, may have been sifted like wheat by evil which caused them to fall. Yet, the sinner will admit he/she is a sinner and realize their shortcomings, and this will create in them a broken heart in which they must cry out to God for mercy. This is the action and words of a broken and contrite heart: *God have mercy on me a sinner.*

The Hebrew word *shabar* (H7665) is translated as *broken* and is also part of the word *brokenhearted*. This is why the Lord from Heaven, who is Jesus, came to save His people from sin and death. He came to *bind up the brokenhearted.* People today lift up the strong of this world; Jesus on the other hand binds up the *brokenhearted* and then grants to them the greatest gift of all, which is salvation:

Isaiah 61:1: The Spirit of the Lord GOD *is* upon me; because the LORD hath anointed me to preach good tidings unto the meek; <u>he hath sent me to bind up the brokenhearted</u>, to proclaim liberty to the captives, and the opening of the prison to *them that are* bound; 2: To proclaim the acceptable year of the LORD, and the day of vengeance of our God; to comfort all that mourn...

440

During His 3 ½ year ministry, Jesus entered into the temple and read Isaiah 61 and proclaimed that He is the fulfillment of Isaiah 61. He, however, left out *the day of vengeance* only because that is reserved for the end of the mirror of the 3 ½ years in our time. We are rapidly approaching the *day of vengeance* in which God will perform a huge reversal.

It is not hard to be dismayed by all the crazy activities going on in this world. A recent report which was reported by many news agencies stated that half of the people in America are taking prescription drugs. Many people are blindly taking vaccines without even asking what is in the vaccine. Billions of dollars are being made by big pharmaceutical companies and people are having serious side effects from all these drugs and vaccines. These topics have excellent YouTube videos for further information[26].

One of the most destructive things to mankind and the earth in the past few years is the increase of spraying in the upper atmosphere (called geoengineering[27]). The *powers in charge* are attempting to either alter weather and natural climate events or block the sun in attempts to stop what they believe to be global warming. This is a worldwide effort without the consent of the citizens of many countries. It is an attempt to act as God but will fail miserably. This so-called atmospheric science is interfering with natural climate events.

A worldwide attempt to geoengineer (chemical spraying) the upper atmosphere comes at a great health cost to everyone on the planet. We should be able to walk outside without an attempt by an evil agenda to deflect the sun by using harmful chemical sprays. We should be able to breathe fresh air and not go outside and worry if we are breathing alumina, strontium, and barium particles, not to mention the effects these particles have on the soil and water supplies.

441

This is a time of evil, but is all lost? The answer is absolutely not. Certain verses in the Bible mention how God is going to *destroy the strength of the kingdoms of the nations.* This is very timely because God declaring this removal of strength or power was within the years of Darius. We are currently living in the mirror of the years of Darius. We are rapidly approaching the time when God *shakes the heavens and the earth:*

> **Haggai 2:22: And <u>I will overthrow the throne of kingdoms, and I will destroy the strength of the kingdoms of the heathen</u>; and I will overthrow the chariots, and those that ride in them; and the horses and their riders shall come down, every one by the sword of his brother.**

Some of these topics (such as geoengineering & vaccines) I mentioned have a corresponding YouTube video title in the endnotes sections. Please take the time to watch these videos. Further Bible studies are also available on the *2011studies* channel (YouTube).

The only thing in this world that is secure is salvation through the Lord Jesus Christ. Salvation and forgiveness by the creator is real; it is needed by everyone because God is going to soon change this world. All that can be shaken will be shaken. The kingdom of the Lord Jesus, which we enter by being saved by His Spirit, is the kingdom that cannot be shaken. This is the kingdom that will stand and stand forevermore:

> **Hebrews 12:24: And to Jesus the mediator of the new covenant, and to the blood of sprinkling, that speaketh better things than *that of* Abel. 25: See that ye refuse not him that speaketh. For if they escaped not who refused him that spake on earth,**

much more *shall not* we *escape*, if we turn away from him that *speaketh* from heaven: 26: <u>Whose voice then shook the earth: but now he hath promised, saying, Yet once more I shake not the earth only, but also heaven.</u> 27: And this *word*, Yet once more, signifieth the removing of those things that are shaken, as of things that are made, that those things which cannot be shaken may remain. 28: <u>Wherefore we receiving a kingdom which cannot be moved, let us have grace, whereby we may serve God acceptably with reverence and godly fear</u>: 29: For our God *is* a consuming fire.

Now is the accepted time; today is the day of salvation. Today is the time to seek God in honesty and sincerity. If you experience the Lord's salvation in these final years or have already been saved by God's Spirit, as fellow believers we are headed for a better tomorrow, an incredible tomorrow.

2 Peter 3:13: Nevertheless we, according to his promise, look for new heavens and a new earth, wherein dwelleth righteousness.

1 Corinthians 2:9: But as it is written, Eye hath not seen, nor ear heard, neither have entered into the heart of man, the things which God hath prepared for them that love him. 10: But <u>God hath revealed *them* unto us by his Spirit</u>: for the Spirit searcheth all things, yea, the deep things of God.

Such Great Love (Agape)

In the study of this book I was re-introduced to the topic of love which is from the Greek word *agape* (G26). When I looked at one verse on this topic, I wondered why Paul placed abiding in love before faith and hope.

> **1 Corinthians 13:13: And now abideth faith, hope, charity, these three; but the greatest of these *is* charity.**

One thing about the study of the Bible is that we are always in the mode of learning new things. The word *greater* really means just that. It is foremost of importance. If our heart condemns us, we must remember that *God is greater than our heart* and He knows all things:

> **1 John 3:20: For if our heart condemn us, God is greater than our heart, and knoweth all things.**

After studying the word love (agape), I believe the reason it is greater above faith and hope is that we cannot abide in faith and hope without God's love first being given to us by His Holy Spirit. This truth is found in Romans chapter 5:

> **Romans 5:1: Therefore being justified by faith, we have peace with God through our Lord Jesus Christ: 2: By whom also we have access by faith into this grace wherein we stand, and rejoice in hope of the glory of God. 3: And not only *so*, but we glory in tribulations also: knowing that tribulation worketh patience; 4: And patience, experience; and experience, hope: 5: And <u>hope maketh not ashamed; because the love of God is</u>**

shed abroad in our hearts by the Holy Ghost which is given unto us.

The love of God which spills forth out of a believer comes from God's Spirit living in a believer. This love allows us to have faith and hope. It allows us to share the good news of eternal life. It has allowed friends in Christ and myself to work on this book in seven short months. Love and laboring in love is important during these final years. Why? Because we are warned that the *love of many will wax cold* during the final years, due to iniquity abounding:

> **Matthew 24:12: And because iniquity shall abound, the love of many shall wax cold. 13: But he that shall endure unto the end, the same shall be saved. 14: And this gospel of the kingdom shall be preached in all the world for a witness unto all nations; and then shall the end come.**

We now are full circle as the *Gospel of the kingdom* will go forth into the entire world for a witness unto all nations. God's Spirit saves many people and love abounds. With this love granted by God's Spirit, faith and hope also follow. All these spiritual fruits are from God's Spirit. I hope many will share the information in this book and carry on with this labor of love.

> **Hebrews 6:10: For God *is* not unrighteous to forget your work and labour of love, which ye have shewed toward his name, in that ye have ministered to the saints, and do minister. 11: And we desire that every one of you do shew the same diligence to the full assurance of hope unto the end...**

A *better tomorrow* is on the horizon, so please carry on with this labor of love. Share the gospel with many people in these final years. We have established some sites so that you can share freely the good news that Jesus is coming in great power and glory:

- 2011studies (YouTube video Bible studies)
- www.1335days.com (blog with Bible text studies)
- www.lettersofpeaceandtruth.com (website with language translator)

A Final Letter to the Reader

Thank you for reading through this study of God's Word. I hope this book has been a help in understanding the time in which we are all living. The information contained in this book should be taken seriously because the evidence of the falling away in the houses of God is occurring worldwide.

God has written His Word in such an incredible way. The patterns of yesterday have become the reality of our day. There is nothing new under the sun. The false worship of yesterday allows us to know that God's judgment is righteous. In all of this, we still witness God's mercy as He reverses *the captivity* of His people.

After the year 2011 and the grand announcement of Judgment Day coming, I became convinced that we are now living in the final seven years of history. This is the time of God's longsuffering. He is not willing that any would perish as they did with the Noachian Flood. The year 2011 was an important marker in announcing the coming of Christ on the last day. This work continues as we declare the same announcement within the seven years of God's longsuffering.

I am grateful for the dedicated teachers saved by Christ who laid the foundation of the study of Biblical chronology. I am also grateful for the studies produced by fellow believers concerning the detailed information of the 8,400 days ending May 21, 2011. The newer information concerning the *years of Darius* and the continued building of God's eternal house is a key to understanding the timeline of the final seven years. God willing, more online studies will be produced for fellow believers in Christ to fellowship together. We do not discard the old, but rather, we add to it to complete further understanding of God's Word. God will make us *fruitful and multiply* us in a great way:

> **Leviticus 26:9: For I will have respect unto you, and <u>make you fruitful, and multiply you</u>, and establish my covenant with you. 10: And <u>ye shall eat old store, and bring forth the old because of the new.</u>**

Like the first Pentecost in 33 A.D., the believers were in *one accord*. My hope is that before and after the second fulfillment of Pentecost in 2015 more believers will be in *one accord*. God and His Word will be magnified in a boundless way. We are months away from this great event. The exciting news of God being magnified and Satan being removed *into a land barren and desolate* will show the absolute power of God. The Lord will *shake the heavens and the earth* and changes are soon to come in the year 2015.

Believers in Christ need to prepare for bringing the Gospel into the entire world. The good news of Jesus Christ, the forgiveness of sins, and His free gift of eternal life will go forth. There is no other salvation and no other name under heaven by which men can be saved:

> **Act 4:10: Be it known unto you all, and to all the people of Israel, that by the name of Jesus Christ of Nazareth, whom ye crucified, whom God raised from the dead, *even* by him doth this man stand here before you whole.**

> **Act 4:11: This is the stone which was set at nought of you builders, which is become the head of the corner. 12: <u>Neither is there salvation in any other: for there is none other name under heaven given</u>**

**among men, whereby we must be saved. 13: <u>Now
when they saw the boldness of Peter and John, and
perceived that they were unlearned and ignorant
men, they marvelled</u>; and they took knowledge of
them, that they had been with Jesus.**

We can only boast in the mercy of Christ and His blessings.
May the Lord help you to be active in bringing the Gospel
with boldness and truth. Time is short, but He is with us to
accomplish the task.

> **1 John 5:13: These things have I written unto you
> that believe on the name of the Son of God; that ye
> may know that ye have eternal life, and that ye
> may believe on the name of the Son of God.**

Timeline Charts

Historical Biblical Patterns of Tribulation

Comparison of Judah's Historical *Tribulation* Period with our *Tribulation* Period	
Judah's 70-year (840 month) captivity occurred from the time the last good king of Judah (King Josiah) died in 609 B.C. until their captivity was ended when Cyrus the Persian and Darius the Mede took the kingdom in 539 B.C.	The first *tribulation* period of our day began on May 21, 1988, and ended on May 21, 2011, for a total of 23 years or 8,400 days.
Judah's historical 70-year captivity totaled 840 months in length.	The 23-year *tribulation* of our day totaled 8,400 days in length. This was a shortened version of Judah's 840 months of captivity.
God divided Judah's 70-year captivity into two parts. The first part consisted of the 23-year period (609 B.C. to 587 B.C.) where Jeremiah was told by God to proclaim to all the Jews to depart out of the land of Judah and go into captivity in the land of Babylon (see Jeremiah chapter 24). The second part began when Nebuchadnezzar, the King of Babylon, destroyed Jerusalem in 587 B.C., and those that went in captivity were ruled over by Babylon until 539 B.C.	God divided our 23-year *tribulation* into two parts. The first part consisted of the 2,300 days spoken of in Daniel 8:14 where the sanctuary and the host were trodden under foot, which was from May 21, 1988, to September 7, 1994. The second part consisted of 6,100 days, which were from September 7, 1994 (Feast of Trumpets and the year of Jubilee), to May 21, 2011 (the 7,000[th] anniversary of the flood in 4990 B.C.).
During the second part of Judah's captivity, King Nebuchadnezzar set up the golden image for all to bow down and worship. Those who	During the second part of the 8,400-day *tribulation* period, Satan sets up his false doctrines in the fallen churches for all to bow down

would not worship the golden image were thrown into a fiery furnace, but while in the furnace, no harm came to them because of God's mighty protection. See Daniel chapter 3.	and worship. Those who did not agree with the false teachings followed the command of Christ to *Come out of her my people.* This command continues into the time of *great tribulation* because of the doubling that occurs: *Babylon has fallen, has fallen.* (See Revelation chapter 18)- It is a time of *furnace testing.*
After the 70-year captivity, the promise of *good and comfortable words* comes from Zechariah 1:13: *And the LORD answered the angel that talked with me with good words and comfortable words.* In Zechariah 1, God speaks of a time of universal rebuilding represented by the four carpenters: Zechariah 1:20: *And the LORD shewed me four carpenters.* This time of rebuilding began in the years of Darius as seen on the chart titled: *The Years of Darius.*	The 8,400 days ended with the announcement of *Judgment Day* coming. The mocking that followed fulfilled the declaration of 2 Peter 3: *Where is the promise of His coming?* God also tells us at this point in Habakkuk 2:3: *For the vision [is] yet for an appointed time, but at the end it shall speak, and not lie: though it tarry, wait for it; because it will surely come, it will not tarry.*
	Continue to chart two, *The Years of Darius.*

The Years of Darius

THE YEARS OF DARIUS			
ACCESSION YEARS OF DARIUS	**B.C DATES- NISAN TO NISAN**	**MIRRORED DATES IN OUR TIME**	**INFORMATION GIVEN IN THE BIBLE CONCERNING EACH YEAR OF DARIUS**
1st Official Year of Darius	538- 537 B.C.	3/24/2012 to 3/11/2013	In the 1st year of Darius, Daniel receives understanding.
2nd Official Year of Darius	537 -536 B.C.	3/12/2013 to 3/31/2014	The 1st day of the 6th month (our 8/7/2013), God gives the command to build His house. On the 24th day of the 6th month (our 8/30/2013), God stirs up the remnant to work. The 21st day of the 7th month (our 9/25/2013), work for God is with us. On the 24th day of the 9th month (our 11/27/2013), the foundation is laid. From this day and upward God will bless His people.

3rd Official Year of Darius	536-535 B.C.	4/1/2014 to 3/20/2015	The command to build God's house continues.
4th Official Year of Darius	535-534 B.C.	3/21/2015 to 4/8/2016	The command to build God's house continues. On the 4th day of the 9th month (our 11/16/2015) God says to: *Execute true judgment, and show mercy and compassions every man to his brother: And oppress not the widow, nor the fatherless, the stranger, nor the poor; and let none of you imagine evil against his brother in your heart* (Zechariah 7:9-10).
5th Official Year of Darius	534-533 B.C.	4/9/2016 to 3/27/2017	The command to build God's house continues.
6th Official Year of Darius	533-532 B.C.	3/28/2017 to 3/16/2018	The house was finished on the 3rd day of the 12th month which was the month Adar (our 2/18/2018).
The mirror of the condensed work of Ezra and Nehemiah by God Himself	N/A	Our 2/18/2018 (Adar) to 10/2/2018 (last day of the Feast of Tabernacles)	The beautification of God's eternal temple (Salvation of believers worldwide).

After the *Tribulation* Ending May 21, 2011

After the First *Tribulation* of 8,400 Days		
Time Period	Length	Jesus' Command
An important time period began immediately after the 8,400-day *tribulation* period on May 21, 2011, which was also the 7,000th anniversary of the Noachian Flood in 4990 B.C. This period ushers in the period of "feed my sheep."	153 days from the end of the first *tribulation* period- May 21, 2011 to October 21, 2011 (Feast of Tabernacles-last day). May 21, 2011 to October 2, 2018 is 2691 days or: 3x3x13x23	After catching 153 great fish, Christ commanded Peter to feed His sheep. This time period is also five months, which was the exact time period the waters increased while Noah was in the ark. Isaiah 54:8-9 tells us that God hid His face for a moment, and God equates this to the *waters of Noah* and this allowed for a worldwide mocking to occur which was the fulfillment of 2 Peter 3:3-4.
Immediately after the 153 days, October 21, 2011, to the anniversary of the cross on April 3, 2015, we have the fulfillment of possibly several time prophecies.	1,260 Days 42 Months 3 ½ Years Time, times, and half a time	These four time periods all feature a 3 ½ year time period. The 1,260 days is 42 months when divided by 30 days. The 42 months when divided by 12 months in a year is 3 ½ years. The *time, times, and half a time* when calculated by years is 3 ½ years. This is the length of time that Satan is given during the *last end of the indignation* (Daniel 12:7).

Continued from previous page…

After the First *Tribulation* of 8,400 Days (Continued)		
From the Feast of Trumpets, which is September 28, 2011, to Pentecost on May 24, 2015, there is a double fulfillment of a major time clue prophecy.	1,335 Days Trumpets to Pentecost-Fulfilled twice in the *years ending* in 33 A.D. and 2015 A.D.	This time period is spoken of in Daniel 12:12: *Blessed is he that waiteth, and cometh to the thousand three hundred and five and thirty days.* On Pentecost in 2015 there will be a double fulfillment of God's Spirit being poured out, but this time it will be worldwide.

The *Great Tribulation* & Biblical Factors from Important Dates

Jacob's *Great Affliction* Years	To 2011 A.D.	To 2015 A.D.	To 2018 A.D.
1879 B.C. (1st year of famine)	3,889 total years-3,889 is prime		
1877 B.C. 2nd year of famine-Jacob goes into Egypt under Joseph's care.	3,887 total years-3,887= 13x13x23		
1879 B.C. (1st year of famine)		3,893 total years-3,893 = 17x229	
1877 B.C. (2nd year of famine-Jacob's family given the land of Goshen to be herdsman)		3,891 total years-3,891 = 3x1,297	
1879 B.C. (first year of famine)			3,896 total years- 3,896 = 2x2x2x487
1877 B.C. (second year of famine)			3,894 total years- 3,894 = 2x3x11x59
3-God's Purpose, 13-Tribulation, 23-Tribulation, 17-Salvation, 11-Christ's Coming-Salvation			

The Noachian Flood to our 7-Year *Great Tribulation*

Noachian Flood Date	To 2011 A.D. (no year zero)	To 2015 A.D. (no year zero)	To 2018 A.D. (no year zero)
4990 B.C.	Years = 7,000 years Factors = 2x2x2x5x5x5x7	Years = 7,005 years Factors = 2x2x17x103	Years = 7,007 years Factors = 7x7x11x13
Noachian Flood (using May 21, 4990 B.C.)	In days = 2, 556,737 days Factors = 37x43x1,607		In days to October 2, 2018 (last day of the Feast of Tabernacles)- 2,559,428 days or 4 x 639,857 The # 4 means universal.

The Noachian Flood to the Cross-The Cleansing Times

The Flood in 4990 B.C. to the Cross in 33 A.D.			
Noachian Flood	To the Cross. (April 3, 33 A.D.) in Days	To the Cross (April 3, 33 A.D.) in Years	
Noachian Flood (May 21, 4990 B.C.) to the Cross, April 3, 33 A.D.	1,834,239 Days= 3x11x11x31x163	5,022 years= 2x3x3x3x3x31	
Note: the number 31 is significant since Josiah reigned 31 years and cleansed Jerusalem's false idol worship (2nd Chronicles 34:1). From Josiah's 1st year of his reign (at 8 years old in 640 B.C.) to the cross of Christ in 33 A.D. there are 672 years. 672 years shows the factors of: 2x2x2x2x2x3x7			

Purim 391 B.C. – The Grand Reversal in the Book of Esther

Purim in 391 B.C.	To 2011 A.D.	To 2015 A.D.
The year of the grand reversal.	2,401 years = 7x7x7x7	2,405 years = 5x13x37

Note: The Feast of Purim is highly significant with the year 2015. Many paths lead to 2015 as being the time of a great reversal by God. I believe this was illustrated for us in the book of Esther.

When the Jews had victory over Haman and his 10 sons who sought to destroy all the Jews in the Kingdom of Ahazuerus, *letters of peace and truth* went forth. *Esther 8:16: The Jews had light, and gladness, and joy, and honour.*

Light, gladness, joy, and honor are all significant when God performs a grand reversal. *Light* is related to God's protection. *Gladness and honor* are related to Isaiah 35:10, Isaiah 51:3, and Isaiah 51:11 when the redeemed of the Lord shall *rejoice with singing.* The word *honor* is related to when judgment sits, and Christ's dominion is given great honor and the believers *consume and destroy* (see Daniel 7).

March 5 & 6, 2015 is the Purim celebration for that year. Is 2015 the year that God is going to reverse the evil of Satan who is seeking to destroy the Gospel of Christ? I believe this is the year so that the Gospel will go forth one last time into *all the world* for a *witness unto the nations.* This parallels the *letters of peace and truth* going into every province of King Ahazuerus' kingdom in Esther's day. God used Mordecai and Esther to bring about this reversal in 391 B.C. Many professed to be Jews in that day of God's honor being known; they had *feasting* and *a good day.* The Hebrew word *tub H2896* (good) is also used in Lamentations 3:25: *The LORD is good unto them that wait for him, to the soul that seeketh him.*

Big changes are coming. We wait patiently for God to perform His grand reversal and to experience a *good day.*

False Worship is Judged- Judgment on Jezebel

Date	Reign	Judgment	To 2015 Factors
842 B.C.	11th year of Joram the Son of Ahab	Jehu enters the city and is mocked by Jezebel- She is thrown over the wall. Jezebel dies and is destroyed by dogs.	2,856 years- 2,856 = 2x17x84 or 2x2x17x42 or 2x2x2x3x7x17

Jezebel's death (842 B.C.) may signify the end of *great tribulation*. Since the *great tribulation* period is patterned after the 7-year historical account of Jacob & his family going into Egypt, the shortening of those historical days can be illustrated to be 3 ½ years. The shortening of the *great tribulation* would line-up with the year 2015. To see the numbers of *tribulation* (42 & 84) from 842 B.C. to 2015 A.D. is significant. The number 17 is a number of salvation, and it is significant since 2015 is also the year of *blessed is he that waits and comes to the 1,335th day*. Jezebel mocked Jehu by proclaiming how he was following in the footsteps of Zimri who killed his predecessor and had a very short reign:

> **2 Kings 9:31: And as Jehu entered in at the gate, she said, *Had* Zimri peace, who slew his master? 32: And he lifted up his face to the window, and said, Who *is* on my side? who? And there looked out to him two *or* three eunuchs. 33: And he said, Throw her down. So they threw her down: and *some* of her blood was sprinkled on the wall, and on the horses: and he trode her under foot.**

This account is significant due to how Jesus relates *great tribulation* with Jezebel:

Revelation 2:21: And **I gave her space to repent** of her fornication; and she repented not. 22: Behold, I will cast her into a bed, and them that commit adultery with her **into great tribulation**, except they repent of their deeds.

The 7-Year *Great Tribulation* Period and Events

Event	Years	Historical Pattern	Verses	Years to Important Time
Historical *Great Tribulation*	Famine starts in 1879 B.C. 1877 B.C. (two years into the famine)- Jacob while in Egypt dwells in the fertile land of Goshen	Original Event- Great dearth in the land of Canaan & Egypt	Genesis 41:54- Acts 7:11	1877 B.C. to 2011 B.C. = 3887 Years= 13x13x23
Current *Great Tribulation*	2011-2018 Shortened to 3 ½ years- Ending in 2015.	Jacob & his family go into Egypt due to the great famine.	Genesis 42- Acts 7:11-15.	3 ½ years to the year 2015-Then a final 3 ½ years to 2018

The famine predicted by Pharaoh's dream of the seven years of plenty and the seven years of famine was managed by Joseph's command to store up for the seven years of famine. Jacob and his family, two years into the famine, travel into Egypt and are helped by his long lost son Joseph. They dwelt in the land of Goshen and certain of Jacob's people (*men of activity*) became rulers over Pharaoh's cattle (Genesis 47:5-6).

When Jesus spoke of the *great tribulation* in Matthew 24:21, He made known that it is not like any since the world began, nor shall be after it. It is a famine of hearing God's Word. It is a time of *false christs* and *false prophets* coming with *lying signs and wonders;* this is the nature of this current *famine.* Like Jacob who was saved out of the famine, the believers during this 3 ½ years will be fed by God's Word.

Timelines Within the Final Seven Years

Year	Event Timeline
2011	• The 7-year *great tribulation* period begins (shortened to 3 ½ years by the Lord). It is known as the time of *Jacob's trouble,* yet *he will be saved out of it.* • 7000th anniversary of the flood and the mocking of *where is the promise of His coming* began after May 21, 2011. • End of the 8,400 Days. • 153 days (May 21, to October 21)-time to begin feeding God's sheep. • Beginning of Elijah's 3 ½ years of no rain 10-21-2011 to 4-3-2015 (anniversary of the Cross). • Historically, Babylon is given to the Mede and Persian (Oct. 539 B.C.). • God hides His face for the duration of 370 days then commands to be *fruitful and multiply* (an illustration of salvation). • The 1,290/1,335 second fulfillment begins at the Feast of Trumpets (9-28-2011). • The *last end of the indignation* begins (*time, times and half time* or 42 months or 3 ½ years. • Historical opposition of the building of the temple/Jerusalem causes ceasing until Darius finds the edict of King Cyrus to build the temple. Note: 539 B.C. when God gave the Babylonian kingdom to Darius and Cyrus to the year 2015 is 2,553 years. 2,553 years is 3 x 23 x 37. 2015 is a time of judgment upon Satan and the fallen houses of God?
2012	• Official 1st year of Darius (month Nisan) - Daniel given understanding. The believers are given further understanding of the final seven years. • Daniel prospered in the years of Darius (Daniel 6:28).
2013	• Official 2nd year of Darius (month Nisan) - The rebuilding of the temple begins. • On the 1st day of the 6th month (our 8/7/2013), God gives the command to build his house. • On the 24th day of the 6th month (our 8/30/2013), God *stirs up* the remnant

464

	to work. • On the 21st day of the 7th month (our 9/25/2013), God says to work for He is with us.
2014	• Official 3rd year of Darius (month Nisan). The command to build God's house continues. While there is no mention of the 3rd year of Darius in the Bible, the temple was not complete until the 6th year.
2015	• Official 4th year of Darius • The command to build God's house continues. On the 4th day of the 9th month (our 11/16/2015) God commands us to do the following: *execute true judgment, and show mercy and compassions every man to his brother: And oppress not the widow, nor the fatherless, the stranger, nor the poor; and let none of you imagine evil against his brother in your heart* (Zechariah 7:9-10). • The Lord performs a great reversal this year as God is magnified after He removes the *Northern* (Joel 2). • Satan (the *Northern*) is removed into a land *barren and desolate.* • We arrive at the second fulfillment of the 1,335 day prophecy and *blessed is he that waits.* • Worldwide Pentecost on 5-24-2015. • Judgment on the fallen houses of God lines up with the anniversary of the cross in 2015; God is magnified. • The Gospel goes into *all the world* as a witness unto the nations for 3 ½ more years. • Once the judgment comes, the believers *consume and destroy* the kingdom of Satan by bringing God's Word (Daniel 7:26). • Daniel is only given information of the *time, times and half of time* (3 ½ years). Daniel did not know of the reversal by God and the "hereafter of these." God reserves that information for the time of the end when knowledge of His Word would increase. We have arrived at that time (2011-2018).
2016	• Official 5th year of Darius. The command to build God's house continues.
2017	• Official 6th year of Darius. Like the 3rd year of

	Darius, the command to build God's house continues.
2018	• The house was finished on the 3rd day of the 12th month which was the month Adar (our 2/18/2018). Salvation is not yet over worldwide. The beatification of the temple must take place according to the historical events. God's short work (logos) could apply to Adar 2018 to the last day of the Feast of Tabernacles which is October 2, 2018. It may also apply to the year 2015 onward since God's magnification will be known worldwide. • The beautification of the temple which relates to salvation in our time should occur from the month the temple is completed in the mirror of the 6th year of Darius (our 2018), to the Feast of Tabernacles (October 2, 2018). • The condensing of what Ezra did with teaching the *statutes and judgments* of God's Word during the reign of king Artaxerxes will be in effect during the final months. • God builds the *wall of salvation* as Nehemiah did to repair Jerusalem. This information was covered beginning on page 359 in Chapter 15. Chapter 15 also covered the *beautification* of the temple, which is all about the salvation of the meek and the praise God receives as spoken of in Psalm 149: **Psalm 149:4: For the LORD taketh pleasure in his people: <u>he will beautify the meek with salvation</u>. 5: Let the saints be joyful in glory: let them sing aloud upon their beds. 6: *Let* the high *praises* of God *be* in their mouth, and a twoedged sword in their hand; 7: To execute vengeance upon the heathen, *and* punishments upon the people; 8: To bind their kings with chains, and their nobles with fetters of iron; 9: To execute upon them the judgment written: this honour have all his saints. Praise ye the LORD.**

Bible Numbers Quick Reference Chart

Number	Meaning	Bible Verses
1	Three are One	1 John 5:7
2	Related to the believers as witnesses/God doubles	Mark 6:7, Genesis 41:32
3	Trinity/God's purpose	2 Corinthians 13:1, John 19:20
4	Universality	Revelation 7:1, Daniel 7:2-3
5	Dual meaning of judgment and grace	Matthew 25:2, Mark 8:19, Revelation 9:10
6	Number of man	Genesis 1:26, 31
7	Perfection or rest/Jesus and the first early churches (7 churches = totality of all churches worldwide)	Genesis 2:2, Revelation 8:6, Revelation 1:20
8	Salvation or Universal Salvation (2 x 4)	1 Peter 3:20-21, Acts 9:33-34, Leviticus 12:3
10	Completeness/tribulation	Revelation 2:10
11	Related to Jesus' coming	Matthew Chapter 1 (77 names-7 x 11)
12	Fullness 12x12x1,000 =144,000	Revelation 14:3, Mark 3:14, Luke 9:17
13	Relates to Paul being the 13th commissioned apostle to the gentiles. End of the world & evangelizing of many nations. Repletion of fullness.	Romans 1:1, 1:13 (1988 = 13,000 yr. since creation.)
15	3x5 (God's purpose for mercy and judgment).	Genesis 17:20, Genesis 7:24
16	1,600 can represent the winepress of God's judgment. 16 x 100. False worship	Revelation 14:20, 2 Chronicles 28,1

	during the reign of Ahaz (16 years)	
17	Salvation/Redemption	Jeremiah 13:9
18	Bound by Satan in years	Luke 13:16
21	Waiting period- 8,400 days is 4 x 2,100.	Daniel 10:13
23	Always judgment-2,300 days, 23,000 fell in the wilderness	1 Corinthians 10:8, Daniel 8:14
31	Cleansing of false worship	2 Kings 22:1
37	Salvation & judgment	From important Biblical dates to the Cross
40	Testing period	Mark 1:13, Jonah 3:4
42	*Great Tribulation* (42 Months)	Revelation 11:2, 13:5
43	Salvation/judgment	From important Biblical dates to the Cross
70	Tribulation/captivity	Jeremiah 25:12, Daniel 9:2
84	2x42 (tribulation)	70 years of Daniel 9:2 is 840 months
100	Fullness of believers/Christ's sheep	Matthew 18:12, Luke 15:4
666	Satan's dominion over mankind	Revelation 13:18
1,000	Completeness of time/generations/elect	Psalm 50:10, Revelation 20:6, Revelation 20:7, Deuteronomy 7:9
10,000 x 10,000	Representing God's elect worldwide past and present (a myriad)-Completeness	Revelation 5:11

Blessed is He that Waits- 1,335 Days

Start Date	Event	To Pentecost
Feast of Trumpets 29 A.D. (9-28-29 A.D.)-The 1,290/1,335 day countdown begins.	Jesus baptized by John and announced by God.	1,335 days- God saves about 3,000 in one day. The gospel is ushered forth. (5-24-33 A.D.)
Feast of Trumpets 2011 A.D. (9-28-2011 A.D.)-The 1,290/1,335 day countdown begins.	The duplication of the 3 ½ years of Christ's ministry and the abomination period of 1,290 days begins.	1,335 days completed on Pentecost 2015 (5-24-2015 A.D.) The Gospel goes into *all the world as a witness unto the nations*.
Bible Verses of these Two Important Feasts		

Trumpets: **Luke 3:21: Now when all the people were baptized, it came to pass, that Jesus also being baptized, and praying, the heaven was opened,**
22: And the Holy Ghost descended in a bodily shape like a dove upon him, and a voice came from heaven, which said, Thou art my beloved Son; in thee I am well pleased.

Pentecost: **Acts 2:38: Then Peter said unto them, Repent, and be baptized every one of you in the name of Jesus Christ for the remission of sins, and ye shall receive the gift of the Holy Ghost.**
39: For the promise is unto you, and to your children, and to all that are afar off, *even* as many as the Lord our God shall call.
40: And with many other words did he testify and exhort, saying, Save yourselves from this untoward generation.

41: Then they that gladly received his word were baptized: and the same day there were added *unto them* about three thousand souls.

***Blessed is he that waits*: Daniel 12:11: And from the time *that* the daily *sacrifice* shall be taken away, and the abomination that maketh desolate set up, *there shall be* a thousand two hundred and ninety days.**
12: Blessed *is* he that waiteth, and cometh to the thousand three hundred and five and thirty days.

Note: At the time of Pentecost, Peter commanded the people to repent (think different) and be baptized in the name of Jesus Christ for the remission of sins and to receive the gift of the Holy Spirit. This command was <u>gladly received</u> as the Word was being proclaimed. While the words *save yourselves from this untoward generation* were used by the King James translators, the truth is that the command of *be you being saved from this crooked generation* is the action of God's Holy Spirit.

With gratification they welcomed the Word that was brought by Peter. In one day about 3,000 souls were saved by God's Spirit. That is the power of God's Word being proclaimed at a precise time in history. We are rapidly reaching the duplication and arrival of the 1,335th day in the year 2015. The good news of Jesus Christ will be in full force.

Isaiah 55:6: Seek ye the LORD while he may be found, call ye upon him while he is near: 7: Let the wicked forsake his way, and the unrighteous man his thoughts: and let him return unto the LORD, and he will have mercy upon him; and to our God, for he will abundantly pardon. 8: For my thoughts *are* not your thoughts, neither *are* your ways my ways, saith the LORD. 9: For *as* the heavens are higher than the earth, so are my ways higher than your ways, and my thoughts than your thoughts.

I encourage everyone to continue with word studies and laboring in the work of bringing the Gospel (good news) of Jesus Christ. Proclaim boldly His forgiveness and the free gift of eternal life to many people. We are living in a time in which God is revealing much Biblical information about this present time and the Lord's soon coming in *power and great glory.*

God bless each reader with the reality of God's salvation and hope of a better tomorrow...

> **Psalm 47:1: To the chief Musician, A Psalm for the sons of Korah. O clap your hands, all ye people; shout unto God with the voice of triumph. 2: For the LORD most high *is* terrible; *he is* a great King over all the earth. 3: He shall subdue the people under us, and the nations under our feet. 4: He shall choose our inheritance for us, the excellency of Jacob whom he loved. Selah. 5: <u>God is gone up with a shout, the LORD with the sound of a trumpet</u>. 6: Sing praises to God, sing praises: sing praises unto our King, sing praises. 7: For God *is* the King of all the earth: <u>sing ye praises with understanding</u>. 8: God reigneth over the heathen: God sitteth upon the throne of his holiness. 9: The princes of the people are gathered together, *even* the people of the God of Abraham: for the shields of the earth *belong* unto God: he is greatly exalted.**

Trumpet-H7782 *Shophar*

> **Nehemiah 4:17: They which builded on the wall, and they that bare burdens, with those that laded, *every one* with one of his hands wrought in the work, and with the other *hand* held a weapon. 18: For the builders, every one had his sword girded**

471

by his side, and *so* builded. And he that sounded the trumpet *was* by me. 19: And I said unto the nobles, and to the rulers, and to the rest of the people, The work *is* great and large, and we are separated upon the wall, one far from another. 20: <u>In what place *therefore* ye hear the sound of the trumpet, resort ye thither unto us: our God shall fight for us</u>. 21: So <u>we laboured in the work</u>: and half of them held the spears from the rising of the morning till the stars appeared.

1Corinthians 15:57: But thanks be to God, which giveth us the victory through our Lord Jesus Christ. 58: Therefore, my beloved brethren, be ye stedfast, unmoveable, always abounding in the work of the Lord, <u>forasmuch as ye know that your labour is not in vain in the Lord</u>.

Personal Bible Study Notes:

References

[1] *E-Sword* with Concordance numbers for the Greek and Hebrew Text- Free download online: < www.e-sword.net> Digital.

[2] Camping, Harold. *Time has an End- The Biblical Calendar of History- 11,013 B.C. - 2011 A.D.*, Vantage Press- New York, 2005. Print.

[3] *The Cyrus Cylinder*: Online: < www.britishmuseum.org> The Conquest of Babylon in 539 B.C. Digital.

[4] Haggai 2:19: *...from this day will I bless you.* King James Bible. Digital.

[5] Anderson, Troy. Article: *Billy Graham Sounds Alarm for 2nd Coming*, <www.wnd.com> Digital.

[6] Camping, Harold, *Time has an End- The Biblical Calendar of History- 11,013 B.C. - 2011 A.D.*, Vantage Press- New York, 2005. Print.

[7] Paramount Pictures. *Noah*-The Movie- 2014. YouTube Trailer. Digital.

[8] Camping, Harold. *Time has an End- The Biblical Calendar of History- 11,013 B.C. - 2011 A.D.*, Vantage Press- New York, 2005. Print.

[9] Camping, Harold. *1994?*, (Pgs. 412-413), Vantage Press- New York, 1992. Print.

[10] *ISA (Interlinear Scripture Analyzer)*-Free download from: www.scripture4all.org. Digital.

[11] 2011studies Publications. *Countdown to the Last Day*- 2011. Print.

[12] Camping, Harold. *Time has an End*- The Biblical Calendar of History- 11,013 B.C.- 2011 A.D. (Pgs. 101-103), Vantage Press- New York, 2005. Print.

[13] Wikipedia.org online. John Nelson Darby. Name entry. Digital.

[14] Wikipedia.org Online. Cyrus Scofield. Name entry. Digital.

[15] *The Cyrus Cylinder*, Online: <www.iranchamber.com/history/cyrus/cyrus_charter.php> Digital.

[16] Camping, Harold. 1994?, (Pgs. 460-461), Vantage Press- New York, 1992. Print.

[17] Tetrad Eclipses. http://eclipse.gsfc.nasa.gov/OH/OH2014.html. Digital.

[18] *Gill's commentary*-http://bibleapps.com/commentaries/Isaiah/16-14.html. Digital.

[19]Wesley, John. *John Wesley Commentary*- http://bibleapps.com/commentaries/Isaiah/16-14.html. Digital.

[20] YouTube Public Video. *Is this Fire From God?* Title entry. Digital.

[21] Camping, Harold. *Time has an End- The Biblical Calendar of History*- 11,013 B.C. - 2011 A.D. (Pgs. 104-112), Vantage Press- New York, 2005. Print.

[22] Bullinger, E.W. *Number in Scriptures*- It's Supernatural Design and Spiritual Significance, Online: <www.biblebelievers.org.au/number01.htm > Digital.

[23] *Online Hebrew Calendar*: <www. Shabad.org> Digital.

[24] Cyrus the Great & the Shahbaz. <https://en.wikipedia.org/wiki/Flag of Iran> Digital.

[25] Camping, Harold. *Time has an End- The Biblical Calendar of History- 11,013 B.C. - 2011 A.D.* (Pgs. 101-103), Vantage Press- New York, 2005. Print.

[26] YouTube Public Video(s). *The Silent Epidemic; The Untold Story of Vaccines*. Title Entry. Digital.

[27] YouTube Public Video. *Geoengineering and the Collapse of the Earth*. Title Entry. Digital.

www.ingramcontent.com/pod-product-compliance
Lightning Source LLC
Chambersburg PA
CBHW071312090426
42738CB00012B/2677